MW00781471

Critical Issues in Organization Development

Case Studies for Analysis and Discussion

A Volume in
Contemporary Trends in Organization Development and Change

Series Editors
Peter F. Sorensen and Therese F. Yaeger,
Benedictine University

Contemporary Trends in Organization Development and Change

Peter F. Sorensen and Therese F. Yaeger, Series Editors

Critical Issues in Organization Development

Case Studies for Analysis and Discussion

Edited by

Homer H. Johnson
Loyola University

Peter F. Sorensen and Therese F. Yaeger
Benedictine University

Information Age Publishing, Inc.
Charlotte, North Carolina • www.infoagepub.com

Library of Congress Cataloging-in-Publication Data

CIP data for this book can be found on the Library of Congress website http://www.loc.gov/index.html

ISBNs: Paperback: 978-1-62396-325-5
        Hardcover: 978-1-62396-326-2
        eBook: 978-1-62396-327-9

Printed in the United States of America

CONTENTS

SECTION II: RESOURCES AND THE BOTTOM LINE

SECTION III: POWER AND ETHICS

SECTION IV: CONFLICT

SECTION V: GLOBAL ORGANIZATION DEVELOPMENT
AND CULTURE

INTRODUCTION

Homer H. Johnson, Therese F. Yaeger, and Peter F. Sorensen

This book has been over 10 years in the making. But, as the field of Organization Development (OD) is over 50 years old, and some of the fundamental concepts of OD are addressed in this case book, perhaps this book has been over 50 years in the making as well.

On a serious note, this book began over 10 years ago in 2002, when Homer Johnson received a request from the *Organization Development Practitioner* to develop cases for the readers of the *Practitioner*, which would be based on a typical and timely situation confronting an OD practitioner or consultant. Soon after, Homer Johnson invited Therese Yaeger as a case respondent, which led to the OD Network inviting Therese and Peter Sorensen to collaborate with Homer in case writing in 2006. Since that time Homer, and Therese and Peter have alternated the development of cases, presenting a total of four cases each year.

The editors owe much to the *OD Practitioner* and the OD Network. The OD Network is the largest professional association for the OD consultant, and it is the *OD Practitioner* that has served over the years as the voice of the largest OD professional association. We would like to express our appreciation to the editors of the *OD Practitioner* for their continued support and encouragement. Dr. Marilyn Blair provided the initial opportunity, and Dr. John Vogelsang, the current editor of the *OD Practitioner*, who has provided his continued support for the development and content of this book.

Critical Issues in Organization Development:
Case Studies for Analysis and Discussion, pp. ix–xiii
Copyright © 2013 by Information Age Publishing

ix

The cases presented here include, although disguised, real situations which are encountered in the practice of OD. These cases not only present the opportunity for professionals and students in the field to read and reflect on these various situations, they also provide the opportunity for giving voice to OD consultants who have lived through these experiences. Consequently, through this book, these consultants share their experiences with the larger OD community.

The book is comprised of 30 cases. Each case begins with an OD consulting situation followed by responses from established OD consultants describing how they would work with the situation. All of the contributors are experienced OD consultants, both independent and internal, some of whom represent the largest corporations globally. The participating consultants come from a wide range of organizations—from global corporations to health care and community service agencies, among others.

The book editors represent more than 150 years of combined experience in OD and OD education. Dr. Homer Johnson and Dr. Peter Sorensen were responsible for establishing two of the first master's programs in the field—Homer at Loyola University of Chicago, and Peter at George Williams College (which later became the Benedictine University Program). Therese and Peter later were responsible for developing one of the first PhD programs in the field, the current program at Benedictine University.

The book divides the 30 cases over five central topics: strategy, resources and the bottom line, power and ethics, conflict, and global and culture. Each section presents cases which characterize today's environment for OD practitioner.

Part I: Strategy

The role of the organization practitioner in the development and implementation of organizational strategy represents one of the relatively new roles in the field. As the field has developed, matured and changed, strategy has become a more critical aspect of what the OD practitioner does. The importance of this relatively new role is reflected in the inclusion of seven of the thirty cases. In the first case "Recognizing the Value … and Values of Organization Development" the key figure in the case, the director of OD for an airline, is confronted with the problem of implementing strategy within the broader and more effective and sustainable values of OD.

In the second case, "Measuring Organization Development's Success: Organization Development and XYZ" a new director of OD is confronted with the problem of how to present the measurable impact of OD in a culture new to the methods and values of OD. In the third case "Exploring Large Group Interventions" an inexperienced OD consultant is faced with the opportunity for implementing one of the most powerful OD methods for developing and implementing organization strategy: large group interventions. In the following case "Prescribing a Healthy Dose of Organization Development for Healthcare," we have a new chief operating officer working with the manager of OD in developing strategies for effective change. Case 5, "Quality Initiative in the Pathology Lab" deals with improving work processes within a critical function in healthcare and presents the collaboration between MDs, pathologists, and the OD practitioner. The last two cases in this section "Anticipating Major Resistance in Metro City," and "Resolving an Human Resources Problem at Metro Transit," represent OD opportunities within governmental organizations.

Part II: Resources and the Bottom Line

The next five cases present issues related to OD's contribution to an organization in terms of effectively building and using an organization's resources. The initial case, "Today's Challenging Times and The Role of Organization Development" presents a particularly important role for OD—how does OD contribute to sustaining a healthy, positive, and effective organization under the stress of a difficult overall economic environment? In "Implementing the Triple Bottom Line" we have an OD consultant given the responsibility by her CEO for implementing a triple bottom line strategy and the issue of how to do it. Next, in "Leveraging Organization Development: Strategies for Limited Resources," we have a successful OD manager who is confronted with the not uncommon problem in OD—how to meet and implement strategies for the increasing demands for OD with limited resources, which is too often the price of success in OD. In "The Case of the Ideal Organization Development Job" we see another frequently encountered situation—how to respond when the company has been acquired by an organization with a culture and philosophy very different from OD. In the last case, "The Sustainability at Metro Charity Hospital," we address the application of OD to the question of sustainability in a healthcare organization with limited resources.

Part III: Power and Ethics

In Part III we have five cases dealing with two of the core values and issues in OD. The field has always been grounded in the concept of power, based on the sharing of power rather than the unilateral and hierarchical use of power. The question of ethics frequently related to the use of power has always been a central concern in the field. These five cases present some of the most difficult issues in the practice of OD. In Chapter 13, "Unethical Use of Power," an authoritarian CEO imposes culturally inappropriate OD techniques upon his global corporation, and executives are fearful to voice their opinions. In the second case, "Some Questionable Practices at County General," the OD consultant is faced with how to deal with fake data reported in a "successful" turn around. In "The Case of 360 Degree Reviews at Electronic Division" the consultant is faced with the ethical question of sharing information gained in executive coaching sessions. In "You Walked into a Political Minefield and I Hope You Survive," we again see our OD consultant confronted with a common situation—the implementation of an unpopular program, unpopular except with the chief executive officer. In the last case in this section, "The Transition Isn't Working," our consultant is faced with a forced executive retirement and a slow, troublesome transition of power.

Part IV: Conflict

Here again, in section four we are dealing with one of the core topics in the field. Conflict seems to be built into the DNA of humans and consequently into the DNA of organizations. The first case, "The Case of Food Service," deals with conflict between cooks and the kitchen staff supervisors. The supervisors, who have requested the help of an outside consultant, have refused to let the OD professional speak with the cooks; the consultant must decide what her next steps will be. In the second case, "Do You Want to Work for a Jerk," the problem is the boss and what the OD consultant should do? In the next case "Resolving Conflict at InSo" we see probably one of the most frequently encountered OD problems: cross-functional conflict. In "Resolving Conflict at Walberg Bank Group" we again see a classic source of conflict: interpersonal conflict- what should the OD consultant do? In "The Case of Competition at Centri-Pharm," we address a topic which has generated much debate in the field: the relationship between HR and OD. Is this relationship possible? Can it happen? Should it happen? And again in "Bad News at Great North Insurance," we have a wonderful example of a frequently encountered situation implementing one of the most frequently used OD methods—survey research and how do you handle "the boss is the problem?" In the last case in this section, we have a situation where the OD consultant must deal with issues related to the police force and the community following a police shooting.

Part V: Global Organization Development and Culture

In this last section and in the last six cases, we present concerns dealing with the most recent work and issues in the field—work and issues dealing with organization culture and more recently the emergence of the application of OD on a global basis. In "A Case of Too Much Diversity," we have a situation of the need for collaboration between diverse cultural groups. What does the OD consultant do? In "No Child Left Behind" we see a situation where the consultant has an opportunity to assist in one of the major initiatives in education of our time. The following case, "The Camwell High School case," again deals with education and change from an authoritarian to a collaborative culture. The book concludes with three cases on global organization development. "Organization Development's Role When Going Global" presents the case of a U.S. based pharmaceutical company expanding into India, China, and Africa and the role of OD. In "Implementing a Global Corporate Strategy: The Role of Organization Development" we have an established global organization in the process of creating a new identity and continuity of operations. And the last case, "Organization Development in Africa: Insights from Experts," presents the role of OD in implementing corporate strategies in countries with significantly different national culture—the new future of OD.

In the above 30 cases we, the editors, have shared with you major and frequently encountered situations by the OD practitioner, cases which span a number of situations in a number of different organizations, and finally in highly different national cultures.

In presenting these cases we also share with you, through the experiences of the editors and our contributors, over 1,000 years of experience in OD.

Thank you again to the OD Network, the *OD Practitioner*, its editors, and publishers for all of their help and support for this opportunity.

Book Editors:

Homer H. Johnson
Therese F. Yaeger
Peter F. Sorensen

SECTION I

STRATEGY

CASE STUDY 1

RECOGNIZING THE VALUE ... AND VALUES ... OF ORGANIZATION DEVELOPMENT

Therese F. Yaeger and Peter F. Sorensen

The field and practice of organization development (OD) is a field characterized by a strong value base—a set of values which were highly influenced by the founders of the field, including Kurt Lewin. As a field, it has always provided a means for creating highly effective organizations. OD has, however, been often characterized as being too soft, as being too people-oriented, and not contributing to the "bottom line." This "soft" perception of OD is where our case begins.

This case involves Goodman Airlines, a large, established airline with numerous national and international routes. Goodman Airlines, similar to the airline industry today in general, has been confronted by a continuous set of serious challenges, including major cost and price squeezes created by significant increases in the cost of fuel, and increased competition from both domestic and international carriers.

Mike, the Director of OD, is responsible for creating a quick improvement in the corporate bottom line in this turbulent organization. Mike, a seasoned OD professional, has worked within various industries, and has been with Goodman Airlines less than 1 year. He has a master's degree in OD, and is grounded in OD values, theories, and interventions. Although

Critical Issues in Organization Development:
Case Studies for Analysis and Discussion, pp. 3–9
Copyright © 2013 by Information Age Publishing
All rights of reproduction in any form reserved.

he enjoys working for Goodman, he feels that there is so much more that OD can do to improve the organization.

Harold, the CEO of Goodman Airlines, has a reputation for being action-oriented, driven by immediate results, pragmatic, and determined to create a successful turnaround. He is very much oriented toward measurable results. The corporation and Harold have a long and established history of success amidst industry challenges.

Recently in meetings, Harold expressed to Mike the need for rapid change, but he appears to be neutral as to the capability of the OD Department to play a meaningful role in the new corporate strategy. In meetings, Harold has used terms such as soft, oriented toward long-term results amidst short-term needs (i.e., "organization change is hard and takes time"), and when or if there are no significant short-term results there will be no long term to even consider. Harold has referred to OD as nebulous, questioning, "Where are the hard measurables and results?" Above all, he is hard-nosed and is highly receptive to anything which he feels will make a contribution to what he perceives to be the need for major change. He is intensely aware of the difficulties in major corporate change and what is at stake for the corporation, its reputation, its employees, and other stakeholders, as well as for his reputation and career.

As Mike became more aware of Harold's thoughts of OD, he realized there is more than just OD work ahead for him—Mike also has to educate Harold about OD contributions to Goodman Airlines. He began to wonder if Harold even knew what OD and its values were. Mike knows he has to make a stronger case for OD with Harold. But where should he start? As Mike realized, he has limited time to demonstrate all of OD's possibilities for helping to improve Goodman's current system. What advice would you provide Mike?

We have asked three highly seasoned, experienced OD practitioners to address what they would do in Mike's situation. First, Bruce Mabee has been a successful consultant for over 25 years and a major contributor to the Chicago OD community. Bruce worked with the Federal Aviation Administration for 5 years and with Motorola for 12 years to develop internal consulting skills globally.

Second, we have Kathryn Kasdorf, the Organizational Effectiveness Manager at W. W. Grainger, who has over 15 years experience managing client expectations in various Human Resource disciplines. She is currently enrolled in the MSMOB program at Benedictine University.

Third, we have invited Deb Orr, PhD, who holds a full-time academic position at Roosevelt University and also has her own consulting practice. Deb brings a more academic perspective to the case and has the distinction of being the first recipient of the Best Student Paper Award given by OD Network. Let's see what these experts have to say ....

Bruce Mabee

I'd love to help Mike sell his CEO on the value of OD! How? There are several potential angles. A sales model may help Mike sort the benefits and costs that Harold may perceive in OD. Mike would need to be clear about the short-term business benefits in his favorite models for rapid change. Mike needs also to have good, hard and actual data about what boosts short-term performance among employees, passengers, suppliers, fuel suppliers, the FAA and other stakeholders so that he can be accurate, as well as articulate with Harold. We could explore the politics of who influences Harold, thus who Mike needs to help him sell OD to Harold.

But this time, I'm going to start by trying to avoid my own trap. This trap is to join Mike in this collusion, to impose OD education on Harold without asking how this is relevant to Harold or the client system. I do not buy the idea that whatever client Mike wants automatically becomes the goal, even if I agree with it. My job is to help my client test, clarify, and reach his goal in the context of his value to Goodman Airlines.

Maybe Goodman Airlines can deal with the fuel costs and competition changes sooner without their CEO understanding OD; maybe Harold's education will be "experiential" if Mike just applies OD to help achieve Harold's goals, rather than getting into a selling game.

Another OD value is relevant: empathy. Is it possible that Harold is right about this situation, and that Mike is the resistant one? Maybe Mike can decide that he needs more education than Harold does education for Mike in understanding how change happens, specifically in the airline business. Could Mike's interest in learning the industry also reduce Harold's resistance to OD?

Tremendous speed may come if Mike can quickly help Harold identify and engage the right team. This Change Team may immediately dive into debating hard numbers. If Mike is allowed to facilitate, and if he makes the numbers discussion effective, then he can also ask, "What else can we do that will get us through this crunch and also build some sustainability for Goodman?" He can ask what will get the unions on board, and what will attract some positive attention from the stock analysts. Mike may increase the total speed of execution by expanding the view of the stakeholders. Harold will like that, and these are compatible values.

If Mike starts getting "soft" and impatient about addressing humanistic values, he might consider Maslow in the discussion. Harold may need to act on his value for survival before he is ready to act on his higher level need to care about people. If you embrace Harold's values for numbers and speed, might that help expose Harold's willingness to serve humanity?

From what values of mine are these angles coming? At an OD Network National Conference a number of years ago, Tony Petrella described an

OD consultant in a way that I find continually helpful: "A companion, not a guide." I hope that this principle can help Mike trust Harold and begin a consulting relationship of companions.

I trust that Mike knows how to make or buy the tools to measure and manage the other issues. Mike knows how to engage the employees, suppliers, regulators and other stakeholders whose lives will be buffeted by the changes that Harold is trying to manage. As an OD consultant, I hope that I can help him get into a position to work his magic.

So, now I have a starting point for how to advise Mike. Hopefully, as my starting assumptions about this situation begin to crumble, as Mike watches my own struggle to make sense of this complex situation, both will help him cope with the volatile airline culture for that is the world Mike needs to navigate in order to sell and perform OD at Goodman Airlines.

Kathryn Kasdorf

Educating a resistant CEO on the benefits and values of OD in one short meeting is a lofty goal. The case implies that Mike is not viewed as a strategic partner and he will need to build this relationship over time. To start, Mike needs to speak in the language of the CEO. As Mike builds credibility with Harold, he can continue to educate him on the value of OD. In the interim, Mike needs to gain some quick wins.

In preparing for the meeting Mike will need to discuss the organization's strategy and operational goals in addition to the external factors that are adversely affecting company profits. Assuming he has developed sound relationships with other leaders in the organization, he should do a quick organizational scan to determine the issues they are facing in their departments that have a direct effect on the bottom line.

Based on what he learns from his research and discussions, Mike should present his findings and a list of services to address the identified results- that is, gaps that would address short-term concerns and which can be quickly implemented. He should emphasize that the value OD can bring is assessing the organization and developing solutions to improve organizational performance. Examples of improved performance in the past would be beneficial. He can show the trend of operational metrics before, during, and after a well-executed change.

Mike should spend time understanding the business problems from Harold's point of view and discuss how OD can partner to address those issues.

It is critical that Mike spends time on the longer-term value that OD can bring. Here he can identify services and solutions that may take a little longer but have a more significant and positive impact on the organization. He may want to touch on the difference between transactional and transformational change.

I would advise Mike to avoid discussing OD's values during the initial meeting. As Mike begins to develop a strategic partnership with Harold, he can begin talking more about values and benefits of OD.

Deb Orr

Animating the values of Organization Development by modeling to others is an excellent teaching tool to demonstrate what the field is about. Teaching by example is one of the strongest ways we can bring our values to life in organization development. One of the most important values that OD puts forth is the idea of meeting people where they are at in terms of learning, in the change process or in their understanding of OD. This is what Mike needs to do in order to get Harold to see the value in what he provides to Goodman Airlines.

In a practical sense, this means using the interaction with the CEO as an occasion to apply the values of the field. Mike has the opportunity to listen actively, act on the information the CEO puts forward and give him the reassurances he needs in terms of quantification of outcomes. By understanding the perspective that the CEO has with quantification, Mike will reduce resistance and make evident the power of the values of the field. Mike should look at the kinds of metrics that have meaning for the CEO and find ways to offer him the quantification he needs. Once the needs for measurement from the CEO are met, Mike can begin a larger conversation about the importance of human beings in a system, developing trust, building team and creating engagement.

Quantifying bottom line value has always been a challenge in the field of OD. Mike should review the strategic plan of the organization and identify where the organization is moving, looking for change or emerging in a new way. By looking at the intersection of human systems, technical changes and organizational outcomes, Mike will find the metrics that will give the CEO the quantification he needs. Mike has a few choices to make about how he wants to measure value. He could:

- Measure the outcome of the strategic plan that most closely aligns with people
- Review the outcomes of similar areas he has worked with versus areas he has not worked with to find the difference in outcomes
- Identify research that closely aligns with the strategic initiatives he is undertaking and determine how it was quantified and then replicate that work in his organization.

As he goes through this process, Mike can begin talking about the unquantifiable pieces of OD, such as the value of a relationship in an organization, the synergy and engagement developed by team and how motivated and inspired people build lasting innovation into organizational culture. These organizational practices and outcomes unquestionably have quantifiable value and produce outcomes. The successful execution of these OD practices is where the real value of OD's unquantifiable values is.

Therese Yaeger and Peter Sorensen Respond

This situation at Goodman Airlines addresses what has been one of the central questions in the history of OD—the question of values and how to effectively align OD values with corporate strategy. Our three experts contribute considerable insights in terms of their approaches. First, Bruce Mabee's response is of special interest because of his background and experience with FAA and also being the senior member of the panel. Bruce is able to draw on his years of experience in the FAA and OD fields, citing OD icon Tony Petrella. Bruce's quote from Petrella that the 'OD consultant is a companion not a guide,' reminds us of the central role of the OD practitioner.

Second, Kathryn Kasdorf brings her corporate experience to bear on her comments and addresses key elements for the OD practitioner, such as being able to speak the language of the CEO, building credibility through demonstration, and the role of quick wins. Kathryn also reminds us of the differences between transactional and transformational change, and the importance of building relationships in preparation for discussing OD values.

Finally, Dr. Deb Orr combines both her academic and consulting experience in addressing the issue, emphasizing the importance of modeling, and the importance of understanding the world in which the CEO lives.

In total, our expert panel has much to contribute about our understanding of what continues to be one of the central issues for the OD practitioner. Thank you Bruce, Kathryn and Deb for your differing insights and perceptive suggestions.

ACKNOWLEDGMENT

An earlier version of this article was published in the *The OD Practitioner*, *40*(2), 47-49.

CASE STUDY 2

MEASURING ORGANIZATION DEVELOPMENT'S SUCCESS

XYZ and Organization Development

Therese F. Yaeger and Peter F. Sorensen

Mary Likert has just been hired by XYZ Company to start-up and build an organizationa development (OD) department. Like most companies, XYZ Company is feeling the turbulent effects of the negative economic environment. As part of their recent strategic review, the company has decided that now is the time to start an OD operation in order to create an increased focus on innovation amidst cost containment.

Mary is an experienced and educated OD consultant with mostly external consulting and only some experience in a large corporate environment such as XYZ Company. In just a few weeks on the job, Mary is excited about her work with the XYZ employees. Already, with initial assessments, she has identified some of the major characteristics of the company's corporate culture. For example, she sees the culture as running a "tight" operation. Success is defined as innovation with good margins and tight cost controls. The company also operates at a fast pace for its products, and that speed is reflected internally as well. In general, XYZ

Critical Issues in Organization Development:
Case Studies for Analysis and Discussion, pp. 11–18
Copyright © 2013 by Information Age Publishing
All rights of reproduction in any form reserved.

Company hires a large number of PhDs, engineers, and scientists. Most of the executive management level has been with the organization a number of years and has seen the company experience high levels of success and growth, which they attribute to the organization's culture.

Mary understands that she needs to work within and contribute to XYZ's culture. She also understands that the new OD function will be dependent upon her ability to deliver on the expectations of executive management. If she fails, OD fails. Mary reports to the EVP of Operations, who is a research PhD. Mary has strong support from her boss, and the executive group in general. She has met with all of the executives and is a member of the Monday morning executive meetings. At these meetings, Mary is expected to give advice and counsel on organizational strategy and organizational change. She is also expected to present regular reports on the status of the OD department.

Mary is enthusiastic but apprehensive about her new position. She is concerned that she will need to deliver measurable results. These OD results must be based on the development of a strong business case for her projects and regular assessment of their progress. She also understands that she needs to develop the appropriate expectations of the executive group. She is also aware that some of her external OD consulting friends insist that good OD takes time, that change does not happen overnight, and that often OD does not lend itself well to quick measurement. Mary is concerned that this approach to OD is not going to be successful at the XYZ Company. In need of a strategy for measurement, a defined process, and appropriate tools, she will need quick, substantial, and measurable results to deliver at the Monday morning meetings.

What advice would you give to Mary?

Jason Wolf

Mary's challenge, while not new, seems more prevalent in these times. In my experience, organizations often identify a need for the OD function without understanding the full implications of that decision or the commitment it requires. Add to this precarious foundation the weight of challenging expectations and we can truly feel Mary's predicament.

But is it a predicament at all? Mary has, as it sounds like she believes, an incredible opportunity to bolster a culture that has led to great results while showing the value OD can bring. I would first call her to reexamine the perspectives that "good OD takes time," a value-laden statement unto itself, and begin to frame a plan that both fits the environment she is in AND honors the impact she hopes to have.

Keys to her success seem clear and emerge from the very language of XYZ—"success defined as innovation," "good margins," "tight operation" and a long-tenured and well-educated employee base. The fact that she also has strong support at senior levels, including access to executive leadership and the expressed desire for her input, already lowers her first hurdle. Many OD departments never get past this first step.

Mary must now act quickly to simultaneously frame expectations and move to proven outcomes. Her opportunity may be rooted in the successes that XYZ has already experienced and should be focused on its desire to drive innovation in the face of cost limitations. For this, and in understanding her audience of PhDs, engineers, and scientists, I would suggest Mary has the unique opportunity to return to the very roots of OD as an applied behavioral science and to the Lewinian foundations of action research. Mary's path to immediate contribution and rapid impact is to help XYZ capitalize on its strengths in people, processes and products that have already led to measurable outcomes.

All too often in business settings, specifically in larger organizations, resources and capital are focused on buying the "best" solutions to address organizational challenges. It is this quest for the "best" that may actually lead an organization in the opposite direction—into a place of commonalities versus competitive distinction—and in doing so an organization will often overlook the best "best" of all, their own internal strength. Mary's opportunity as OD leader is to stress the importance of looking inside XYZ to the human capital, processes, and know-how that have helped them achieve great things every day. Her ability to be both a valuable contributor and strategic partner will come from her willingness to discover the strength that lies within.

While I do not dismiss Mary's need for a longer term development strategy, the opportunity for a quick and impactful launch to her OD efforts is in working with teams via an action research process to determine what people, products, and processes are most successful at XYZ. She has a chance then to "deconstruct" these findings with active working groups of leaders and employees to propose clear models of "proven" practice for leadership, product development, production, and so forth, and work with these teams to both share and then implement these findings as appropriate throughout the organization.

With this process she has already created a link to measurable results as the focus of the action research is on areas successful in both innovation and cost management. In engaging the organization around its successes and helping to broadly deploy these ideas, Mary emerges as a true strategic contributor, with a focus on expanding competitive strategy and a commitment to building an organization capable of achieving and sustaining significant results with the very resources they possess.

Mary has the opportunity to contribute in one of the most strategic ways OD can. More than simply helping to frame the strategy through facilitation, or develop capacity through training, her role raises the level of awareness of organizational strengths, and ultimately results in a quick and valuable contribution to the company's strategy of innovation.

Amy Alfermann

Mary has quite an opportunity to start up and head an OD department, but it will not be without its challenges. While some of the challenges are ones that all new OD departments face, some will be specific to XYZ Company. Mary sounds like she works for a company that is similar to many companies with their emphasis on running "tight" operations, controls, and focusing on innovation and speed. Mary's understanding of XYZ's culture is a huge first step and one that is important not to be overlooked. Recognizing the culture and values of the company not only positions Mary to speak to the company's values and what is important to them, but it can help point her in the areas in which she chooses to focus on first. Mary should be very grateful that she has the strong support of her executive management, that they include her in their meetings, and look to her for input. Now it is time for Mary to step up to the plate.

Mary could first look to the organization's strategic plan for the next one, three, and five years to see how OD can help in accomplishing the company's goals. This should also be compared and contrasted to what she heard in each of her individual meetings with the executives. Mary can then create OD's strategy, making sure that it links to and supports the overall business plan.

The measurable outcomes should, once again, be linked to what is currently being measured and to what is of importance to the strategic plan, but Mary should keep an open mind that there may be some metrics that could be captured that are overlooked. One thing Mary must do is to capture what these metrics are currently, so that she has a baseline for comparing the impact the OD department has had and the value it has created. Some example metrics could include employee engagement scores, 360 feedback scores, customer satisfaction results, accuracy and reduction of errors, speed and time to market, new ideas, and so forth. Once it has been determined what the overall goal is and how it will be measured, realistic milestones can be created. This helps establish the expectations of the executive team on what the OD department is focusing on and is also good for Mary. Having these predetermined milestones will help remind Mary of the progress she has made when she might feel that she should be doing more. Some companies prefer to have a balanced scorecard or a dashboard visual that can highlight, at a glance, the progress that OD has made.

The biggest issue that Mary must remember in establishing the OD department at XYZ is to keep communicating with the executives not only on what the OD department is doing, measuring, and its progress, but also to stay open to listening to what the executives feel the company needs and the direction it is headed. After all, without the organization, there would be no OD.

George W. Hay

The success or failure of measurement is rarely determined by measurement itself, but rather the larger organizational context in which that measurement takes place. Successful measurement comes from the alignment of the social system of the organization with the technical system of measurement. Foundational to any success that Mary may have in leading the new OD department, therefore, is her active leadership in creating a favorable measurement culture.

My advice is based on general observation. Four recommendations for Mary flow from this perspective:

1. Study the past. I would advise Mary to learn the history of the organization by reading any relevant material in the company's archives and by interviewing the tenured managers who have seen a couple of business cycles and corporate initiatives come and go. Aside from becoming familiar with "insider's knowledge," this allows her to identify best practices and failure patterns. This will allow her to contribute to the Monday meetings based not just on the wisdom of her prior experience, but on her detailed knowledge of XYZ.

2. Collaborate with gatekeepers and stakeholders. I would advise Mary to continuously meet with the key gatekeepers and stakeholders in and around the organization. Although this is a way to build support and influence, the primary objective for the meetings—at least in the beginning— is communicative. The objective for Mary is to find the words and concepts that create shared meaning and aligned action. Although this might sound simplistic, we often underestimate the unique professional microculture that shapes our personal vocabularies and how we make sense out of the world. The same words (i.e., quick, substantial, and measureable) can mean different things to different professional microcommunities. In order for her insights to be understood and valued, she will need to translate them into the language of the organization.

3. Analyze power. Measurement rarely occurs for the sake of learning within organizations. Measurement takes place to influence decisions that ultimately allocate resources. Thus all organizational measurement activities have the potential to change the power within an organization as the measured initiatives are stopped, started or continued. Mary needs to think through how her department and its measurement activities may change the power relationships within the organization. There are two additional power maps to create:

(a) Map the power relationships of her boss so that she knows when, where and how they can be allies; and

(b) Map the power relationships of the company as a whole so that she knows the sources of power that are inside versus outside her sphere of influence.

4. Gain recognition for small wins. Seek some early wins by demonstrating how OD adds value to current activities. One option is to link OD as a support function to the start of an initiative in another department. For example, partner with those responsible for innovation to demonstrate how OD knowledge can improve the early phases of new product development. Another option is to enrich the current organizational performance scorecard with content and techniques from OD. Can more reliable and valid metric of employee engagement be piloted? Can more sophisticated statistical analyses be conducted that prioritize the people metrics in terms of their contribution to organizational functioning? In sum, focus your measurement activity on smaller, more manageable areas of OD application. Avoid the big research project that tries to prove how essential OD is for the success of XYZ.

Therese Yaeger and Peter Sorensen Respond

Each of expert panelists contributes relevant and critical insights to Mary's situation. For example, Jason Wolf calls attention to the applicability of Kurt Lewin's action research as an approach to measurable outcomes. He also addresses the "good OD takes time" issue, and Mary's essential role of raising the level of awareness of the organization's strengths.

Amy Alfermann provides some examples of the metrics that might be used to assess the outcomes of OD. She also identifies a number of approaches for establishing appropriate expectations and establishing her role with executive management. Our third contributor, George Hay, raises the important issue that successful measurement is determined by the larger organizational context or culture in which that measurement takes place. He provides important steps for establishing Mary's success, such as understanding the culture by studying the past, identifying and working with key gatekeepers and stakeholders, analyzing and understanding the power structure, and the importance of small wins.

Measurement is now more important than ever for the credibility of OD and its continued success. This is particularly true in a culture which is as metrics-oriented as XYZ. Thank you to our panelists, who each provided a wealth of experience and understanding to the importance of this increasingly critical component of OD—measurement of outcomes.

ACKNOWLEDGMENT

An earlier version of this article was published in *The OD Practitioner,* *41*(4), 57-60.

CASE STUDY 3

EXPLORING LARGE GROUP INTERVENTIONS

Therese F. Yaeger and Peter F. Sorensen

Kerry slumped at her desk in need of an organization development (OD) mentor. As a young OD consultant with her recently received master's degree in OD, Kerry is the only official OD person in her firm, Levelco. Having just left the CEO's office 5 minutes earlier, Kerry wondered if she was in over her head with the assignment the CEO Stanley just gave her. Apparently, Stanley heard about the success of "large group interventions" from other CEOs at a Wall Street executive meeting last week, and so he thinks "it would be a great idea to do a large intervention here at Levelco regarding our new initiative."

Kerry felt overwhelmed. Her success at Levelco and her past jobs involved OD projects on building successful project teams, dealing with executive conflict issues, and leading some technical pieces of strategic changes. Kerry's shortcoming is in the large group/search conference/OD summit work.

At Levelco, Kerry's work has always been appreciated—she had been a welcome addition in many senior team issues, and even with up and coming young executives who appreciated her approach to change initiatives. But in her past OD work, and her 2+ years at the firm, she ran the OD

Critical Issues in Organization Development:
Case Studies for Analysis and Discussion, pp. 19–25
Copyright © 2013 by Information Age Publishing

19

department as a solo internal consultant, and her OD expertise proved measurably successful.

Levelco, like so many Wall Street firms these days, was planning for change. A new initiative was being planned for a roll-out within a month. Like most Wall Street issues, any message of a failure regarding rolling out this change initiative would cause a rumble on Wall Street in these challenging times. Kerry was aware that failure was not an option, but if the CEO wants it, she must deliver the upcoming change initiative as a large group intervention.

Kerry needed to roll up her sleeves and get an initial plan to Stanley's executive team with appropriate timelines. She knew as a one-person OD operation that she would need support. Also, Kerry had just attended the annual OD Network conference and remembered a session that discussed the topic of OD summits and large group efforts. She quickly checked her notes from the conference and found three contacts—Angie, Gina, and Eric—who may be able to help.

Kerry quickly started to jot down some questions that would need answers:

(a) What are the top ten tools and techniques required for this effort? How can she map out the time line, and people power required for this effort?
(b) Beyond large group interventions, are there particular approaches that can provide positive aspects to change, while still keeping a business imperative for Levelco?
(c) How can Kerry define success on this initiative? What data should she use to measure the outcomes?

Perhaps with counsel from her OD Network colleagues, this large group intervention roll-out for Levelco's change initiative might have a greater chance for success. Let's see what advice Angie, Gina, and Eric can provide.

Angie Keister

Along with large group interventions, Kerry should strongly consider **her** strengths and past successes in determining various large group intervention approaches. Given Kerry's technical project management success, I would strongly recommend she consider a collaborative management research (CMR) approach or sociotechnical systems (STS) approach.

If Levelco is interested in Six-Sigma or Lean technologies, then an STS approach will parallel and complement those efforts and utilize the embedded organizational knowledge. Additionally, with Kerry's tactical experience and success of change efforts this would be a great way for her to help guide and facilitate the team.

Also, measuring outcomes for success is critical. I would recommend clarifying performance measures according to what matters to the CEO, most often in terms of the business performance. For Levelco, I would take a multilevel approach to measure, including some or all of the following:

1. Personal change stories. Team members and change recipients capture these and make them public in a safe way.
2. Employee survey data. If there is a standard measure, use it and see if it changes before, during, and after the change.
3. Measure the impact of the organization's social network. For example, by involving 10 people on the research team, how many people did they interact with regularly and map those connections out visually or put them into numbers that can translate to a percentage of involvement (e.g., 50% of the employees across the organization participated at an involvement level of 3% or greater).
4. Measure the impact and connections made of the change communications. Find a way for the communication to be two-way and measure the number of people who engaged in the change discussion.
5. Account for the time invested by each research team member and alongside that graph/measure their level of engagement in the organization to help justify their growth, learning, and time spent on the project.
6. Measure the outcomes of the change team several times throughout the process (including any in-house survey tools, ideas, common way to work together, or training) and produce an outcome report that classifies each outcome as a competitive advantage, sustainable resource, or appropriated resource (do or can you own it?). This translates outcomes into strategic and economic terms which will be a language that is understood by the C-suite.

My last piece of advice would be to recommend a shadow consultant; someone who has experience in the intervention approach that you choose and can serve as your coach and adviser. Specifically, it would be helpful to have a shadow consultant with a research background, easily obtained from a local PhD program, as this person will have access to the latest academic research and can help inform your process as well as assist you with the write-up and contribution of knowledge to the OD community. A shadow consultant can remain unknown to the large group team members, and often is never even on site.

Gina Hinrichs

Kerry poses an excellent question in wanting to go beyond large group interventions (LGI) to additional approaches that can provide positive aspects to change. Before I address her specific question, it is appropriate to reflect on the larger context.

Kerry's situation is enviable for those who have struggled to gain awareness and acknowledgment for OD. It bodes well that her CEO has learned about LGI from colleagues on Wall Street. LGI, as an engagement approach, is being seen to have the capability to positively impact a bottom line. Knowing that Levelco's top leadership is willing to risk and support an OD engagement approach to change is hopeful.

I would first acknowledge Kerry for reaching out to her OD community. Then, I would caution her to understand my insights are based on my experience and research. She must connect my suggestions to Levelco's context. She is the cultural expert to fit to Levelco's reality.

Kerry can go beyond LGI by focusing on broader OD engagement approaches. The term "Intervention" in LGI indicates to non OD's that there is something to be fixed. With engagement approaches, there is a focus on moving from good to great. Engagement approaches are designed for engagement, alignment, and commitment of diverse stakeholders. These powerful OD approaches utilize holistic and strength-focused perspectives to achieve innovation and faster cycle times for change. Instead of dealing with resistance to change, an organization will achieve engagement with change.

To meet Kerry's need for a design, a phased approach is offered below. The first three phases should occur over 3-6 months.

Phase I (2 days needed)—provide clarity, connection, and commitment—define the "What."

- (Day 1)—Conduct a SOAR (see Stavros, Hinrichs, & Hammond, 2009), *The Thin Book of SOAR; Building Strengths-Based Strategy (Strengths, Opportunities, Aspirations, Results)* strategic visioning session with leadership. This leadership session may involve 8 or 80 depending on Levelco's situation. Leaders still need to lead and they have the unique role to provide a broader and external perspective. They must provide the "What" of the new initiative. From this session, clarity and concrete results for the new initiative are defined.
- (Day 2)—Specifications to critical areas of the new initiative should be identified. This can be accomplished through a process that systematically investigates what is needed for organizational structure,

systems, culture, and process as they relate to the new initiative. Kerry should employ a model that fits Levelco's culture. For example, McKinsey's 7S or the Burke-Litwin change model helps to organize the conversations.

Phase II (~1 day needed)—Design Levelco's engagement approach. *The Change Handbook* (see Holman, Devane, & Cady, 2007) is a useful resource to determine what approach would be appropriate for Levelco's change initiative. To learn and improve the odds of a favorable outcome, Kerry should engage an external consultant for this first experience. Levelco's goal should be to make engagement approaches part of the culture; not just an event.

Phase III (2-3 days needed)—Conduct the LGI. The approach will afford diverse stakeholders engagement, alignment, and ownership of the identified projects for new initiative. The stakeholders determine the "How" of the new initiative.

Phase IV (Ongoing)—Provide follow up. As an internal consultant, Kerry can effectively support the teams and projects with dashboards, celebrations, and learning.

Again, Kerry must review and refine the above approach for Levelco's culture. She needs to take a deep breath and realize the risk to Levelco that doing nothing is greater than the risk of experimenting with a new OD approach. The potential rewards of engagement approaches are infinitely greater. Good luck.

Eric Sanders

Kerry has a great opportunity here, as both she and Levelco have a clean slate regarding the Large Group Intervention process. She has been running good interventions for 2 years, and has credibility across the firm. Now it's time to scale up a bit. I'd recommend she approach this process in four general steps: set expectations, review her own "tool kit" and resources, design the intervention, and show results (based on the agreed-upon expectations).

Set expectations. One point to remember, especially on Wall Street, is that leaders tend to focus on problems. It's our job in OD to help them look past those problems and envision a positive future, whatever techniques we might use.

Kerry needs to determine what goals need to be accomplished, and when. Business results generally fall into four categories: output (e.g., revenue), speed (e.g., processing time), quality (e.g., client satisfaction), and cost reduction. Levelco is sure to measure items in all of these categories.

Which does the CEO want to improve, by how much, and how soon? A good conversation should clarify that.

The CEO gave her a tight timeline. Once the need is clarified, an intervention technique can be chosen and a timeline created, which may require more than 4 weeks to be done well. When presented with a timeline to achieve the desired result, the CEO might find more time to implement the change. Kerry should do her research, and come back to the time restriction if necessary.

Tool kit and resources. Kerry has proven herself good at team-building, conflict resolution and strategic change. What else can she do? Data analysis? Applying systematic processes? Putting local change in systemic context? There are bound to be many transferrable skills Kerry can apply to this context, which will build her confidence further. As to human resources, Kerry has many available: previous clients, colleagues and faculty members from her OD master's program, and contacts in the OD Network could provide both conceptual help and assist in running events of whatever size.

Plan the intervention. The first two steps were necessary to see what needed to be done and what resources Kerry has available. Here's where the rubber meets the road. A large group intervention might be a summit using appreciative inquiry, future search, world café, or another process, depending on what Levelco wants to accomplish. All of these interventions collect and process a lot of qualitative data quickly. This nonnumeric data is then collected into themes and brought to life by the power of the collective voice of the people. There are two key considerations, regardless of which process you use. First, in the design, don't ask a question if you are not willing to act on the results. The disappointment from unmet expectations by the participants is worse than if you had not asked the question to begin with. Second, involve as many people as possible in the process. If the entire population cannot attend the large-group event, have leaders at various levels interview their direct reports beforehand, so they are vested as their representatives. Keep communications open in the action planning process and implementation of the plan agreed upon. Transparency is critical for any OD work.

Show results. If she's done the first three steps well, this part is relatively easy. Go back to the expectations, and jointly with the clients, set reasonable milestones toward achieving them using the information from the large-group event and follow-up. Celebrate successes early and often, as that will create momentum toward more and greater success.

Therese Yaeger and Peter Sorensen Respond

What exceptional advice for Kerry we have received from our expert panelists—thank you Angie, Gina and Eric! We would like to follow-up and reinforce a number of comments made by the panel. There are a number of very important, even crucial themes that run through the advice given by our panel. First, to team with an external person skilled in the intervention (the evidence is very strong that external/internal OD partners and teams contribute significantly to the success of OD). Second, the importance of expanding beyond the intervention itself and to evaluate the intervention over time, using both quantitative AND qualitative measures. Third, our panel sets forth several alternatives in terms of choosing an appropriate large group intervention, an intervention matched to the objectives to be accomplished within the situation. Fourth, is the specific suggestion that the OD term "intervention" itself reflects or implies the situation is being defined as a problem, "something to be fixed," while large group interventions in fact are oriented toward building on strengths and successes, moving from good to great. Fifth, OD is recognized, by Levelco (a culture with a strong orientation toward success and accomplishment) as an important vehicle for successful organization change with important implications for "bottom line" results.

What a great opportunity!! We are sure that Kerry, with the advice of her OD panel colleagues, will continue her successes at Levelco. With an exceptional OD career ahead of her, perhaps Kerry may be reporting at a future OD Network meeting and publishing in the *OD Practitioner* as well.

ACKNOWLEDGMENT

An earlier version of this article was published in *The OD Practitioner, 42*(3), 53-56.

REFERENCES

Holman, P., Devane, T., Cady, S. (2007). *The change handbook: The definitive resource on today's best methods for engaging whole systems* (2nd ed.). San Francisco, CA: Berrett-Koehler.

Stavros, J., Hinrichs, G., Hammond, S. (2009). *The Thin Book of SOAR: Building Strengths-Based Strategy.* Bend, OR: Thin Book.

CASE STUDY 4

PRESCRIBING A HEALTHY DOSE OF ORGANIZATION DEVELOPMENT FOR HEALTHCARE

Therese F. Yaeger and Peter F. Sorensen

Tremendous changes have occurred in both healthcare and organization development (OD) since OD guru Marvin Weisbord wrote his classic 1976 article "Why OD Won't Work in Healthcare." Healthcare is now undergoing the most extensive changes the field has ever experienced. OD too has changed, moving from its historical roots of small group interventions, to major large group interventions, strategic OD, Appreciative Inquiry, and other major changes. OD has also established itself as a highly successful field with an exceptionally high success rate, as documented by Dr. Bob Golembiewski. So let's combine OD and healthcare for this case history.

This case involves Karen, an experienced hospital administrator who has just been recruited from her position at a small, successful hospital, to become a chief operating officer of a large healthcare system. This large healthcare system has been experiencing a number of problems including decreased morale, turnover, and difficulty recruiting top-rate personnel.

Critical Issues in Organization Development:
Case Studies for Analysis and Discussion, pp. 27–35
Copyright © 2013 by Information Age Publishing
All rights of reproduction in any form reserved.

Karen is a bright, successful healthcare professional with a number of her early years as a nurse. Over the years Karen has moved upward in various administrative positions to this chief operating office (COO) role, which has always been her aspiration. Karen is highly regarded, well liked, and competent. This COO position, however, is her first executive position in such a large system. Karen is questioning what she should expect as she transitions into this new position and how she can successfully implement change, which will result in a changed culture with enhanced hospital effectiveness.

Karen, from her past healthcare positions, has knowledge of the potential contribution that OD can make to help improve an organization's performance. In the new healthcare organization, however, OD is not well understood and/or has been ineffective on a large scale. Regardless, Karen wants to connect with the OD manager to discuss opportunities for OD work.

As the OD leader in this healthcare operation, what recommendations would you give to Karen for opportunities with OD in this organization?

We asked three OD/healthcare expert consultants—Rosa Colon-Kolacko, Corinne Haviley, and Aimee Stash—to share their healthcare insights on what OD can do assist Karen in her transition.

Aimee Stash

Serving as an internal OD consultant within a healthcare organization presents unique challenges and opportunities. Assisting Karen during her transition into the COO role is a perfect opportunity for the OD practitioner to form a solid working relationship with the new COO, show the value of OD in the organization, and help improve the health system on both a micro- and macrolevel. The OD leader is well-positioned to serve as an assimilator for Karen, and to facilitate the cultural integration that must take place when a leader joins a new organization. The process of absorbing something new into something existent takes time and has inherent challenges, and the transition of Karen into her new role will require focused attention from the OD leader to help Karen, and the organization, achieve success. To help assimilate Karen, the OD leader should develop a transition plan that focuses on three key areas: opportunities for listening and learning, identification of big rocks, and assessing, aligning, and accelerating leadership talent. In each of the three key areas, there are specific actions steps the OD leader should take.

Opportunities for Listening and Learning: Identify key formal and informal leaders for Karen to meet with early in her tenure. Help Karen understand who she needs to have successful relationships with in order to be successful in her role (key medical staff leaders, product line leaders, key partnerships in community, etc.). Facilitate opportunities for Karen to listen to the staff and learn about the organization, such as employee forums, focus groups of leaders, and rounding in key departments. Support Karen as she implements "management by walking around" to get a feel for the climate of the organization. Encourage Karen to listen to the words used, the way people interact with one another, and to remain intellectually curious about the people, their roles, and the operations of the organization.

Identify Big Rocks: Help Karen work with her leaders and her peers to identify the key priorities for her to focus her energy and attention on. Weeding through the myriad of ongoing projects, outstanding issues, and operational objectives will be an important process for Karen so that she can gain a clear understanding of what matters most, and what needs attention first. After knowing the key priorities, the OD consultant can assist Karen in identifying intended outcomes and measures of success. Knowing what success looks like at three months, six months, and one year will help Karen create a plan for addressing the key operational challenges that face the organization.

Assess, Align, and Accelerate Leadership Talent: Here the OD consultant can help Karen evaluate key leaders in the organization, especially those reporting to her as COO. Develop a process so Karen can assess the leaders' capabilities, competencies, emotional intelligence factors, past successes and failures, education and work experience, and current roles and responsibilities. Knowing the depth and breadth of the leaders on her team is integral to Karen's success, as she can only be as successful as those around her. The OD lead can be a sounding board for Karen as she processes through the decisions about who to place into which roles, and how to handle those who are not meeting expectations. OD can help Karen determine the most appropriate organization structure for her area of responsibility, support her as she identifies leaders who are overleveraged or underleveraged, and facilitate the alignment of individuals into the appropriate positions. OD can also aid Karen in developing clear and consistent charters for the teams that she is responsible for to ensure an understanding of the groups' functions and responsibilities. Finally, support Karen and her team through various leadership development offerings that help them function on an individual, team, and system level.

An effective OD leader knows their organization well and understands both the culture and the climate. An incoming COO needs to be brought up to speed very quickly in order to assimilate effectively into their new role. Serving as an assimilator during the transition of an executive level leader is a prime opportunity for an internal OD practitioner to be a valuable resource to their organization.

Corinne Haviley

Understanding organizational culture is an intriguing and revealing process which may serve Karen well as a first step in addressing deficiencies, morale, and recruitment challenges. Culture, often defined as the expressed values, beliefs, norms, and artifacts, is dependent upon a construction of events, experiences, and staff relationships over time. Culture is a deeply engrained "way that we do things around here" that provides insight into behaviors, decisions, and organizational performance outcomes. Studying culture is a way of looking backwards and understanding what has led up to and what has been influential in the past. As environments change and new demands evolve, the learning and adaptation from the past may not work in the present or future. Deteriorating staff satisfaction, retention, and consumer satisfaction are often symptoms of deeper issues embedded within the culture.

There are several approaches to exploring organizational culture. One of the fastest means is to survey staff perception of their existing culture. Because organizational members may be unaware of their culture, self-administered questionnaires may prompt bringing employees to a consciousness of underlying values and assumptions.

There are multiple tools available that bring to light inter- and intra-organizational comparisons, dominant culture characteristics, and sub-cultures or cultures within a larger culture. These subcultures may be seen in different nursing units, within hospital departments, or among specialties such as nurses, physicians, pharmacists, and leadership staff. Most importantly, presenting the information gained from assessments of staff and leadership begins the process of culture first, and subsequently, change management.

Organizational culture in some organizations has resultant gaps between the culture that is expressed by individual members and those expressed within subcultures. When these gaps are wide, then the environment suggests that it will be more difficult to launch improvement strategies and initiate change.

Healthcare organizations can benefit from gaining an understanding of existing departmental or unit-based culture styles and determine what components of the culture can be released to increase capacity for change, leading to improved organizational performance. Karen can use several strategies to learn more about the strengths of the hospital's culture which takes time and support from "going down and in," meaning asking questions of the staff to realize the underpinning of daily operations. Most administrators have been trained to ask staff in small group sessions about "What is working well and what is not working well?" as the standard approach to assessing environments. This presents an avenue to paint a black and white picture of what is right and what is wrong. Frequently, what has been identified as wrong is what is focused upon while what is working well is ignored and falls out of focus. Another method is to incorporate an appreciative inquiry approach such as asking questions illuminating the positives, including "What are the most outstanding moments from this organization's past that make you proud to be a member of your department?" or "What should we try to preserve about our program and our unit- values, traditions, best practices-even as we change into the future?" or "If you had three wishes for your unit, can you describe what they would be?"

The most important intervention is spending the time to understand the quantifiable (survey) or the qualitative (feedback from work group sessions) data that reflects the existing organizational potential. Relying on your OD manager to gather this information will afford a more meaningful and objective method to determine the history behind the roots of this organization and the potential for the future.

Rosa M. Colon-Kolacko

I have been in my role of vice president of system learning for 3 years. One of my key lessons learned in healthcare is that business strategies and/or people-related functions are not that well understood. The term organization development comes across as "soft" and too much a part of the human resources world. I spent my first year defining the term organization development and how all our leaders are responsible to develop our people so that in return we can develop our organization capability. I recommend Karen and her new organization use the new emergent approach to OD called dialogic OD (Bushe & Marshak, 2009). Dialogic OD tends to rest on an opportunistic-centric approach, that is, social constructionism, which starts from common aspirations and shared visions, making engagement in the change process more appealing. I have found that in a healthcare setting this approach is more appealing to different cultures including the nurses, physicians, and administrators. In dialogic OD, change comes from changes in meaning-making and new, associated decisions and actions that people can and will take as a result of those changes in meaning. This will allow healthcare teams to move away from the traditional OD diagnostic approach that focuses more on a problem-centric approach, where the assumption is that the organization is broken and needs fixing. This can create a lot of resistance versus allowing conversations that can create positive energy and move people to action.

I also recommend paying attention to two areas: The first is leadership. Here, define the role and expectations of leadership within the health system. Effective leadership in organizations can have a great impact on organizational performance, as has been demonstrated across industry sectors. There is even more diversity of opinion on how leadership can be applied in different industries. I have found in healthcare that we tend to promote great clinicians into leadership positions. In the majority of the cases, these great clinicians have not been educated in leadership skills and/or do not have the background in behavioral change to be good at leading others. We also recognize that in almost every case where organizations fail, whether that organization is a surgical team, a hospital unit, a company, or a country, it is rarely the consequence of one leader's actions, but may well be that the overwhelming issue is the power of leadership and the hierarchy of leaders. We can also argue that each leadership situation is so unique that it requires more than one alternative model to explain them all. According to change management expert John Kotter, "Leaders don't make plans, they don't solve problems, and they don't even organize people; what leaders really do is to prepare organizations to change and help them cope when they struggle through it." To transform healthcare we need to harness the best thinking, the most productive collaborations, and the active engagement of every employee. It must start with the people on the front line of the transformation: its leaders. For Karen and her OD consultant, I recommend the development of a leadership program to re-define expectations and behaviors.

The second key area to address is culture at different levels. As Ed Schein (1985) describes, "culture is a pattern of basic assumptions, invented, discovered, or developed ... that has worked well enough to be considered valid and, therefore, is taught to new members as the correct way to perceive, think, and feel." In healthcare, this issue is more aggravated because one attempts to implement change in a setting where three key different cultures interact everyday: physicians, nurses, and administrators. These three cultures have different expectations, different mental models, and language. They perceive the patient and employees around them in a different way. In many cases, among these three cultures there is no understanding of such differences, and the only way to make this visible is to develop interventions and/or opportunities for them to come together to learn and get consensus on differences. Once this is done, the diverse group of collaborators can come together to find solutions and approaches to implement change successfully. It is amazing how much you learn as a leader and how much you enable learning by addressing internal cultural differences in an organization. This can make a great difference in the way to implement change and also can accelerate transformation.

Therese Yaeger and Peter Sorensen Respond

How well these respondents bring to light the numerous opportunities for OD in healthcare! It is quite clear things have changed since Marvin Weisbord reported the challenges for OD in healthcare. The situation for new COO Karen is very real in many healthcare organizations today— executives must get up to speed quickly in their new position. Collaborating with an internal OD consultant helps provide opportunities for good OD work and potentially more effective outcomes for Karen as COO.

For our experts' recommendations, each contributor provides similar and different suggestions on how to capitalize on OD knowledge. Aimee suggests the three areas of listening/learning, finding out what matters most (big rocks), and addressing leadership talent through assessing, aligning, and accelerating. We most appreciate Aimee's concept of using the OD leader to serve as an assimilator.

Corinne raised the issue of culture and the importance of gathering quantifiable and qualitative data to determine the history of the organization. She also suggested an appreciative inquiry method to illuminate the positives in the organization's traditions and programs, as healthcare often focuses on only the right and wrong.

While Rosa also mentioned culture, important too is her suggestion of Dialogic OD in that it is more opportunistic-centric. Rosa also addressed leadership issues, and while all three experts addressed the concept of leadership, Rosa specifically addressed leadership and the different challenges with power and behaviors in healthcare.

What we most appreciate in these three responses is the real healthcare knowledge and expertise that these OD practitioners bring to this case. Thanks to Aimee, Corinne, and Rosa for providing true expert advice for OD opportunities in healthcare.

ACKNOWLEDGMENT

An earlier version of this article was published in *The OD Practitioner,* *42*(3), 53-56.

REFERENCES

Schein, E. H. (1985). *Organizational culture and leadership.* San Francisco, CA: Jossey-Bass.

Weisbord, M. (1976, Spring). Why organization development hasn't worked (so far) in medical centers. *Health Care Management Review,* 17-28. (Reprinted in *Organizational diagnosis: A workbook of theory and practice.* Reading, MA: Addison-Wesley, 1978.)

CASE STUDY 5

QUALITY INITIATIVE IN THE PATHOLOGY LAB

John Nicholas and Homer H. Johnson

Bayside University Hospital and Medical School had recently introduced a lean Six-Sigma quality initiative throughout the hospital. One of the units specifically targeted was the hospital's pathology lab, which had been plagued by a number of somewhat serious internal quality problems. Marge Wilson had recently taken over as director of the lab, and her first priority was to reduce the number and quality of problems, hopefully to zero. Marge had worked in the lab and had also taken Six-Sigma green belt training, as well as courses in managing change, so she seemed to be uniquely qualified to address the issues.

The main function of the pathology laboratory is to prepare and diagnose specimen samples that arrive from different areas of the hospital (e.g., operating room or gastro/intestinal lab). All specimens follow a five-stage process through the lab:

- Accessioning—information about specimens arriving at the lab is entered into a computer.
- Grossing—specimens are visually examined and an overview description is written.

Critical Issues in Organization Development:
Case Studies for Analysis and Discussion, pp. 37–47
Copyright © 2013 by Information Age Publishing
All rights of reproduction in any form reserved.

- Processing—specimens are processed through a number of steps and ultimately put on slides and stained.
- Reading—pathologists view the slides microscopically and dictate the diagnoses.
- Transcription—the dictated diagnoses are transcribed into written reports.

The stages are virtually identical for every specimen sample, although the time at each stage varies depending on the type of sample.

The laboratory has 40 workers that range in educational background from high school (accessioning and transcription stages) and AS/BS (processing stage) to MS (grossing stage) and MD (reading stage). About half the workers are members of the laboratory staff and report to Marge, and the other half—the MD pathologists—are faculty members and belong to the pathology department.

Complaints regarding quality problems in the lab had been building for some time. Among the problems were misplaced specimen samples, inadequate or incorrect information about specimens entered into the computer, high variability for processing times and lack of standardization in procedures, mislabeling of slides, and poor quality of specimens on slides. To address the growing number of issues facing the lab, Marge developed what she thought was the perfect plan: for each of the stages in the lab process she would form a small team to investigate its problems and make solutions. Since most of the problems occurred in the accessioning, grossing, processing, and transcription stages, she created four teams each consisting of a champion, a facilitator, and three people who worked in the stage. Each team's champion would be someone well-respected by the team, usually an MD that people knew and liked, and its facilitator would be someone trained and experienced in Six-Sigma and lean production methods. The remaining three members would be workers from the lab, selected for their motivation and capability. Their place in the team would be crucial to ensuring the correct issues were addressed and for gaining buy-in from other workers for the solutions to be implemented.

Marge planned extensively for the initiative. She sent a small group of select people from her staff to receive training at a medical center well known for its innovative quality and continuous improvement efforts. She carefully chose the champions and facilitators, and rounded out each team with motivated, enthusiastic workers. Before starting the program she wrote a one-page newsletter and sent it to everyone in the lab. Her intent was to send the newsletter once a month thereafter to provide updates on progress and further rally support for the initiative.

The program commenced with a kick-off meeting attended by everyone in the lab. The chairman of the pathology department spoke briefly and voiced his complete support for the program. Marge gave an introduction to Six-Sigma and lean production methods and introduced the team members. Everyone seemed energized and ready to move forward.

The first task of the teams was to flowchart their assigned stages, and to identify the most significant defects or quality issues. There were many perceived problems, and it would not be possible to address all of them at once. Thus, early on the teams would have to prioritize the problems so the most important ones could be attacked first.

The teams were readily able to create the flowcharts, but when they began to look for quality problems they immediately ran into a roadblock: although everyone seemed to be aware of a wide range of quality problems in the lab, no one could say which were the most pressing or important because there was no data. The solution, it seemed, would be rather easy: gather data about the kind and frequency of quality problems or defects, and after a trial period identify which of them occurred most often or had the biggest consequences.

To track quality-related problems, Marge created a form on which to keep a record. Since most of the complaints about quality problems came from the pathologists (which made sense since they received specimen samples late in the process, and by that time, defects have accumulated from the earlier stages) they would use the form to record any quality problems. Marge attended a meeting of the Pathology Department, and with the support of the department chairman gave every pathologist a form with instructions to record every quality issue or defect they encountered. They were to do this for one week, during which time about 10 pathologists would be on duty. Marge felt that data collected by 10 pathologists for a week would be sufficient to determine which quality problems were the most important.

When Marge collected the forms at the end of the week, she got a big surprise. Seven of the pathologists didn't return the forms because they said they hadn't encountered any problems. For the remaining three who did turn in their forms, there were very few recorded problems. During the week the pathology group had reviewed about 500 specimens but noted only 14 problems; most of them were not even quality-related, but rather complaints about other issues. It was clear that the pathologists had simply not taken the data-gathering seriously.

Marge talked to the chairman of the pathology department about the results. He apologized but added that the pathologists probably had been very busy during the week. They decided to try it again during the next week, and at the next departmental meeting the chairman encouraged the pathologists to keep track of and record all quality-related problems they might encounter.

A week later when the forms came in the results were almost the same: only 3 of 10 pathologists turned in forms, although they were not the same three as in the previous trial. And just like the time before, the number of problems on the forms was very small. Each pathologist had reviewed roughly 50 specimens, yet one form listed 13 problems, another listed 6, and another only 3. Marge knew the success of her program hinged on getting reliable data from the pathologists, but she was at a loss on how to get their participation. Although they had always been quick to complain and point out defects, they seemed to have no interest in gathering data that could lead to eliminating those defects. Getting data was essential to resolving the problems, but that required commitment from the pathologists. They did not report to her, so she couldn't "order" them to gather the data, though she knew that likely wouldn't work anyway. The chairman of the pathology department had offered his support and "encouraged" his people to gather the data; although, looking back, Marge now felt that his support had been rather limp. Everyone on the teams was waiting for the data.

Marge was now extremely frustrated. She thought she had followed all the rules of effective change and of quality management. But it was not working! In search of an answer, Marge sought the assistance of the director of organization development (OD) for the medical center. If you were advising Marge, what would you suggest she do? Would you advise her to drop the initiative to resolve quality issues in the laboratory? What would you say about the apparent resistance of the pathologists? How can Marge get them aboard? Or should she find another way to address the quality question? Are there any general principles for dealing with situations like this?

We asked three expert OD consultants to assist us with this case and to give us their analysis and suggestions as to how Marge might resolve her dilemma. Dorie Ellzey Blesoff resides in Oak Park, Illinois and has extensive OD experience as an internal consultant in the healthcare, manufacturing, and service industries, and now is an independent consultant. Jay Morris has a strong OD and change management background in Fortune 100 companies, including healthcare, and is currently at the Yale-New Haven Health System in New Haven, Connecticut. Marilyn Blair is a Senior Consultant and principal of TeamWork in Denver, Colorado and was editor of the *OD Practitioner*, during which time she served as mentor to many in the OD profession.

Dorie Ellzey Blesoff

Should Marge drop the initiative to resolve quality issues in the laboratory? My answer: "No way!" What a great time to declare a "pause" in the process to review the approach so far and glean what can be improved going forward. This moment provides a twofold opportunity—to get back on course in the lab and to share the lessons learned so that others in the Bayside system become more capable of enacting the new organization-wide quality initiative.

What about the approach so far? The basic Six Sigma process is DMAIC—*define, measure, analyze, improve* and *control*. Perhaps the path lab initiative might have benefited from a sharper *define* phase, which includes identification of specific problems and measures (in addition to process mapping). While a clear conclusion had been reached that the pathology lab had "somewhat serious internal problems," there was absence of clarity about the basis for that conclusion: which problems recur, where, to what degree, how often, and so forth. In a more thorough *define* phase, this lack of data could have been discovered earlier in the game.

Even with a thorough *define* phase, it is sometimes learned that there is not an existing baseline from which to measure improvement of a process. If this is the case, it is important to begin tracking the process, using key measurables, such as turn-around time, quantity of errors, cost, and so forth.

In her effort to collect data, Marge's approach depended upon pathologists completing forms. Although the results were not considered significant enough, I am not ready to assume that the physicians were not committed or did not cooperate with the study. To establish meaningful data collection, other approaches worth considering include a "hotline" (single number) for pathologists to call and report specimen issues (from which a regular report could be generated), or a focus group with a cross-section of pathologists to help zero in on the most meaningful data to establish a baseline.

Are there some lessons learned? I'm guessing Bayside has a set of organizational values that likely include patient/customer service, quality, and excellence, among others. How could this project be positioned as an embodiment of the values? For example, perhaps the pathologists could be considered internal customers of the path lab since they owe timely and accurate specimen readings to other MD's (who owe results to patients). The pathologists need to be able to rely on predictable best practices in order to deliver their piece of the patient care puzzle. Would this help inform the best approach for collecting data?

I applaud the holistic planning on how to set up smaller teams across the lab. With a clearer definition of the baseline and improvement objectives, I think the project could have done well with an initial focus on just one process stage, implementing the Six Sigma steps, and developing capability in how to use the tools, and so forth. Growing from there might be more practical for managing the initiative overall, in the lab and in the entire system.

Jay Morris

Marge Wilson has a strong background in quality and Six Sigma, and has done a commendable job in addressing the issues facing the laboratory. She has put together what seems to be a logical approach to solving the problem. However, it appears that some of the key stakeholders have not been fully engaged in the development of her strategy.

Since she is new to her position, I would recommend that she meet with her department head to discuss her frustrations, review her progress and discuss the plans she has proposed. One of the areas where she might need some assistance is maneuvering through the political landscape and culture of the hospital. Although the pathology chair spoke at the kick-off meeting, it appears that his commitment, along with the pathologists', was not strong. I would also recommend that she identify and engage key stakeholders including the departments that rely on the specimens. At the end of the day, patient safety is at risk.

Marge received a number of complaints from the few Pathologists who had taken the time to provide input. In order to get their buy-in, perhaps she could have designed the strategy and obtained their input before communicating publicly. Marge drove all of the activity by: (1) giving an overview to the lean process, which was probably magnificent, (2) putting together a newsletter, (3) identifying teams, (4) sending people to training, and (5) determining the course of action. It appears that most of the activity identified in the case has been driven by Marge. The sponsors, whoever they are, and the pathologists were not involved in the upfront planning.

Marge has direct control over three stages of the five-stage process. I would recommend that she begin working in the areas where she has more control. She could have her team develop process maps for misplaced specimen samples, inadequate or incorrect information about specimens entered into the computer, high variability for processing times and lack of standardization in procedures, mislabeling of slides, and poor quality of specimens on slides. These areas are within the scope of her authority. The pathologists identified these areas, so why not narrow the scope to focus on these areas and engage the Pathologists after applying lean methodologies?

Hospitals, like other organizations, have a culture and a way of getting work done. The relationship between the lab and the faculty could be sensitive. Understanding the dynamics between the two groups is critical in order to move the work forward. I would recommend that Marge review the strategy with her department head and then meet with the Chair of the pathology lab to identify outcomes, define his role, and gain his full support.

Marilyn E. Blair

Marge ought not to drop the initiative to resolve quality issues in the laboratory as the matter of quality is more than important in such an exacting environment. Marge needs data from the pathologists. Professionals often resist "another project" when their plates are continually overloaded, or when some part of their work is not proceeding as expected. Breaking through that resistance is one of the primary skills of an OD practitioner.

There might also be some hidden conflict that needs to be brought into the consultation where it can be dealt with by a third party (consultant) working with client group members to resolve or manage.

Four action steps for dealing with the situation:

1. Establish a contract for OD work.
2. Schedule individual face-to-face interviews between the OD consultant and each pathologist and small group interviews with the lab staff that reports to Marge.
3. Provide an interesting and accurate data feedback session for everyone in the work unit.
4. Develop a NEXT STEPS Agreement with the client group at the data feedback session. Identify four or five group members who would like to work with the Consultant and assist in moving the project forward.

Establish a Contract for OD work: Marge and I need to contract for her role as client sponsor and mine as OD consultant. We need to talk about both roles with regard to our initial and ongoing responsibilities. An exploration of the client group responsibilities also must occur and the two of us need to come to agreement on that matter so that we can lead and support those responsible for doing the quality lab work. Desired

Outcomes of the consultation need to be a part of this contract. The contract should be in writing for future memory.

Individual face-to-face interviews between the OD consultant and each pathologist: I believe that individual face-to-face interviews between the OD consultant and each pathologist will yield the most truthful, thus useful data. Marge ought to be interviewed in this manner also.

Questions need to be the same for each interview; I do not share these questions prior to the interviews and I ask each interviewee not to do so either. Maintaining as much confidentiality as possible in the initial data gathering is an important step for developing consultant-client relationships, and in moving the consultation forward.

I will interview the executive to whom my primary client reports, that is, Marge's vice president, and any other executives whom I believe will benefit from being part of the interview process can be included also.

Small group interviews with the remaining lab staff need to be scheduled. These are as important as the pathologist interviews and the small group interview is very useful with staffs, primarily because the verbal interaction is lively and often provides the interviewees with a different view of the situation and their role in it.

Provide an interesting and accurate data feedback session for everyone in the work unit, including the pathologists and the executives involved: The most important part of the consultation is the data feedback; here is where the die is cast. I make sure that the client sponsor and interviewees, including executives, hear the message of the criticality of this time. I send everyone involved two or three e-mail message reminders of the session.

The presentation of the data can be a challenge. What is most important to me is to chart the data, structuring it to an organization model. Weisbord's 6 box model is my favorite because it is clear to the client group what organizational factors are being considered. I pass out the Data story in two forms when the session is concluded: (1) As charted and (2) the consultant data analysis.

Craft a NEXT STEPS Agreement with the client group at the data feedback session: Identify four or five group members who would like to work with Marge the project manager and the consultant to do the work of moving the project forward. I need to remember that Marge and I are joined at the hip. It is most important that the client group and the executives identify and experience her as the project manager and me as the consultant.

The primary OD principle I utilize in my consulting is active client involvement throughout the consultation process. Like most OD consultants, I love the social construction paradigm and the resultant interventions that have been designed and utilized widely in the last 15 years.

After experimenting for several years, I believe that where there is considerable resistance and/or conflict holding a work group back from accomplishing its goals, it is more effective and timely to utilize the traditional four to six step consultation process.

John Nicholas and Homer Johnson Respond

All of the members of our expert panel advised Marge to push on with the quality initiative. As often happens with change projects, the first attempt, even if well planned, does not have the expected effect. So, move on to Plan B. This is one of those "good" projects that all parties likely agree is important and critical to the hospital and the patients. So, it has a good chance of success if only they can get beyond this barrier.

But there is no obvious best way to approach Marge's dilemma, and beyond agreeing that Marge should press onward, the panel members each offered a somewhat different approach. Dorie posed the question about whether Marge had adequately defined the major problems facing the lab. While the consensus was that the pathology lab had "somewhat serious internal problems," it is not clear what the problems are or the measures used to identify them. Rather than rely initially on the pathologists to provide all the data, data could be gathered elsewhere at other stages of the process, of the process as a whole, or at the end of the process at the delivery of diagnoses to the "customer" physicians who made the request. Such data would provide a better understanding of the nature and magnitude of the problems, and of their effect on lab customers. Also, Dorie suggests that if data must be gathered from the pathologists, alternative means of initial data collection could be used, such as a hotline for them to call and report specimen issues or a focus group with a cross-section of pathologists. These might be adequate to determine the most prevalent or serious quality problems.

Jay offers good advice when he says that Marge might need assistance "maneuvering through the political landscape and culture of the hospital." Bayside University Hospital and Medical School likely represent at least two cultures: Marge and the lab represent one culture—the hospital; the pathologists represent another—the medical school. Culture and perceived status differences within groups can pose big barriers to changes that require everyone's involvement. One possible way to gain commitment from the pathologists, despite such differences, is to reference the lab's customers, anyone who relies on the lab for specimens and diagnoses. Ultimately, patient safety is the number one issue, and what must be driven home here is that data is needed from the pathologists to eliminate problems that put patient safety at risk.

Alternatively, Jay points out that Marge has direct control over three stages of the five-stage process, and rather than start data collection at the stage where she has the least control (pathologists reading the samples) she could begin in the stages where she has the most control—the first three. The quality initiative could then move forward, and results obtained from the data might be sufficient to suggest solutions to many or most of the lab's quality problems. A decrease in the pathologists' complaints would be a crude measure of the degree to which quality problems are being resolved.

Marilyn's approach is to determine the source of the pathologists' resistance—is it simply they are being overburdened with more work, or is it a potential conflict with Marge or someone else? To reveal the source of the resistance, she would interview each of the pathologists individually, members of the lab in small groups, and other stakeholders individually, such as Marge's boss and other affected managers. She would then present the data collected and her analysis to all participants at a structured data feedback session using, for example, Weisbord's 6 box model. Following discussion of the issues raised and reaching consensus on which are the key ones, the session would conclude by forming a small group to determine next steps to address the issues and to move the quality initiative forward.

The suggestions of our expert members address Marge's dilemma from different perspectives, though in our opinion they are all valid and represent additional or broader issues not included in Marge's original plan. As a next step, Marge could choose to adopt any one of them, or to create and implement a strategy that uses aspects of all of them.

ACKNOWLEDGMENT

An earlier version of this article was published in *The OD Practitioner,* *42*(1), 48-52.

CASE STUDY 6

ANTICIPATING MAJOR RESISTANCE IN METRO CITY

Homer H. Johnson and Tony Colantoni

It was difficult to miss the latest scandal in Metro City. The newspapers were having a field day with their exposé on the political hiring by the city government. Today's headline in the *Metro News* focused on the uncle of one of the city councilmen, who was hired by the city about 6 months ago. It was unclear as to what his job duties entailed, but it did not make much difference because he only showed up once a week in order to sign his time sheet and to pick up his pay check. The newspaper estimated that the effort took at most 20 minutes, which allowed him ample time to work (on city time) at a dog grooming business that he owned.

The scandal was the topic of conversation throughout Metro City, and that extended to the group of organization development (OD) consultants who were having a light snack just prior to the monthly Metro City OD Network meeting.

"What a hornet's nest! They have been trying for years to clean up that mess, but it keeps resurfacing," commented Bobby Wong, who had lived in Metro City most of his life, and who also had an OD consulting practice in the city. "What happened to the last court order?" Bobby was referring to a court order 4 years earlier that ordered the city government to end political hiring.

"Nothing happened. It's business as usual," commented his partner Carol Veron, "I don't see how the system is going to change, but my

Critical Issues in Organization Development:
Case Studies for Analysis and Discussion, pp. 49–57
Copyright © 2013 by Information Age Publishing
All rights of reproduction in any form reserved.

understanding is the court is going to make another attempt to institute change because of the recent publicity in the newspapers and television."

"Hey, how would you like to be an OD consultant on that project?" Bobby asked, which brought a roar of laughter from those seated around the table.

"It's not an OD project," someone said quickly when the laughter subsided. "The key to a successful OD project is client involvement, and this means that the client wants to cooperate with the change effort at least somewhat. It is pretty obvious that the level of cooperation is less than zero, given the history of failure here."

"Why should the employees want to change?" added Bobby, "Most of them got their jobs through political connections. The patronage system works well for them."

"And the mayor and the council persons love the patronage system because they can reward their political supporters with city jobs. Not a bad deal. They tell their supporters, if you get me elected, I will get you a job on the city payroll," Carol added. "So, why change a good thing?"

"Talk about resistance to change," Bobby said. "I think the court needs a magician, not an OD consultant!"

That statement brought on another round of laughter as several at the table repeated the statement, and with that they all got up and headed for the meeting.

Fast forward 6 months. Bobby was sitting in his office and received a phone call. The caller identified herself as an officer of the court and said she would very much like to talk to Bobby about undertaking a consulting assignment. She went on to explain that the court had issued a new order that specified the city must cease and desist hiring based on political consideration, and that it had 2 years to demonstrate the city was in compliance with that order. She had been appointed by the court to see that the order was carried out.

Bobby was listening intently and wondering what that had to do with him. He had nothing to do with the court or the city.

The court officer went on to explain,

> I think we need some help from you OD people on this. We don't think we can force change down the throats of the city. This didn't work last time. Rather, we need someone to work with the city agencies and help them get involved and committed to the change efforts. We can't whip them into compliance. Bottom line is that they need to implement the change themselves, and they need to take responsibility for making this work. That's why we need help from you OD change experts.

Bobby was speechless, and sat there stunned for a moment. All he could think of was the conversation he had with his fellow OD consultants 6 months ago. He finally recovered enough to thank her for thinking of him, and to say that he would have to think about her offer a bit more and would get back to her within the week.

In the next couple of days Bobby tried to find out as much as he could about the city's employment practices. The city government was large and complex, which one might expect for a city of 900,000. There were some 9,000 city employees who were assigned to 18 departments including the Department of Streets and Sanitation, the Water Department, Traffic Control, Building Permits, Health, Human Services, and even Rodent Control.

The city did have a centralized Human Resources (HR) Department that apparently was the beginning point for all hiring. Here all jobs were posted, applications were accepted, testing given, eligibility determined, and so forth. However, the final hiring decision was made in the individual departments from a list of three qualified candidates that was forwarded from HR to the department. On the surface this looked like a standard process that many companies use; however, somehow applicants were receiving jobs for political service, rather than based on their other qualifications. And from what Bobby could gather from the court officer, the court had already placed onsite monitors in the HR Department who were observing the application procedures, interviews, and eligibility reviews.

Bobby was not sure what to do regarding this possible engagement. On one hand, it was a unique challenge. On the positive side he thought that he could help make the city run a lot better, as well as to ensure fairness in job hiring and city services. On the other hand, he wondered if OD had any role in this project. Maybe the city isn't ready for an OD approach to change and the best strategy would be for the court to wield a big stick and to try to force compliance again.

Assuming that Bobby decides to go ahead with the project, what approach would you recommend he take? Where would he start? What would be some of his key interventions or change initiatives? What advice would you have for OD consultants that face a situation in which the client (indeed the whole system) seems to be very reluctant to change?

We asked a panel of experts what advice they would offer Bobby. Christopher Worley, Research Scientist, the University of Southern California and Associate Professor, Pepperdine University, together with Raymond R. Patchett, City Manager, City of Carlsbad, and Val Brown, Communications Manager, City of Carlsbad, combined to provide our first response. Eileen Gomez, the Human Resources Director for the City of Boulder, Co, provided the second response. Chris Pett, Director, Organizational Effectiveness and Leadership Development, Exelon Corporation, provided our third response.

Their advice follows.

Christopher Worley, Raymond Patchett, and Val Brown

There's a saying: "If you visit China for a week, you will think you know everything. If you live in China for a year, you will know that you know nothing." I've worked with government organizations enough to know better than to address the issues in this case without help. That's why I asked my coauthors to "shadow" me on this response—and boy am I glad I did. Government organizations are political systems, and any OD practitioner that does not recognize the role of power will be wondering which way is up. Are you listening, Bobby Wong?

First, Bobby needs to get a complete and confidential briefing about the legal and criminal matters under investigation. Quid pro quo and patronage hiring are illegal and nonnegotiable in most circumstances, yet the case suggests that prior court orders have been toothless and ineffective. It's inconceivable that a city, or any city official, would fail to respond to the Court. If the Court is concerned about giving the briefing, it's likely there is more here than meets the eye, and a poor time for an OD intervention.

Second, Bobby needs to know the answer to "Who is my client?" If the court is the client, then what sort of relationship are they expecting? Does Bobby feel comfortable being an "agent" of the court? That is, however far-fetched, the court may be asking Bobby to work confidentially (internal informant) on the investigation. Such a role would prove to be an interesting ethics test for the OD consultant. If the city is the client, then the client could be the mayor, the city council, or the city manager—or all of them! Knowing the form of government in Metro City will be a big determinant of this issue.

Third, if the legal and client questions can be answered, Bobby should determine "what problem is being solved?" For example, the hiring process described in the case is a common one, and the court has already installed an inspector. Are all jobs posted in the system? Can a department manager ignore the three names offered by the HR organization? Is the hiring authority protected by city charter or code? Perhaps most importantly, what percentage of hires has been outside the three names or could be considered patronage? It's entirely possible that the court is spending valuable time and money on one illegal hire, in which case there would be no need for an OD intervention at all!

Eileen Gomez

Background to Local Government: As an executive change agent new to the public sector, it was hard for me to understand the strong resistance to change and the slowness of processes until I took a local government class. The internal organization is a microcosm of the community and employees expect the same process as the community receives: having a voice, open government, and transparency. These are principles on which our country was founded to serve the people. Local government is a complex and evolving system with more pressure being put on local government from federal and state government, as well as from the people being served. The "system" consists of city council (the policymakers), city management (the implementers), and the community (the customer).

Case Review: This is a classic OD-type of project on one hand, as it requires a whole system approach to change. We know that change occurs for several reasons, vision and pain being two of those. The change didn't work last time because "it was shoved down their throats" (the pain factor). But what's missing is the accountability part. There was no enforcement to the last court order four years ago and this court officer doesn't seem to want any part of it this time.

On the other hand, and to echo one of the consultant's points, "The key to a successful OD project is client involvement and this means that the client wants to cooperate with the change effort at least somewhat." So who is the executive sponsor of this change? What are the consequences if there is no change in two years? What are the rewards for change?

Court orders, policies, and procedures are all tools, but meaningless without oversight and enforcement. The stakeholders, representing systems, that need to be involved are: the community to express their displeasure and, if necessary, elect new council members; the council who can create policy around the issue; city management; HR to ensure current job descriptions and sound hiring practices; and, managers who need to hold employees accountable to meeting their goals, enforcers, auditors and the court system.

If "the scandal was the topic of conversation throughout Metro City," there must be some energy around change, at least at the grass roots level.

As the OD consultant, Bobby needs to:

- Do some homework and find out what happened last time that was unsuccessful. It could be because a systems approach wasn't taken that it keeps resurfacing.
- Determine if he can find an executive sponsor. Who has the most to gain or lose from this change? Who has the ability to influence other key stakeholders?
- Help the executive sponsor develop a compelling vision for change.

- Mobilize other key stakeholders, including some key resistors. Use some of the energy created by the press.
- Help them develop a plan of action, including a public relations plan that includes a timeline, accountability, and evaluation.

My primary advice would be if you can't find a reliable executive sponsor, don't take the work, and if you can, prepare for a long engagement. Systemic change in a public sector environment is slow and rewarding.

Chris Pett

Most of us would likely agree at the outset that there is no OD "solution" to this situation. Coming from an organization with a compliance-driven culture, this case demonstrates the limitations of compliance as only a short-term strategy for enduring change.

But that is the question. What is the real change Bobby is challenged to facilitate? How might that change be characterized?

- Dismantling the belief system that this is politics and the way it's always worked?
- Redesigned hiring and personnel practices?
- Driving a shift to an accountability culture?
- Cleaning out City Hall—regime change?

In actuality, no one will truly know what the real change is without a collective effort of all the stakeholders who determine that there is a better way to run a city and keep in balance the needs of its stakeholders. We are now in search conference territory, which is an intervention that is far out ahead of what is possible at this point in time. Bobby's opportunity is to find the right entry points of the right influencers in this system to sell the idea of the leadership opportunity that buys the mayor a solution that comes not from advisors or political expediency, but from a true representative group of all the city's stakeholders.

More specifically, Bobby could take these actions towards a longer-term change:

- Do the research on governmental interventions that addresses the systemic drivers of the behaviors and attitudes.
- Break the systemic realities into workable pieces that, combined, will create critical mass; for example, support efforts to get some integrity into the hiring process and help the HR function operate more strategically versus just being a personnel function; also,

build an aggressive and robust communication plan that quickly gets key leaders out in the community delivering key messages about change.

- Leverage the oversight functions that lead to building the case for an accountability culture; research indicates that noncompliant (read illegal) activities in a corrupt system are reinforced by a belief that there are no real consequences to doing the wrong thing—this belief system needs to be dismantled to remove any meaningful rewards and benefits to sustaining these behaviors.

- Partner with community organizers to build broad alliances to advocate for and frame the needed changes; leverage prior change efforts, such as school reform, to better understand what it takes to sustain this kind of process.

- Find out who has leverage with the mayor and other behind-the-scenes advisors or people of trust within the influence structure and engage them in a way that builds some trust and line of sight to what a preferred future might look like; what serves some purposes (e.g., political capital) for making changes to how the system is currently operating.

- As this line of sight becomes more real and leads to a road map for change, link this work to some significant milestone or initiative that becomes the anchor for making changes—almost helping to save face, but in reality, makes change more easily communicated to a broader base of stakeholders.

While there may be consensus across broad segments of the city that the system is corrupt and of course, it needs to change, the scope and difficulty of intervening in a highly entrenched political and social system is extreme and long-term. A consultant asked to take on this work would benefit from taking the quick-hit, high-impact actions first to create a sense of movement and intentionality, and then work specific change efforts, segment by segment, on a longer-term basis while engaging as many stakeholders as possible, even the mayor!

Homer Johnson and Tony Colantoni Respond

Great suggestions from the panel! This is very obviously a difficult assignment for an OD consultant, as noted by all members of the panel. And this is probably something Bobby might decline given that he thinks his approach will not be of help. It is important for a consultant to understand his or her limitations (including the limitations of the methodology), and be honest with the client when it does not appear that his or her efforts will be of value to the project.

Without repeating the panel's insights, a couple of points deserve emphasis. Chris Worley and his associates nicely advise Bobby to do his homework before jumping into this project. As they note, governments are political systems and this one may be more political than most. Determining the client identity is also a key question here. Is it the court, or the city, or the council? Interesting question! Moreover, what problem is to be solved? The answers to these questions are not as obvious as they might first seem.

We like the background information Eileen Gomez offers, particularly how local governments differ from other systems. She also emphasizes the need to do one's homework on this project, particularly understanding what happened the last time this was attempted. Why didn't the change take? There should be some important learnings here. She gives a hint of what might have happened in her discussion of the need for the client system to cooperate in the change. You can't force someone to do something they don't want to do, because as soon as you aren't watching, they will revert back to the old behavior. And she follows this by talking about the need to find an executive sponsor, to mobilize the key stakeholders, and then (a very critical point) have them develop the action plan, not Bobby, nor the court.

At the risk of putting words in Chris Pett's mouth, he has made a very significant point when he suggests using multiple leverage points. The more leverage points used, the better the change will take, and the more it will become a continuing part of the culture. For example, leverage the oversight function (court) to build the case for accountability. That is, make sure the city knows that there are serious consequences for continuing illegal behavior. Also, partner with community activists, the business community, and the press. Great change strategy! Chris also emphasizes the need to engage the mayor and other key stakeholders. Somehow he or she, and they, have to get behind this effort.

Many thanks panel for very insightful advice. This case is part of an ongoing change project. Reader suggestions on how to proceed on the project would be gratefully appreciated. E-mail Homer Johnson at hjohnso@luc.edu or Tony Colantoni at tony@sgcconsultinggroup.com.

ACKNOWLEDGMENT

An earlier version of this article was published in *The OD Practitioner,* *40*(1), 47-50.

CASE STUDY 7

RESOLVING AN HUMAN RESOURCES PROBLEM AT METRO TRANSIT

Homer H. Johnson and Michael F. McGovern

Monday was not going to be a good day for Ahmed Das, the Vice President of Human Resources (HR) at Metropolitan Transit System. Before he had a chance to taste his morning coffee, Ahmed received a call from Billy Watson, the Vice President of Operations, who didn't bother to say "hello," but instead blurted out, "What the hell is going on with you guys in HR?" Billy's normal demeanor was to be blunt and a bit gruff; however, Ahmed could tell that Billy was really irritated about something this morning.

It turned out that Billy said he had been receiving complaints from Rail Operations regarding the quality of candidates in the *rail operations manager* pool, and for some reason he thought the problem was with HR's training area. "How come your training program is not delivering the people we need? What's wrong with the training anyway? You guys in HR need to get with it! We're expecting some retirements and we need qualified people to fill these positions."

Billy went on to explain that of the cohort of eight management candidates who had completed the manager training 11 months ago, only four remained. Two candidates had been removed from the "pool" at the request of the rail operations director due to their inability to perform the

Critical Issues in Organization Development:
Case Studies for Analysis and Discussion, pp. 59–67
Copyright © 2013 by Information Age Publishing
All rights of reproduction in any form reserved.

job, and the other two had resigned, complaining that they hadn't been adequately trained or informed about what the job entailed.

Metro has an extensive and complex rail system that covers both the city and suburbs in the Metro area. This system includes underground (subway), ground level, and elevated rail service.

Rail operations managers are a critical part of the rail system. Their major responsibility is to ensure that the trains are running on schedule. Probably the most difficult of their duties is dealing with disruption in service, which might be caused by any number of problems including equipment failure, crew shortfalls, weather problems, fires, attempted suicides, bomb threats, and so forth. Since trains are not easily or quickly rerouted or replaced, it takes considerable ingenuity and skill to maintain the integrity of the rail system operation.

The training program for new rail operation managers is one of the last steps in the process for selecting and training new managers. First, there is a call for applicants for the manager position. This call is open to all Metro employees, and it usually results in a large number of applicants from various parts of the organization, including employees without rail experience, as the rail managers are well-paid. The first cut is made by the HR staff, which eliminates employees who are recent hires or who have had attendance or disciplinary problems.

From the remaining pool of candidates, HR narrows the list to 15 or 20 candidates by reviewing the applicants' annual assessments, work performance records, as well as soliciting evaluations from the candidates' supervisors. The remaining applicants are interviewed by a panel of three or four interviewers, the composition of which varies from interview to interview; however, it always includes a representative or two from HR and at least one manager from the instruction department. They are joined by a current rail operations manager, although lately scheduling problems have made managers' attendance difficult. HR then picks eight candidates based on panel ratings.

Usually a cohort of eight manager candidates is trained every 12 or 18 months, or when the manager pool is running low. The week-long training covers the basic rules governing the running of the rail system, but also puts considerable emphasis on the service disruption problems noted above by using simulated incidents. The candidates are then placed in a manager pool from which they are called on to temporarily replace the regular rail operations managers who are sick or on vacation. Their performance in these temporary assignments is evaluated, and those whose performance is acceptable are eventually promoted to become a regular rail manager.

Ahmed was initially a bit irritated at Billy's demeanor on the phone. However, he realized that Billy had a serious problem and that he was counting on HR to solve it quickly. Ahmed had his suspicions that the training program might not be the problem, but he did not know for certain. The training program had been designed collaboratively with the rail operations managers who had approved, and even praised, the content. It was basically the same quality program that had delivered a group of highly qualified management candidates two years ago. The same folks voicing concerns now had been delighted then. However, something was obviously not working now.

While Ahmed didn't know where to begin to sort this out, he had a good idea as to who might help, and he immediately put in a call to Sharon Woo, the Metro Transit Systems Manager for Organization Development. Sharon was well-respected among the people at Metro, and she was also part of the HR function. One of Sharon's strengths was that she was a "systems person," and Metro was a giant transit system with complex interrelated parts, each of which could have a profound effect on the total system.

In fact, Sharon had just completed an assignment with rail operations in which she had led a task force designed to make it much easier and quicker for customers to use the bus/rail transit system by focusing on coordination at "transfer points." While Sharon did not have the subject matter expertise in many of the areas she was involved in, she was very good both at helping the subject matter experts identify the critical points in the system and also in conducting a diagnosis of how these points affect one another. Moreover, she had developed a model for implementing change at Metro that worked quite well by involving the right people on the right tasks in the right sequence.

Assuming you are Sharon, what advice would you give to Ahmed? What approach would you take to solve this problem? How would you start? Where should Ahmed and you be looking? Who should be involved? More generally, how might the OD approach and/or OD practitioners assist HR? What are some areas in which HR/OD collaboration would be most valuable? What are some areas in which HR or OD should be working separately to help ensure success? What dilemmas or challenges do you anticipate that HR and OD might face on this project?

We asked three consultants who have expertise in both the HR and OD areas to assist us with the case and give us their analysis and suggestions regarding the current problem as well as advice on HR/OD collaboration. Kathleen Buchman is currently Managing Partner, Buchman Consulting Partners, LLP, and an adjunct professor at Benedictine University. Anthony Buono is Professor of Management and Sociology and founding coordinator of the Alliance for Ethics and Social Responsibility at Bentley University. Donna Hapac is a Performance Consultant with Health Care Service Corporation.

Kathleen Buchman

What an incredible opportunity for OD and HR to chart a course for highly collaborative work between OD, HR, and Operations!

Sharon is fresh from a project in which she has quickly been able to articulate how critical components of the system behave, while also helping people better understand and successfully implement change. While these skills will serve her well in this new endeavor no doubt, her greatest advantage is that she's already established herself as a trusted resource in rail operations.

Since Ahmed initiated the request, Sharon will want to talk with him first to be sure that she fully understands his perspective on the situation. Areas that could be explored include the selection process, composition of the interview panel, and the information candidates are given regarding the job itself. It will be important for Sharon to listen attentively, ask clarifying questions, and to let Ahmed know that she'll be soliciting Billy's perspective on the situation as well. In addition to exploring the current process and perceived issues with Billy, Sharon will have some specific questions about this year's candidates and the circumstances surrounding the situation. She will also want to learn more about the retirements Billy mentioned in his call. Meeting with both VPs will help Sharon understand the bigger picture and the relationship between the two vice presidents (VPs).

Following one-on-ones, Sharon will want to facilitate a conversation between the two VPs to ensure that both have an integrated look at what's happening and that both participate in the improvement discovery process. She should be prepared to facilitate emotional ownership and problem identification disagreements. Taking a "let's look at the facts first" approach may help disseminate some of that and pave the way to having both VPs identify short-term, immediate steps to be taken, people to be involved, and resources on hand that can be utilized for a transitional fix of the problem. Longer term, the challenge will be that of working to implement a program that ensures the pipeline for skilled manager candidates is full and fluid.

HR, OD, and operations will be collaborating on process and content expertise. Sharon will use her process examination, change management and facilitation skills to explore improvement opportunities, while Ahmed will use his knowledge and experience as a strategic HR expert in considering people, practices, costs, and potential legal implications that exist as improvement ideas surface. Billy will provide real-time operations insight and experience that will enhance the overall design of an effective candidate training program. In addition, he may be able to leverage the retiree talent bank, by creating a reduced-hour mentoring role for successful, experienced rail operations managers to mentor new, inexperienced candidates. Understanding, accepting, and managing the changes necessary for success in this endeavor will be the responsibility of all.

There is no doubt that this is an opportunity for OD, HR, and operations to capitalize on a mutual crossing over of skills!

Anthony F. Buono

Based on the information provided, which, as is the norm, raises more questions than it answers, Sharon should begin with an exploratory conversation with Ahmed. The concerns about training and frustration expressed by Billy Watson could very well be due to some missteps by Metro Transit's HR group or a reflection of much deeper and more problematic challenges faced by the transportation system.

The best place to start is a fact-finding discussion with Ahmed in which Sharon raises possibilities and questions that need to be explored. Much of the problem could lie in a poor explanation of the job and failure to adequately prepare newcomers for what the position actually entails. The attractiveness of the well-paying position is perhaps drawing people who are not really equipped for the job, especially those without any rail experience.

Noting that the training program was one of the last steps in selecting and training new managers, Sharon should explore whether realistic job previews are included early on in the process. A reality is that many job applicants have relatively little insight into the job for which they are applying, often with significant misconceptions about what it actually entails. And despite scheduling difficulties, it is imperative that a rail operations manager be part of the final interview process. It is important to stress that developing a highly skilled transportation system work force requires a collective effort.

A second possibility concerns the content of the training itself. No real information is provided as to how the training was devised. Training is a complex activity; and even when programs are designed by technical experts, all too often little thought is given to design and delivery. It's not clear that any training needs assessment or evaluation was conducted that would have helped the organization to focus on the critical issues involved in success. Drawing on the experience of the last cohort of successful managers, it would be useful to have them evaluate the development process, drawing out what worked, where they found gaps in their training, what else might have been useful, and so forth. Just because a particular program might have appeared to be successful in the past, without such evaluation there really isn't any basis to determine the factors that actually facilitated that success.

Beyond the immediate concern, a potentially deeper and endemic issue in many mass transit systems is the safety and reliability concerns that have been escalating due to deferred maintenance of existing systems. Given Sharon's system orientation, she needs to help the organization explore if its problems might be a function of aging equipment and infrastructure, overly-strained resources, a lack of capital investment, and related challenges. Despite a good training program, the system itself might be structured for failure.

A potential problem is that, as with many HR Departments, at Metro Transit OD appears to be seen as a project-oriented function, focused on specific interventions and called in when problems arise. Sharon will be challenged to show that OD must be a strategic partner with HR if Metro Transit is to be successful. Billy's "blunt" and "gruff" manner, which tends to be the norm rather than the exception in transportation systems, reflects a culture that is likely to be skeptical at best about OD. However, building on her past successes and exploring possible challenges—from realistic job previews, to more thorough training needs assessment and evaluation, to an assessment of the broader complexities that might be involved—should provide Sharon and Ahmed with a good foundation to start their work with Billy and other key stakeholders in the system.

Donna Hapac

This case study presents an excellent example of just how interrelated the parts of a complex system can be. It appears that Sharon's task force on coordination of transfer points may have introduced significant change into rail operations at the Metro Transit System. One of my first questions for Sharon would be, "On your task force, did you include anyone responsible for the design and/or updating of the training for new Rail Operations Managers?" If one had been involved, I wonder if that individual recognized the changes that might have to be made to the program to incorporate the new process.

This case generates many questions; Sharon and Ahmed could pursue several avenues of inquiry to seek root causes. What else in rail operations may have changed since the last time a cohort was trained? The program, which is scheduled approximately every two years, obviously worked well to prepare the previous cohort for success.

Has the most recent cohort been brought up to speed on the new model for implementing change? If this model applies to any kind of change, including service disruption, everyone who has to be involved needs to understand the model. Perhaps the manager's role in the coordination is overwhelming or unclear.

As OD manager, Sharon may need Ahmed to get background data about the last two candidate pools. Are they members of different generations, differing numbers of years of experience, differing experience with solving complex problems, and so forth? If the screening process does not consider essential traits like ingenuity, candidates without that trait might burn out regardless of their ability to meet the other mentioned requirements.

One point that shocked me was that HR makes the final decisions on which applicants go into the candidate pool (even if scheduling problems may have prevented a current rail operations manager from participating in the interviews). Did that happen? The case does not make that clear, but seems to imply that it could happen.

Another question that Ahmed or Billy needs to answer for Sharon is about the expected retirements. Could the potential retirees be ambivalent about retiring and be sabotaging the new managers? Or are other workers in the system making life difficult for the latest cohort out of envy?

A final question I have is about the level of problems for rail operations managers to deal with. Has there been a significant uptick in disruptions? Did the new coordination of transfer points have an exponential impact on the number of disruptions or the difficulty in resolving them?

These questions require both cooperation and separation of HR and OD. Traditional HR has had the role of establishing policies and enforcing them, and ensuring that labor laws and union contracts are followed. OD, on the other hand, has a different focus and often manages and/or facilitates projects to address specific issues. But, we cannot forget that operations personnel are another key stakeholder group in resolving the attrition problem with the rail operations manager pool. Looking at systems and how to make them work often requires the sharing of multiple perspectives not bound by anyone's day-to-day role. In any case, these three professions need to confer and share regularly to understand how their roles are interconnected in the larger system and to recognize how their actions may impact each other's roles.

Homer Johnson and Mike McGovern Respond

Nice job, panel! Some great observations and suggestions!

One key observation by the panel that impressed us was that the resolution of this problem requires the collaboration of not only OD and HR, but also rail operations. Both HR and OD are support functions in an organization, and as such, they are not there to serve themselves but rather to serve another unit- in this case, rail operations. Thus the collaboration with HR and OD is also in collaboration with rail operations. The relationship of OD to HR is best assessed and oriented in the context of what serves the client business or organization.

Kathleen nicely points out that Sharon's primary role is to facilitate the efforts of HR and rail operations in examining the current situation to determine the possible causes of the problem, to develop and implement appropriate solutions, and ultimately to ensure that the desired outcomes are achieved.

The OD consultant should not own the problem. The integrity of selection, development, evaluation, and placement are rightfully the responsibilities of HR as stewards of these processes. It is also critical that these processes involve the active partnership and participation of rail operations, who are ultimately responsible for the effectiveness of the rail operations function and will ultimately live with the consequences of these HR processes. Key decisions at each point should be made by rail operations consistent with HR process requirements.

The panel also offered some great ideas as to where the group might begin to look for the root causes of the problem. Tony targets the possible problem area of the managers having poor insight into what the job entails, and also the fact that rail operations people were often not part of making the crucial decision at final interviews. Related to the first point, Donna suggests looking into the background of the recent cohort group (versus previous groups), and also raises an interesting question as to whether the recent system changes in the coordination of the transit points necessitated a change in the training of the managers.

Many thanks to Kathleen, Tony, and Donna for helping sort out this very complex problem and clarify the role of HR and OD in the process.

ACKNOWLEDGMENT

An earlier version of this article was published in *The OD Practitioner,* *42*(4), 51-55.

SECTION II

RESOURCES AND THE BOTTOM LINE

CASE STUDY 8

TODAY'S CHALLENGING TIMES AND THE ROLE OF ORGANIZATION DEVELOPMENT

Therese F. Yaeger and Peter F. Sorensen

Insuranco is a large insurance corporation with a 100-year history. The organization has experienced continued growth until recently. During the last 6 months, the company has become vulnerable to the deteriorating nationwide economic environment. Sales and profits are down significantly. The company has done well in the past during economically challenging times, but this time it is different as the organization attempts to cope with declining sales and profit margins. The company has a history of competent leadership and strong human resources orientation, but it now appears that management is confronted with the possibility of the necessity for significant reductions in personnel costs. The company has an established organization development (OD) function, which receives strong support from management. The President of the company has called a meeting with Susan, the Director of OD. The meeting agenda will focus on the role and strategies of the OD function in dealing with this situation.

Critical Issues in Organization Development:
Case Studies for Analysis and Discussion, pp. 71–79
Copyright © 2013 by Information Age Publishing
71

The president is very much aware of the potential long-term harm that can be done to the corporation if the financial situation is not dealt with in the best possible way to meet the short-term economic and financial crisis, and at the same time maintaining a strong human organization with a highly productive system for the longer term future.

Susan, the director of OD, is in the process of preparing for the meeting. This is a different situation than Susan has faced in the past. Previously, all the OD activities have been focused on providing support for the organization in terms of sustaining and strengthening a highly positive and productive culture. Susan understands that this is the first time that the OD function has been called on to develop strategies for sustaining the existing culture under highly speculative and unfavorable conditions. Susan also understands that the OD function has always had the support of the President. This support has been built over the years through a history of always being able to deliver and being proactive in developing supportive strategies. This time, however, both Susan and the corporation were caught by surprise, as the economic situation had deteriorated at a pace clearly unanticipated—not anticipated by the corporation and clearly not anticipated by its competition. Susan now is thinking about how she is going to respond to this new situation of crisis. How will OD be able to contribute to the reduction in cost and personnel and still sustain the positive culture which has been the hallmark of the company? Finally, how does the OD operation continue to maintain its status as one of the most highly regarded OD operations in the field? There is truly so much at stake for the short-term, for the long-term, and for the status and reputation of the OD function.

Susan wonders what she can do to prepare for this meeting with the president. Perhaps the president does not know what OD's contribution can be? Ultimately, what can OD do for the organization in these challenging times? What advice would you give Susan?

We have asked three highly seasoned, experienced OD practitioners to address what they would do if they were in Susan's situation, or what kind of advice they would give to Susan if they were asked to do so. First, we have advice from Rob Kjar who is at a large Japanese Pharmaceutical company. Recently Rob returned from a year in Japan and has the opportunity to reflect on his experiences there and some of the consequences of Japan's economic difficulties of the past decade. Second, Dawn Newman of Boeing, provides her thoughts on what Susan can address going forward for Insuranco. Finally, an external OD consultant, Neesa Sweet, brings an external/internal view of possibilities for Insuranco.

Rob Kjar

This timing could not be better for experienced OD practitioners. This is a great environment to show the benefits that can come from maintaining a strong focus on both culture and operational soundness. Many of us in OD grew up having to defend why a corporation should engage in a major change initiative or a cultural renewal, for example. I can't think of a better time than this to focus on what made the corporation great, and what will keep it great. This is the time to reenlist the workforce to do jobs that will add greater value at less cost. The internal OD consultant is the best value at a time when you need to look across the board at all external projects, new systems, and infrastructure improvements.

In Japan, where the economy has been on a slow burn since the bubble burst in the 1990s, what is still dragging on growth has a lot less to do with the new so-called J-SOX rules for financial governance, and much more to do with the institutional inertia that slows the entire system. Many of the Japanese institutions are staggering under the weight of their own traditional views regarding the workforce, such as legacy prerequisites, life-time employment, and predominantly male management systems. I am not arguing that traditional views are necessarily bad, only that if our ideas are limited to one way of envisioning the future, we may not have the core organizational capabilities to flex and adjust as conditions change.

Failing to ask the right questions during a time of crisis can lead to structural shifts—even strategic shifts—that fail to achieve the material benefits promised. Skilled OD people can raise the difficult questions, such as:

- What is the organizational capability to rally behind a vision when that vision is not about growth and expansion?
- What trust have we built so that once compensatory incentives are decreased or removed, we can lock arms and move the company forward?
- How can our organization shift from profitable prosperity to energizing support for efficiency initiatives?

OD professionals can demonstrate leadership in these times by rolling up their sleeves and engaging the organization in a new conversation. In the past, we have handled sticky change initiatives, have supported new leadership directions, and have aligned the organization to common goals—so what's different now? I would characterize the main tasks into these buckets:

- **Right talent**—what are you doing to communicate with the leaders and high-potential successors whose brains and brawn are going to be needed to weather the storm? What can you do to lock them in with longer-term incentives to share the ownership accountabilities that are felt at the top? Reenlisting your top performers does not have to be about promotion—it can be about shared risk and shared profit.

- **Right focus**—what can you stop doing now, and how quickly can you stop it? What initiatives, programs, and projects are you pursuing that have not shown promise for too long, and need to be killed? Seize the opportunity to refocus people on their core responsibilities and alleviate some of the wasted efforts thrown after chronic problems. This will also help you see what initiatives are worth saving, and the case becomes stronger as you lay everything open to closer scrutiny.

- **Right process**—while refocusing your team, look to your customers, your products, and your stream of work that supports your core business. What can you do with little cost or no cost to eliminate inefficient protocols, redundant paperwork, and clogged communications, and to improve decision making? This is not the sexy work of growth and expansion, but it is a way to achieve meaningful efficiency and positive cultural change.

Times of crisis call for skilled OD practitioners to do what they do best—to develop within the organization the capabilities it needs to survive and thrive.

Dawn Newman

Susan and the OD department have a great opportunity to exercise strategic business partner skills they have developed. It is important for Susan and her team to get ample information about the current state of the business before formulating options. Most likely, she will need to involve multiple departments and follow a structured process to properly assess the situation.

While it is important to compare Insuranco's situation to competitors', I recommend a deeper exploration of the internal business. In light of the environment, they could start by verifying relevance and priority of existing strategies and company vision. If change is needed, the OD group can help leadership create an effective and timely approach to communicate the future direction and path forward.

Before concluding that personnel cuts are the answer, highlight what is really contributing to Insuranco's bottom line. Focus on issues such as measures, processes, costs, involvement, suppliers and funding:

Markets and Measures: Are sales and profit margins consistent in all markets, or are there some areas of growth to leverage? Insuranco may choose to get out of certain markets that are not profitable and invest in specific growth areas.

Internal Processes: What are the core internal processes and how are they performing? Identify and eliminate waste to improve productivity and help the bottom line. Consider both short-term efforts and those requiring a longer time horizon to improve. Simplify work processes to reduce non-value-added steps and create open capacity to take on new work, perhaps from competitors who don't survive the economic downturn. Consider outsourcing or eliminate noncore processes in order to stay viable.

Personnel Costs: What are the major components of personnel cost? Before downsizing, consider addressing other cost areas. Insuranco may opt to freeze salaries, limit executive compensation, offer early retirement packages to stimulate natural attrition, and reduce medical and education benefits rather than choosing layoffs.

Involvement in Creating the Solution: If given the right forum, Insuranco could involve the employees in coming up with innovative ideas to cut costs immediately and grow the business. By including a representative sample of impacted employees upfront in the process, the organization's leaders gain credibility and demonstrate open, honest communication. This organization has succeeded in the past because it values people and has a culture of inclusion. A high-engagement approach reinforces the stated values and encourages employees to be part of the solution.

Suppliers and Customers: What are end customers saying about Insuranco? Identify key differentiators that promote customer loyalty and build upon those. Insuranco could leverage strong supplier relationships to generate options for creative cost-sharing, global supplier partnerships, and entry into new markets.

New Funding Sources: Identify any external funding opportunities within the supply chain or at the federal, state, or local level to help the company emerge from the downturn.

In tough times some companies overreact and immediately turn to layoffs as the first response. By combining a thorough business assessment, stakeholder-generated solutions, and an effective change management approach, Insuranco improves the likelihood of short and long term gains and minimizes negative impact on people.

Neesa Sweet

Have you seen the picture of Albert Einstein riding his bicycle through Princeton? "To keep your balance," he said, "you must keep moving." This is the essence of Susan's advice, both to herself and to the president. She, he, and Insuranco are about to steer their bikes over a bumpy cobblestone street.

Susan has worked in the good years to develop trust, rapport, and support which will serve her well in the time ahead. She will prove the value of OD by actions and results rather than by attempting to "make the case" for OD. What she can do is present a plan with sound suggestions, processes, and tools that strengthen the culture through the crisis, so that the president considers her a strong partner.

She should make sure she has a thorough grounding in the changed business situation and pressures, and emphasize that she and her team can help discover new solutions from within the company.

She should emphasize that the president's visibility and presence in company offices, as well as his willingness to be honest, forthcoming and transparent are among his most important priorities as changes occur. She and her team may offer useful strategic thinking models, for example, Barry Johnson's polarity management, so that steps are not taken under stress without considering ramifications of particular actions.

Communications are key. She should offer to take a leading role with internal communications to create and facilitate a series of interactive events around the company. It may be that solutions for cost cutting and layoffs come from employees that understand the situation and are energized to be involved.

Advances in brain chemistry give us a "left brain" reason that "right brain" strategies work. Under stress, the company needs people to operate with positive brain chemicals that lead to new perspectives and opportunities, rather than with a flood of negative chemicals that can be paralyzing.

People need to know that they are receiving accurate and up-to-date information and that the company cares about them, even if it must take drastic action. The fact that the economy is changing is no secret but that won't make it easy or less disruptive. If there are layoffs, attention to those who are staying is as important as the attention to those who are going, as they are likely taking on more work. OD can work to make sure people understand their loss and the normal passage through the grief cycle, as well as to help managers understand their own stress and the stress of their people so that performance expectations are realistic.

Susan should also offer to take a leading role with legal, HR, and unions (if present) to make sure that all options are considered and that the values of the company are upheld. For example, people who are laid off are often walked out of the building with little chance to say goodbye. While there are legal considerations that account for this practice, it is devastating to both the people involved and those that stay behind.

Therese Yaeger and Peter Sorensen Respond

The situation at Insuranco is unfortunately a situation which is being faced by too many organizations today. But, it is a situation in which OD professionals have an opportunity to demonstrate real contribution to the organization. A fundamental issue is how OD can help organizations through this difficult time, and at the same time help the organization build for the future. Our three experts contribute considerable insight and sensitivity to both the short-term and long-term needs of the organization and its personnel.

Our first expert contribution by Rob Kjar is of special interest because of his experience in Japan and his firsthand knowledge of the economic situation there, which is not too different from the current situation here in the United States. Kjar combines his economic insights with meaningful strategic suggestions for Insuranco. His focus on both short-term and long-term is captured in the final comment "survive and thrive," the battle cry of a true OD professional.

Our second expert, Dawn Newman, draws on her experience as an internal OD consultant for a major, and one of the largest, global organizations. Dawn takes a highly relevant macro approach to the case, using the situation as an opportunity to assess the organization's strategy, to review the external environment in terms of measures and markets, to review costs combined with mainstream OD activities, working with stakeholders, and to provide high-involvement strategies for creating solutions.

Our third and final expert, Neesa Sweet, brings to her analysis experience as both an internal and external OD professional. She begins her analysis with the analogy of Albert Einstein riding his bike over the bumpy cobblestone streets at Princeton and the quote "to keep your balance you must keep moving." Neesa stresses the importance of supporting the president in terms of maintaining visibility, the role of openness in communications, and supporting both employees who leave the organization and those "left behind." Her strategy provides strong support for employees by working with human resources, legal and unions. Neesa's comments round out the insights of our invited experts related to OD strategies acquired from extensive experience in a wide range of organizations. Thanks to Rob, Dawn and Neesa—a great response by all!

ACKNOWLEDGMENT

An earlier version of this article was published in *The OD Practitioner,* *41*(2), 50-53.

CASE STUDY 9

IMPLEMENTING THE TRIPLE BOTTOM LINE ... OR NOT?

Homer H. Johnson

Ann Telland joined Acme Manufacturing about 5 years ago as the corporate organization development (OD) specialist immediately after Jack Hopper took over as the CEO. Ann was one of Jack's first hires as part of the "change team" at Acme, and much of her work was introducing new initiatives to the 16 manufacturing plants Acme operated. Acme seemed to be always introducing a new initiative—Six Sigma, just-in-time inventory, lean manufacturing, automation, and so forth. So her change agenda was always filled, and she was not surprised when she was told that it was important for her to be at the next staff briefing.

Jack's weekly briefings for the key corporate personnel always started precisely at 7:00 A.M. Monday morning. Coffee and rolls were served at 6:15 for those who wanted a bit of a breakfast. Jack showed up at 6:45, greeted everyone personally, and started the meeting at 7:00. The agenda was always the same: intro remarks by Jack regarding the state of the business, followed by very brief announcements by some of the key vice presidents (VPs) regarding changes everyone should know about. Then the floor was opened to questions, and finally Jack gave out awards to one or two people in the room who did something noteworthy the previous week or so. The meeting ended precisely at 7:50.

Critical Issues in Organization Development:
Case Studies for Analysis and Discussion, pp. 81–89
Copyright © 2013 by Information Age Publishing
All rights of reproduction in any form reserved.

However, this Monday things started out differently. While the meeting did start precisely at 7:00 A.M., instead of talking about the business, Jack started talking very excitedly about a conference he just attended in Aspen with 20 other CEOs together with several guest speakers. The focus of the conference was the triple bottom line. And for some 50 minutes Jack very passionately shared his Aspen experiences with the group.

As the meeting drew to a close Jack kept repeating that, "This was the way we need to go," and "Acme needs to be the leader in the triple bottom line," and "We have to start this right away." And he finished by saying that, "I am asking Ann to draw up our implementation plans, and when I come back from South America in 3 weeks we are going to kick off Acme's triple bottom line initiative." With that pronouncement the meeting ended, Jack gave Ann the thumbs up, and headed for the airport.

Ann sat for a moment in disbelief. She was used to having Jack spring initiatives on her and the other staff members. However, this was a bit different. While she had heard of the triple bottom line, she really didn't understand what it was all about and wasn't sure that many people in Acme did. In fact, she overheard several of the staff ask, "What's he talking about?" as they were filing out of the conference room.

Her fears were further confirmed as she talked with several of her colleagues and key officers during the next week. Most had heard the term but only had a vague idea as to the details. However, there were a couple of people who seemed fairly knowledgeable and positive.

One staunch advocate of the triple bottom line was Sigrid Olson, Acme's Marketing VP, who was rumored to being groomed as Jack's successor. Sigrid had volunteered to brief Ann on the triple bottom line, and was so enthusiastic about the idea that the scheduled half hour meeting ran to 3 hours. Sigrid explained that the triple bottom line looks at (and measures) three areas. The first bottom line is the environment and focuses on what the company is doing to improve the environment. The second is the human capital bottom line which looks at the people aspect. And the third is the economic bottom line, which looks at the economic viability of the company. And as she pointed out it is all about "The Three Ps—Planet, People, and Profits."

According to Sigrid, probably a majority of the Fortune 500 companies were currently implementing the triple bottom line. And she further stated that she thought that within 50 years every major company would be on board and practicing the triple bottom line—in fact, in the future it will be a requirement for being in business.

After leaving Sigrid, Ann really felt pumped up and was convinced the triple bottom line was the wave of the future and quite doable at Acme. However, her elation was short lived when she contacted a couple of the plant managers she knew fairly well. Ann realized that the support of the general managers of each of the Acme facilities was the key to the success of any initiative, and she wanted to sound them out on this one. Their response was lukewarm at best. They had heard of the triple bottom line, but really didn't know what it was or what it was supposed to do. The positive thing they said to Ann was that they would "have to look at it."

The pay and bonuses of the general managers are based on a set of metrics that include overall plant costs, quality, production, and so forth. The managers are usually 100% supportive of any initiative that will improve the numbers on these metrics (such as the Six Sigma initiative did), and that, in turn, will add to their annual bonus. However, they could be a major source of resistance with any initiative that takes up their time and doesn't contribute to improving the key numbers that will make them look good.

Ann is really conflicted at this point. Jack will be back from South America in a couple of days and is expecting a somewhat detailed plan from her for kicking off the triple bottom line initiative. Should she tell him that this is one of those good ideas that won't work at Acme, and to forget about it for now? Or maybe lay out a plan for rolling out the initiative across the corporation and let Jack worry about implementing it?

If you were Ann, or if you were advising Ann, what should she do? Would you advise dropping the idea? Or if she decides to move forward with the project how should she proceed? What are her first few steps? How should she handle Jack? What about the plant managers and the anticipated resistance? How would you handle them?

More generally, what advice would you give to an OD consultant who is asked to implement an initiative that is only vaguely understood in the organization and for which you anticipate resistance from some of the key players?

We asked three expert consultants, Terry Terranova, Kathy Woodrich, and Nancy Ashworth to tell what advice they would give Ann in handling this difficult situation. Terry is a senior organization development consultant at Sun Microsystems in Broomfield, Colorado; Kathy is an independent consultant in Venice, California; and Nancy is an independent consultant in Denver, Colorado.

Charles "Terry" Terranova

For Ann, this change will be different from the other changes she has implemented at Acme. Six Sigma, just-in-time, lean manufacturing all played into the "sweet spot" for the plant managers and Ann likely encountered little resistance implementing these changes. This change requires that Ann first determine if there is a reason to implement the triple bottom line. In other words, she needs to answer "Why are we making this change?" There are other questions to answer as well. Specifically, Ann needs to consider four aspects about this change.

Why is Acme implementing the triple bottom line? "Because our CEO went to a retreat in Aspen" is not a compelling enough reason to change. Ann needs to identify the problems they are trying to solve or the opportunities they hope to take advantage of. She also needs to assess what it is about Acme's business environment that makes them a candidate for benefiting from the triple bottom line? With this information, Ann can build a compelling business case for the change.

What is the change being contemplated? In other words, what are the specifics of the triple bottom line—what will it replace inside of Acme?

Where will the change take Acme? Ann needs to paint a picture of the benefits of implementing the triple bottom line. This picture should address the change from multiple perspectives—employees, partners, customers, shareholders—and state what each group gets and what each group would do differently. If this picture is attractive, it will cause dissatisfaction with the current state and the organization will want to move to the future.

How will the organization get to this future state? Ann needs to consider the training and other experiences that will establish the employees' new behaviors and mindsets. She must also identify systems inside of Acme that will help or hinder implementing the change. It seems that the plant managers' bonus plans will hinder implementation.

Finally, Ann needs to manage Jack's expectations around a swift implementation of the triple bottom line. If a compelling business need can't be established then she needs to get Jack to accept that assessment. Unless she can impress upon Jack the importance of establishing a compelling business need, then Jack may force the change on Acme. That path usually has dire consequences—and Ann may pay the price for this misstep.

Kathy Woodrich

Acme's triple bottom line (3BL) initiative has the enthusiastic leadership support of two key players: Jack, the CEO; and Sigrid, the VP of marketing. However, Jack's habit of regularly springing initiatives on Ann may indicate a precedent of "flavor of the month" change efforts and a resultant change resistant culture.

After educating herself, Ann should get Jack to articulate a compelling vision for the change and to assure her of his long-term commitment to championing it. How does he see 3BL aligning with and supporting Acme's values and strategy? Why change, and why now? What will success look like? For example, what does "being a leader" in 3BL mean to him? Is the leadership team committed to making foreseeable changes such as adding financial reporting staff and aligning the reward system to gain the plant managers' (and potentially others') support? Although benefits from 3BL initiatives can be difficult to quantify, Jack should still be able to state his business case—if only in qualitative terms.

Assuming Jack is committed and still convinced that it makes sense to move forward, Ann could recommend building awareness amongst the plant managers and other key players by involving them in the change effort and sharing with them the business case for change. She could then assess the wisdom in moving forward using Beckhard's change model: Is the organization's dissatisfaction with the status quo × vision × first steps greater than its resistance to the change? If the answer is "yes," Ann should recommend engaging the stakeholders in action planning that further defines needed actions, their impacts, and the capacity of the organization to embrace them. Key objectives for the action planning process might be to:

- Identify opportunities for Acme to:

    o Build its culture and brand
    o Attract, develop, and retain talent
    o Mitigate risk exposure (environmental, social, regulatory)
    o Improve energy efficiencies
    o Reduce waste
    o Satisfy stakeholders' interests
    o Increase its capacity for change
    o Ensure sustainable growth

- Identify reporting metrics most important to Acme's stakeholders
- Create an action plan for adopting 3BL and building it into Acme's culture including needed resources, accountabilities, and a timeline

Simply put, Ann or any OD consultant asked to implement an initiative that is only vaguely understood and, for which they might anticipate resistance, should first ensure strong leadership support, strategic alignment and business case for change. If those exist, involve stakeholders early in assessing change readiness and often throughout the implementation process.

Nancy L. Ashworth

Ann is confronting a dilemma representative of the initial stages of many organization change efforts. Senior executives attend a conference or read a book that inspires them to try a new business model, in this case, implementing the triple bottom line.

What should Ann do? Although Ann has reservations about this change, she runs the risk of being seen as an impediment if she doesn't create an Implementation Plan. At the program level, Ann could propose the following five phases for the change.

Assess Organizational Readiness

- Benchmark other organizational approaches
- Identify readiness and/or resistance
- Potential Impacts
- Link to organizational vision
- Mobilize and design change concept
- Identify key sponsors/stakeholders
- Develop sponsorship model
- Establish change team
- Define roles and responsibilities
- Define program goals

Design and Plan

- Define desired results (organization, plant, department)
- Create detailed plan
- Timeline/Milestones
- Resources
- Deliverables
- Costs
- Develop communication plan
- Design pilot, select pilot location

Pilot the Change

- Pilot in one department or plant
- Feedback during/after pilot
- Revise change plan

Implement the Change

- Finalize approach based on pilot results
- Follow communication plan
- Track to detailed plan
- Ongoing communication of results
- Celebrate and reward efforts

Rationale for Approach

Organization change has become a business constant, and yet it is often poorly managed. Most commonly, changes are pushed down from the top, rather than being designed in concert with multiple organizational levels. This is further compounded by the fact that rarely do new changes overlap or integrate their approach with former initiatives. Continual change is exhausting, and runs the risk of negatively affecting productivity and morale. Employees respond to constant change by questioning their leaders' ability to lead, or to see the impact change has on them. Diminished trust brings out resistance or cynicism, "Here we go again" thoughts. Confusion may follow along with fear (Why are we changing? What aren't they telling us? Will I lose my job?).

For this change to succeed, Ann needs the CEO to slow down, build buy-in with Plant Managers and other primary players, and develop a communication strategy to mitigate resistance and/or confusion at the supervisory and employee level. Her approach minimizes potential resistance by:

- Linking triple bottom line change to past changes
- Designing collaborative management approach
- Partnering with plant managers
- Developing metrics linked to profitability
- Establishing rewards for successful implementation
- Piloting the change

Homer Johnson Responds

Nice job panel! Great advice!

I really like the way the responses of the expert panel complement one another. I will not try to summarize all their comments; let me highlight a couple of things that jumped out at me.

Terry nicely posed the big questions that Ann needs to ask herself or needs to ask Jack. Probably the most important is why are we doing this? What are the compelling arguments for this change effort? If Ann and Jack can't answer that question, the effort is dead. Terry then follows up by asking the what, where and how of the change.

Kathy adds some detail to Terry's questions. How committed is Jack to this effort? And can Jack articulate a compelling vision that will sell this effort? What will success look like and how will it link to Acme's values and strategy? Key questions! I also like Kathy's discussion regarding the question of the leadership team's commitment to provide the resources and (really key) to align the plant managers' reward system to this initiative. Kathy also gives us some leads as how to further proceed, including identifying the opportunities that this initiative might provide Acme.

Nancy then provides an excellent change template for Ann - a nice model of the key steps that Ann needs to cover if this initiative is going to be a success. The template begins with assessing organizational readiness, moves to the mobilization stage (the key here, to me, is who are the sponsors and who is the change team), then to design, then pilot, then implementation. Nice flow, nice template!

I urge the reader to look at the details of each of the panel member's responses. I really can't do justice in my comments to the many insights they offered Ann.

Thank you Terry, Kathy, and Nancy! Great job!

ACKNOWLEDGMENT

An earlier version of this article was published in *The OD Practitioner*, *41*(1), 50-53.

CASE STUDY 10

LEVERAGING ORGANIZATION DEVELOPMENT

Strategies for Limited Resources

Peter F. Sorensen and Therese F. Yaeger

As in our last case, this case deals with an increasingly critical issue for organization development (OD), namely the rapidly expanding demand for OD knowledge and services with very limited resources. There is no question that the role of OD and its contribution to organization effectiveness is becoming more recognized. The need for organizational capabilities related to effective change management, resistance to change, conflict, innovation, and the creation of effective teams is increasing the demand for OD services and competencies. This is particularly true for large global organizations working in highly diverse cultural environments. The increased recognition of the contribution of OD comes as a mixed blessing. Although the increased recognition for OD may provide greater job security, it comes with sharply increased demands—increased demands which, all too frequently, do not result in increased resources. It has been our experience that even large global organizations with thousands of employees internationally are still characterized by small OD departments, sometimes as small as one to three OD professionals.

Critical Issues in Organization Development:
Case Studies for Analysis and Discussion, pp. 91–101
Copyright © 2013 by Information Age Publishing
91

Again as in our previous case, this case is real, but rather than a single organization, it is a composite of several organizations that are dealing with this dilemma of expanding OD without expanding resources. We have asked three expert panelists to comment on the case. Each of the panelists has a great deal of empathy for our OD Director in the case, and each is well positioned to comment. Our panelists bring to the case three different perspectives from three different industries; namely, healthcare, not-for-profit, and the food industry: Dr. Ghazala Ovaice, Manager of Strategic OD at Abbott, one of the largest health care companies in the world; Dr. Vince Pellettiere, former Human Resources Vice President for a Global Food Processor and Distributor, now faculty at Aurora University and Director of POD Consulting; and James Dunn, Vice President of HR and OD for the American Cancer Society. The case and the comments of our panelists are of particular interest to Dr. Therese Yaeger, now that she is the Director of Global OD for Motorola, Inc.

Case

We again revisit the same organization in our last case. thanks to our previous panel, our same highly successful OD director has not only established a place at the table as a partner in developing the corporation's future strategy, but in some ways she has been a little too successful in gaining a major role for OD, since the desire for OD knowledge and competencies has rapidly escalated throughout the organization. but our OD director has not been as successful at increasing OD resources and continues to work with a highly competent, but very small, staff.

Let's briefly review the characteristics of the organization. It is a 100-year-old enterprise with a reputation for high-quality manufacturing products. Thirty years ago the company began international activities, and now has manufacturing and sales operations in 20 different countries including the United States, Scandinavia, Central Europe, Africa, and Asia. Each of the regions has its own sales, marketing, and production operations, and has operated on a fairly autonomous, decentralized basis. The organization has been successful in each of its regional operations. Recently, however, each of the regions is facing a number of environmental changes. The environment has become more competitive, the economic environment is more volatile, and the rate of environmental change has escalated, all of which is placing increased demands on the organization for greater capability to cope with change and to manage change effectively. In other words, more OD knowledge and competencies are needed.

Our director has secured OD a place at the table but she may now be having second thoughts. Now our director has the responsibility not only for facilitating and helping management shape strategy, but also for aligning and shaping an organization capable of delivering the strategy—a task that includes significantly increasing the organization's capacity to identify change needs and to manage change successfully. The regional managers are exceptionally competent at managing job content as they have known it in the past, but managing change is a whole new concept to them. They perceive the Director of OD and the OD staff as competent, but they are not at all sure what this function called OD is all about.

The OD function is still relatively new and considerably smaller than the HR and Training and Development departments, which to some extent are decentralized to the regions.

What advice can our panelists give to our Director of OD?

1. Go for more resources?
2. Create an alliance with HR and education and training (E&T) to create ways of delegating OD to line managers and increasing the line managers' OD competencies?
3. Create formal coursework as an alternative? Training courses are used extensively in the organization, but management education is offered only on a limited basis.
4. If coursework is desired, what courses should be offered, and what consideration should be given to the roles of OD, HR, and E&T?
5. What other alternatives are there?

Again, the basic dilemma confronting our OD director is how she should build OD knowledge and competencies throughout the organization.

Now let's learn from our expert panelists.

Ghazala Ovaice

Now that our OD director has laid the foundation for OD in the organization, there are several considerations for moving forward. As is the case with many organizations, resources are limited for OD work within the organization. Consequently, the organization needs to view OD systematically. By systematically understanding the strategic needs of the organization, then identifying the necessary OD interventions to help achieve that strategy, the OD resources will be prioritized and streamlined.

Assess Strategic Needs: As a result of identifying the overall business strategy and the necessary organizational performance activities required to achieve the strategy, OD will be well-positioned to meet the needs of the organization. An organization-wide assessment of culture, followed with a review of necessary skills, competencies, and activities to achieve the strategy, will highlight and prioritize the needs of the organization. As a result the OD activities will be aligned with the organization's business needs. Consequently, the support, funding, and resources for OD activities should come from the business locally (and not necessarily from Human Resource [HR] centrally).

Assess Capabilities: In the event that HR business partners do not have the necessary skills or competencies to help achieve the business needs of the organization, OD can then partner with HR to determine the competency-building activities necessary to help the business facing HR partners meet the needs of their clients. Thus OD's internal clients would now also include HR. Moreover, the best means to help the business achieve their objectives, with limited OD resources, would be to leverage the existing HR business partners as internal OD consultants to their respective client groups. Therefore, the most efficient and effective means for the OD group to meet the needs of the organization would be through the old adage of "teaching a man to fish." If OD can teach its internal client, HR, the necessary OD skills needed to help the business, OD is then disseminating the skills needed throughout the organization by utilizing existing resources (i.e., HR business partners).

Design and Implement Curriculum: In order to best prepare the HR staff for their role, OD will need to serve as subject matter experts (SMEs) for an OD curriculum. A working knowledge of assessment, feedback, diagnosis, planning, implementation, evaluation, and change management is crucial in successfully driving OD down the organization. As such, a core part of the HR career development curriculum should include OD. This curriculum could also be utilized with business leaders to build their competency on managing change within the organization.

As SMEs, OD can work with instructional designers to develop the necessary OD workshops, action learning, and self-guided OD curriculum.

Specifically, the OD curriculum for HR would include general OD overview workshops, "lunch and learns" on specific topics related to action research (e.g., conducting evaluations of OD interventions), toolkits for managing change (e.g., sample stakeholder charts, communication plans, assessments), or special hot topic seminars on specific OD interventions (e.g., managing culture change during a merger).

Institutionalize Strategic OD: Several opportunities exist to institutionalize this effort to be strategic and systematic about the organization's OD activities. As mentioned earlier, a regular process for aligning OD activities to help achieve business strategy must be established. Second, HR business partners should be leveraged as internal OD consultants. Third, should education be required to bring HR up to speed on OD, an OD curriculum can be established by using the existing OD resources as SMEs. Fourth, this OD curriculum could potentially model the Six Sigma certification approach. That is, use action learning as a method to certify HR (or even business leaders) on OD projects, under the guidance of master OD consultants (i.e., establish OD greenbelts and blackbelts). Fifth, align the existing OD professionals as internal experts with different parts of the business. OD staff would serve as expert internal consultants to HR when they need additional help, support, tools or expertise related to specific OD needs within their client groups. OD is now available to focus on strategic enterprise-wide initiatives, while HR can focus on business specific initiatives, and consequently, it is able to meet the OD needs of the organization at the individual, team, and organizational level.

By systematically reviewing the strategic needs of the organization and leveraging the existing resources within the organization in terms of knowledge, human capital, experience, and expertise, our OD director can establish a structure that meets the OD and change management needs of the organization.

Vincent Pellettiere

The key role of the OD director as outlined in the case study is: (1) facilitating and helping management shape business strategy, and (2) aligning and shaping her organization to be able to deliver and sustain that strategy. The organization is faced with a number of competitive challenges, and based on these external factors, the organization needs to make changes to sustain its success. The OD function needs to establish itself by determining what value-added services it can provide to the organization's regional operations that are faced with these competitive challenges.

I would recommend the following strategy for the OD director based on challenges the organization and OD are facing.

1. It is vital for the OD director to first develop her own strategy. She must seek to understand the external and internal factors that the regional operations must deal with in order to assist them to compete effectively in their environments. It is also vital to know these factors if her role at the table is to help shape the company's strategy, along with designing, developing and implementing that strategy. I feel her first action step is to establish an alliance with the leaders of each of the 20 regional operations. Her role and function needs to be established with each regional operation if she is to become recognized as a value-added service. The OD Director will need to demonstrate the value she could bring to regional operations, so that OD can help the regions and thus help the organization deal with its competitive challenges and achieve and sustain its short- and long-term objectives.

2. Once the alliance has been formed, the OD director and the regional operation partners should work together to conduct an external and internal analysis to determine the need, readiness, and risks for a planned change initiative. The OD director should also introduce an OD intervention tool to the leaders of regional operations when conducting this type of analysis, and instruct them about how to conduct a self-assessment of their business and internal resources. This OD tool can be used throughout a region as a practical OD intervention to (a) help the region better understand what it would need to emphasize and change in order to become more effective, and (b) increase the regional managers' OD knowledge and competencies. Ideally, the OD director should work with each regional operation to conduct this analysis since each region may have unique challenges not faced in other regions. The external analysis would focus on the opportunities and threats each region is facing, and the internal analysis would focus on the strengths and weaknesses of their internal resources.

3. The next stage would require the OD director and her regional operations partners to jointly determine what needs to change, based on the outcome of the external and internal analyses. This decision about what needs to change would then lead to the development of a strategy for change, including where it would be focused, how and when it will be achieved (along with timelines), and who will be accountable. The strategy would also outline an assessment of the readiness and risks for change, including a recommendation for the resources, training, communication needed prior to the implementation of the change strategy, and a risk analysis based on the level of change anticipated and the organization's current state of readiness. I feel that at the conclusion of this stage the OD Director is in a better position to help the organization manage

this strategy for change successfully. She has now also established herself as a business partner and begun the process of enhancing the OD knowledge and competencies within the regions.

4. The next stage involves forming an alliance with HR and E&T to discuss what resources they can provide to help the regions achieve their strategies as determined in the preceding step. Discussions would center on how the alliance would help the organization and the regional operations achieve their strategic objectives by determining:

1.   What training and development is needed to help the regions and the organization?
2.   Is it available internally?
3.   What external resources are needed (universities, consultants, etc.)?
4.   What role would each part of the alliance (and regional operations) play in this initiative?
5.   What other resources are needed from the organization to help the alliance deliver these resources?
6.   What timelines must be observed by the organization during this process of planned change? Can regional operations fulfill these expectations? Can alliance members deliver in a timely fashion?

The purpose of these discussions would be to provide feedback to the regional operation leaders and the executive team, and to seek their guidance, recommendations, and approval. A tactical OD strategy, on a short-term cycle, should be developed to accomplish objectives that have more immediate time constraints. Strategic objectives should also be created for change initiatives that have a more long-term perspective, incorporating coursework, workshops, and internal development programs. These objectives would be mutually established by the alliances formed between the regions, HR and E&T, and the leadership team.

Jim Dunn

Amidst growing public scrutiny regarding appropriate management and allocation of donor dollars, the task of implementing organization-wide change initiatives with limited resources is all too common to those of us working within nonprofit systems. Sharing common experiences with the director of OD, I believe that the cardinal step is creating very strong alliances with other functional areas (i.e., human resources, training and development, IT) in order to foster strategic alignment with the overall change effort. These alliances offer significant benefits: creating collaborative working groups and/or teams, providing broader support for the initiative, and allowing for the potential of shared resources, which lessens the pressure on the small OD staff.

There also exists a certain timeliness to the director of OD's present challenge. At a time when the HR discipline continues to struggle with its ability to play larger strategic roles within many organizations, a well-positioned alliance could allow HR an opportunity of engaging the change agent role. A 2004 survey conducted by the Society for Human Resources Management (SHRM) indicated that only 34% of senior executives viewed the HR function as a "strategic partner." Additionally, a similar survey of HR practitioners cited managing change as the main area of HR competence in which respondents felt they were least effective.

My next set of questions about this challenge relates to the perceived value proposition of the OD department and staff. How clear is leadership about the hard gains from internal OD services? OD appears to be doing fairly well in this case study, since OD now has a "seat at the table." Well, why is OD not eating while seated at the table? Was the decision to provide OD a seat at the table an organic one, or driven by present strategy? The challenge is similar to other organizational efforts like diversity and inclusion strategies. While the premise of engaging diverse groups and individuals sounds good to both senior leaders and organizational stakeholders alike, the return on investment (ROI) on these efforts remains soft and often difficult to express in financial terms. What is the overall value to this global organization that its managers are able to manage change more effectively? Can this value be turned into a hard dollar benefit? What are the advantages to the organization for building this internal capacity versus recruiting line managers externally skilled in managing change efforts?

Finally, as a 100-year-old organization with a reputation for high quality manufacturing products, one can assume that the organization subscribes to a differentiation marketing strategy—an approach requiring increased innovation and creativity on the part of line managers, particularly those involved in R&D and quality efforts. How can OD position itself to enhance this overall strategy?

A differentiation strategy not only provides for unique products and services in ways that are widely valued by buyers, but this is usually achieved through extraordinary service, technological capability, or an unusually positive brand image. By way of example, Toyota Motors has succeeded in differentiating itself from its competitors by gaining a reputation of exceptional quality in its cars. The Toyota Camry, for example, is widely recognized as a very well-built car with excellent reliability and dependability. Consequently, it sells at a substantial premium above other cars of similar size, and the depreciation on the price of a used Camry is also much less than normal. Why is this important? The overall strategy for Toyota was developed from an alliance between marketing and their internal OD staff. When OD can have such a positive impact to the bottom line, as in this example, we will sit and eat at the table as the value proposition becomes clear and measurable.

In short, the OD director must consider options for creating strong cross-functional alliances, building and developing the intellectual capacity of current line managers, and implementing long-term strategies for creating OD value with stakeholders as in the Toyota example. While the current OD staff may be small in number, the charge is huge. OD should not seek to own the issue of managing change alone, but explore avenues for building organizational capacity through the use of subgroups. Although employee development is essential to the long-term success of this global organization, organization leaders generally classify expenditures for employee development as a cost on financial statements. OD professionals charged to create an employee development process must address this incorrect mindset from the outset. Organizations should note that they either pay now or will pay later. The "pay later" will manifest as unprepared employees, lack of talent brought on by less ability to attract and retain exemplary performers, and a reduced knowledge base across the organization.

Peter Sorensen and Therese Yaeger Respond

Each panelist provides helpful insights to an increasing OD dilemma created by the recognition that OD has a significant role to play in implementing organizational strategy. This recognition can be a mixed blessing, creating more to do without additional resources.

Each of our panelists presents a unique contribution. Ghazala emphasizes understanding the business strategy followed by an assessment of the organization's capabilities and competencies. She recommends leveraging of limited OD resources by partnering with HR and developing OD knowledge within HR by creating an OD educational curriculum, using OD personnel as subject matter specialists.

Vincent places more emphasis on creating alliances with leadership of the regional operations. Like Ghazala, Vincent would then create an alliance with the E&T and HR functions.

Jim brings a perspective from the non-profit sector, a perspective with a real appreciation for working with limited resources. Jim differs from our other two panelists in that he focuses more on a differentiation strategy, that is, working with marketing and new product development. He provides an illustration of an internal alliance at Toyota Camry between marketing and OD. Jim also raises the opportunity for correcting an inappropriate mindset that not investing in the development of organizational competencies now has its costs in the future, that is, "pay now or pay later."

Although each panelist brings their own experiences and background to bear on the case there are also striking similarities:

1. It is critically important for the OD professional to understand corporate strategy, and to see the implications of corporate strategy in order to identify and develop organizational competencies in alignment with that strategy.
2. Creating multiple alliances with management, human resources, education and training, and other functions is a key to building and developing the necessary strategic competencies.
3. Effective organizational change is a shared responsibility, and a major responsibility for the OD professional is to leverage OD knowledge through alliances.
4. It is vital that the OD function is seen as adding value.
5. Now that OD is at the table, the real test is developing strategies for coping with success.

ACKNOWLEDGMENT

An earlier version of this article was published in *The OD Practitioner,* *39*(1), 52-56.

CASE STUDY 11

THE CASE OF
THE IDEAL ORGANIZATION
DEVELOPMENT JOB

Homer H. Johnson and Chris Pett

It was about 15 months ago that Bill Demski was asked to give a guest lecture to a graduate class in organization development (OD) at a local university. Bill is the Manager of OD and training at Package Goods Corporation (PGC), a $5 billion per year consumer packaged goods company with 7,000 employees worldwide. The instructor of the course had asked Bill to talk to the class about what an internal OD consultant does in a major corporation. In planning for the presentation Bill thought a lot about his past experiences as an internal OD consultant in several major companies and also reflected on his current position at PGC. Planning for the class made him very aware of how satisfied (and fortunate) he was in his current position. In fact, he felt so positive about his work that he decided to title his presentation to the class, "The Ideal OD Job."

Bill had joined PGC about 7 years previously to rejuvenate the OD function in the company. PGC was an ideal company for a person with an OD orientation. The company was nonhierarchical, team-based, informal, very collaborative, and had a strong ethics and values orientation. Moreover, the company valued OD principles and techniques and used them extensively.

Critical Issues in Organization Development:
Case Studies for Analysis and Discussion, pp. 103–110
Copyright © 2013 by Information Age Publishing
All rights of reproduction in any form reserved.

The work responsibilities of Bill's unit focused on three major areas—general consulting services to the business units, professional skills training, and management development programs. The OD unit at PGC was small, only four consultants; however, they made extensive use of external consultants. In fact, Bill and his OD colleagues were very proud of the network of highly skilled external OD and training consultants that helped them out on a regular basis.

As part of his OD consulting, Bill had developed strong relationships with several of the leaders of the business units, and much of his work and that of another internal consultant focused on assisting those units with their change efforts. "It took a long time to get the trust of the business unit leaders," Bill said, "but once we did we became a critical part of their change efforts." It was this part of his work that Bill really loved.

Not long after his presentation on "The Ideal OD Job," rumors began circulating that PGC might be up for sale and the suitor was a much larger beverage and snack corporation (Beverage, Inc.) with a very different culture and management approach than that of PGC. Initially the employees at PGC thought that, given the dramatic differences in the cultures of the two companies, the beverage company would realize that this was going to be a bad fit and would move on to other acquisition targets. However, much to their surprise and dismay, the acquisition went through, and the question became whether PGC would be left alone to continue as they had been, or would they be absorbed into the Beverage, Inc. culture.

The culture of Beverage, Inc. is very competitive, both in the market place (kill the competition), as well as internally. It is growth-driven at any cost, very numbers-driven, intense, and hierarchical. And of particular concern to Bill, Beverage, Inc. did not have much use for consultants, either internal or external. "Good managers don't need consultants to tell them what to do" was the philosophy of the company. Using a consultant, except for those consultants with highly technical skills, was seen as a black mark on a manager's record.

In the first few months after the acquisition, PGC went along as it had in the past, without much interference from Beverage, Inc. However, about 4 months into the acquisition, a new structure was instituted in human resources (HR). Bill's unit had reported directly to the corporate vice president (VP) of human resources at PGC. Another layer of management was added with the OD and training unit reporting to a vice president of core services (who came from Beverage, Inc.), who, in turn, reported to the PGC vice president of human resources (who also came from Beverage, Inc.).

Shortly after the new VPs came on board, the priorities of the OD and training unit changed. Although Bill had asked to continue the consulting efforts to the business units, the direction chosen by the VPs was that the unit would focus its efforts almost solely on training and development initiatives including professional skills training, management development, and, as a new initiative, conducting 360 degree reviews with follow-up coaching/training. Some "OD opportunities" continued to be available, including assisting with leadership team development and meeting facilitation. However, these latter efforts constituted a minor part of the unit's time and effort. The services of the external consultants who had supported the unit were terminated.

While Bill and the members of his unit were adjusting to the new structure and priorities reasonably well, other parts of the organization were experiencing considerable difficulty. In particular, the clash of cultures and the changes in leadership were causing serious problems in the business units. Morale was down, turnover was high, and, while the data was not public, Bill suspected that sales and productivity were slipping.

The problems caused by the acquisition were of major concern to Bill and his colleagues. Initially, they had been good corporate citizens and had tried to make the best out of their new duties. However, they sincerely believed that they had much to offer the organization in assisting the integration of the two cultures. After all, they were experts in change strategies and had an excellent track record in doing such in the business units. Moreover, they believed that the organization was at risk—the acquisition was not going well, and they, as OD consultants and change experts, could have a significant impact in improving the situation.

What would you do if you were Bill and his colleagues? Would you offer your OD services to facilitate the acquisition? To whom? What would you say that might get the attention of the leadership in the new culture? How would you engage the organization to facilitate the integration of the two cultures? What OD models and techniques would be most effective in this situation?

Or would you, as one of the old PGC managers told him, "just suck it up" and focus on the training and development activities as that is where your new bosses think you can best add value to the organization?

We asked two expert OD consultants, Kathy Carmean and Linda Rasins, to tell us what they would advise Bill to do. Homer and Chris also add their comments following those of Kathy and Linda.

Linda Rasins

Oh, Bill ... this is a sticky one. In the midst of all this change and the accompanying emotional roller coaster, there are so many things to think about ...

Have any intentions regarding the culture, leadership practices, or strengths of PGC been stated by Beverage executives? Sometimes the strategic reasons for an acquisition (implicitly) include maintaining the organizational strengths that make for a successful product line. Why did Beverage buy PGC? Perhaps you can show that maintaining and building on the core strengths of PGC (including the culture and team-based practices) is critical to the return on Beverage's investment in the acquisition. A case might be made for helping Beverage execs understand the core business practices that have made PGC successful, so they don't unintentionally kill the goose that laid the golden egg—perhaps some "best practices sharing" sessions.

Who are the PGC executives with whom you have the best relationships? What's happened with their positions? Have they lost power and influence, or are they seen as high potentials with a big future at Beverage? If there are some previous clients who are being given more responsibility, broader roles, or are consolidating parts of Beverage's organization into their units, they are apparently viewed as "keepers" by Beverage. So they would be good targets for some merger-focused OD services such organization design, assimilating new team members, role clarification, or getting their leadership team aligned. And if they are close colleagues, you might even confide in them about your concerns for your own political positioning. Then they could provide some air cover, putting in a good word about your work to your new boss.

How does your new VP view you and your future with the company? What's your sense of how she or he defines your success? How risky is it for you to pursue OD work that may be critical to the business, yet viewed negatively by your new boss? Only you can assess how far you are willing to push the envelope. If you must survive in this organization, it may well be safer to "suck it up" and play the role that Beverage wants you to play. If it's likely that you and your group will always be seen as "them" and not "us," it may be that no matter what you do, your career with Beverage will be limited. Ouch, the pain of acquisition!

Do you still want to be there, now that the job has changed? Is Beverage the right place for a talented and values-focused OD guy like you? Since Beverage has put two of "their own" people in the key HR leadership positions at PGC, it appears that Beverage intends for their culture to dominate.

Be sure to take some time for yourself, to reflect and get support and advice from trusted colleagues, so you can stay clear on your own needs, goals, health, and values during this challenging time.

Kathy Carmean

At first blush, Beverage, Inc.'s management does not seem to have a clear understanding of what OD consultants do and the kind of impact on business results they can help affect organizations, as evidenced by their cultural norm, "Using a consultant, except those with highly technical skills, was seen as a black mark on a manager's record." Beverage's leadership has been operating under an assumption that internal consultants (and externals) try to "tell business unit leaders what to do." The OD maxim, "meet the client where he is" needs to be demonstrated here by Bill and his colleagues and they must have a plan if they are to survive the acquisition and continue to add value to the company.

Clearly there is a clash of cultures between the acquired and the acquirer, with the former, in OD parlance, being "high maintenance" and the latter "high task." Nonetheless, Bill Demski and his colleagues have a wonderful opportunity to help with this transition. The key will be in the approach and the language used. The new organization, like so many in corporate America today, has a short-term focus, with emphasis on quantitative measures. No doubt PGC also focused on metrics, performance, and results; otherwise, they would not have been an attractive acquisition for Beverage, Inc.

The key for Bill and his colleagues is to focus on the similarities and strengths of both organizations and build trust over time. While an appreciative inquiry approach would be ideal at this juncture for some speedy change and discovery of shared values among the merged employees, it is doubtful that senior leadership would buy in at this point. Nonetheless, Bill and his colleagues are at an advantage in that current leadership (the Beverage, Inc., folks) has (1) retained their services for the time being, (2) given them a list of priorities in the areas of professional skills development and management development, and (3) directed them to conduct 360 reviews with follow up coaching and training. Since external consultants' services have been terminated, there will be greater dependence upon the internal consultants. This may actually be good news as Bill and his colleagues can use these initiatives as entry points to understand the new leaders' focus and exert some influence.

In addition to getting clear from the start about what success would look like and desired outcomes from these initiatives, attention to semantics will be helpful as they launch their new management directed efforts.

While complying with new management, they can simultaneously conduct an internal marketing campaign. As part of this internal marketing effort, Bill Demski and his colleagues would be wise to elicit success stories from PGC's business unit leaders that can demonstrate quantitative improvements or successes that had an impact on sales revenues, cost reduction/avoidance, contributed to growth, or employee development, attraction, and retention. By leveraging earlier relationships with internal business unit clients and gathering stories, data, and statistics that were the result of past successful interventions, they can demonstrate that PGC's management can be just as results focused as Beverage, Inc. By using more business oriented language, a redoubled focus on organizational effectiveness, and seeing themselves as business unit partners, Bill and his peers will begin to engender trust with the new management team.

If met with resistance, they can cite past success stories supported by quantitative data, the language with which Beverage, Inc., is most comfortable. Once tangible results from their new partnership efforts become clear and the trust grows, what can naturally evolve will be discussions with leaders about the human side of the organization. Through this process, Bill and his colleagues will not be forcing themselves on business unit leaders but rather will be doing as originally charged by Beverage, Inc.'s leadership. Through parallel processes-one stated, one unstated-they will slowly but surely transition two cultures into something new that celebrates the best of both that bring about great business results and engaged employees.

Homer Johnson and Chris Pett Respond

This scenario seems to appear more and more frequently given the mergers, downsizing and takeovers occurring in organizations. Traditional OD functions seem to be increasingly at risk and this raises questions as to the role that OD people will play in the new and emerging structures. Linda Rasins and Kathy Carmean have done a nice job in summarizing the issues that Bill and his group have to deal with. A couple of their points triggered some additional thoughts from us, which we provide in the text that follows.

Linda Rasins' advice regarding spending time in reflection is well taken, particularly pondering her questions as to where Bill and his group fit in the new structure and culture. It seems fairly obvious that Beverage has a definite plan for PGC, and the quick replacement of PGC people in key VP positions is a clear signal that PGC will be made over in the Beverage image. Bill and his colleagues need to know whether they also are to be moved out, and, if so, what is the time table. If they are given some assurances that their jobs are safe, then Bill and his colleagues have to decide whether they are comfortable with the role that Beverage has designated for them.

If they are to stay, or if the issue is still being debated, both Linda and Kathy point out that Bill has built up a lot of "political capital" (our term) over the years. This would be a good time to use these contacts to convince Beverage that the OD group has much to contribute.

Bill certainly could use Kathy Carmean's suggestion of using more business oriented language and having Bill and his group focus on data and statistics that relate their interventions to those outcomes that would resonate with the Beverage, Inc., leadership, such as cost reduction, sales revenues, and market growth. This would bring the efforts of the OD group more in sync with both the language and the strategy of Beverage, Inc.

In a sense, Kathy is advocating one of Marv Weisbord's pieces of advice for successful OD consulting, which went something to the effect of "never swim against the current" (or was it "never swim upstream?"). Bill and his group have been trying to "swim against the current" and will quickly exhaust themselves without making any progress. Kathy gives the group a strategy for "swimming with the current," which offers the potential of keeping OD alive while achieving the company goals.

But Bill has another great opportunity to keep OD alive by "swimming in the current," and that is through the work that Beverage, Inc. has assigned his group in management development, administering 360 reviews and doing follow-up coaching. These activities all lead very naturally, and very frequently, to work with executive teams (e.g., leadership team alignment as Linda suggests), product development teams, sales teams and the like. These assignments also frequently lead to work with groups initiating change efforts. Bill's group is doing some of this already and this would seem to be a partially open door to do much more OD. Thus Bill might stop trying to force his version of an OD agenda on Beverage and instead go with the flow, accept the agenda imposed on him. Through that agenda he might actually accomplish many of the things he hoped to with his more traditional OD agenda (but please don't call it OD). If you find one door locked don't try to break it down, but go through whatever door is left open.

ACKNOWLEDGMENT

An earlier version of this article was published in *The OD Practitioner*, *36*(1), 30-33.

CASE STUDY 12

THE SUSTAINABILITY INITIATIVE AT METRO CHARITY HOSPITAL

Homer H. Johnson

Metro Charity Hospital is a 400-bed hospital located in a major metropolitan area. As its name implies, Metro accepts all patients regardless of their ability to pay for the services. Metro's funding comes primarily from government sources, such as Medicaid and county funds. While the medical service is considered generally good, the hospital is often overcrowded and operates with a limited number of staff. It has a large emergency room, and although emergency room patients are never turned away, there is a waiting list for nonemergency admissions.

Given the situation at Metro, Mina Panos was feeling considerably frustrated when she found out that she had been "chosen" to head up a sustainability initiative at Metro. New initiatives were not very popular with the Metro staff. In fact, it had been difficult to receive much cooperation in the past for new initiatives, as the staff was already stretched to the limit in providing basic medical service. However, this was not something that could be ignored, as Metro had to demonstrate progress in sustainability in order to meet a requirement for hospital accreditation in two years. The Metro Board and the staff had many discussions regarding development of sustainability projects over the years. It was something they very

Critical Issues in Organization Development:
Case Studies for Analysis and Discussion, pp. 111–119
Copyright © 2013 by Information Age Publishing
All rights of reproduction in any form reserved.

much wanted to do, however; other priorities always got in the way. Now was the time to get serious about sustainability.

This was Mina's fourth year as the Administrative Vice President at Metro, and prior to that she held a similar administrative position at a major academic medical center. Metro was certainly a very different experience than the medical center. Perhaps most notable was that the medical center practiced highly specialized medicine, and had limited emergency room services. Another glaring difference was that the medical center was never lacking for funding. The medical center attracted individual donors who gave substantial contributions in addition to the federal and state funding the medical center received.

While at the medical center, Mina had been involved with several sustainability projects. The medical center had received much media attention for its ambitious sustainability goals, such as reducing carbon emissions by 25% in 5 years and by 50% in 10 years. However, much of the medical center's efforts were focused on the construction of new or remodeled facilities, usually funded by generous donors, with an emphasis on "green buildings" and renewable energy sources. All of these efforts involved considerable capital funding, which was lacking at Metro.

Every time Mina mentioned the medical center's sustainability initiatives to Metro's CEO, he was quick to tell her, "Don't even think about it, and definitely don't mention it to the board of directors. They are having problems finding enough money to cover next month's expenses." That was probably a gross exaggeration but the message was clear—construction or remodeling was out of the question.

As her frustration began to build she decided to call Jen Han, a friend and an organization development consultant with whom she had worked at the medical center. Jen was an "independent" with considerable experience on sustainability projects.

"Don't worry, you can do it," Jen responded, "The first thing you have to do is to forget about the medical center initiatives. They are in a totally different situation than you are in at Metro. Rule #1 is to not try and copy what someone else did. Begin by thinking about how you can get into sustainability given the situation at Metro."

"Another rule of change is to start with something that is doable. Pick things that are easy to do—something that is not complex and that does not involve a lot of people's time. Can you think of anything that might fit those criteria at Metro?"

"Well, the first idea that pops into my mind are recyclables," Mina replied. "A lot of the medical devices used in the hospital could be recycled, such as some catheters, inflation devices for angioplasty, and cardiac stabilization devices. And that would be easy to do—just throw them into a recycle bin. Right now they all end up in landfills. Recycling those items will keep them out of landfills and prevent some air pollution. Moreover, it will also cut our waste disposal costs, which will save us money. The Board will love that part. As a related idea, we could also contribute to sustainability, and again reduce costs by purchasing recyclable devices. Or by purchasing devices that are more environment-friendly. These projects should be fairly easy to do."

"You have got the idea," replied Jen, "There are probably several initiatives like that at Metro. Since this is a fairly new initiative at Metro you probably are going to have to make a few suggestions to people on what areas are likely targets. However, another rule in change is to have those who are affected by the decision help make the decision. They will figure out a way to do things that you would have never thought of."

Mina was feeling a lot better after her conversation with Jen. She was beginning to think that the initiative was manageable. And, Metro probably could make some serious strides toward improving the environment and also could save some money while doing so.

But, what's next, she thought. How do I organize this initiative? Do I need some sort of organizational structure for this? How do I get people involved? Who should be involved?

If you were advising Mina on the sustainability initiative at Metro what would be your advice to her? First, do you think the advice she got from Jen was good advice? Could it be used for most sustainability projects? Or would you have suggested something different? Next, briefly outline how she might organize the process. Who should be involved, and so on?

We asked a panel of experts, all of whom have background in both sustainability and change management, what advice they would offer Mina. Tony Colantoni is a senior organization development consultant and principal in the SGC Consulting Group in Rolling Meadows, Illinois; Carol Silk is the Vice-President and Chief Learning Officer at New York-Presbyterian Hospital in New York; and Sharon Fletcher is the manager of learning and organizational development and an independent consultant in the healthcare industry.

Tony Colantoni

My first reaction to hearing what Mina is going through is to ask about the scope of the initiative. Is it merely an attempt to comply with the minimum standards of the accrediting agency? Is it truly time to get serious about sustainability? Is there some middle ground to consider? One of the challenges of any project is to avoid jumping into the water before being clear about how deep and cold it is and how far one is expected to swim. When I add to that the possible mixed messages I hear ("time to get serious" versus "not enough money to cover expenses"), the importance of a clear project scope becomes highlighted. This critical work—the first cornerstone of effective project management—involves identifying the key stakeholders, including the Metro Board and its CEO, and then understanding their expectations and requirements. It also involves identifying project sponsors and champions. Finally, it leads to the second and third cornerstones—budget and schedule. Once Mina gets a sense of project scope, expectations and requirements, budget and resource allocations, and timelines for implementation and completion, she will have a better idea about how to approach and organize the initiative.

Jen's advice to "forget about the medical center initiatives" may be sound in reminding Mina to not try and replicate initiatives that are better suited to what appears to be a much different situation. However, one of the most valuable resources Mina has is her experience. I would encourage her to reflect on and tap into that experience as appropriate to guide her thinking and actions here.

In that regard, and whether the initiative's scope is broad or limited, it may be useful to consider a large systems change framework to help organize and structure this effort. This framework for change includes articulating the case for sustainability, building consensus for action among the stakeholders, using multiple levers to drive change, and communicating and educating the system about both sustainability and the process. The framework would help Mina begin to answer some of her questions and provide the structure she desires.

For example, working with the Metro Board, its CEO, the initiative's sponsors if different, and other critical individuals and groups to set out the "why here, why now" of the initiative will help focus the effort and paint a clear picture for all to see. Ideally, this process will show why Metro is embarking on this initiative now, how the initiative is linked to the hospital's strategy, and what successful implementation will mean to the long-term viability of the hospital. This will also serve to galvanize and underscore leadership support. As education and communication are essential to any sustainability effort, this work provides Mina with an invaluable tool and talking piece to "take on the road" to Metro's many staffs, departments and constituents, both internal and external. A well thought out communication plan will be immensely helpful in educating people, answering questions, collecting data, and beginning the process to build consensus.

This in turn will give Mina the opportunity to identify and recruit people throughout Metro to assist in the effort. No change effort can succeed through the efforts of a few people alone. The communication process will give Mina a vehicle to connect with people throughout Metro who will "make it happen" and "help it happen." Thought should be given to both formal and informal leaders, and subject matter expertise as well as people who are interested and energized. She may then create a sustainability team and/or a guiding coalition to help formulate, direct, implement, and communicate/educate about various initiatives and projects.

What we know about lasting change that is large in scope is that it typically does not happen as the result of one or even a few projects or programs. There should be many things going on, and they should be happening all over the system. If that is the case here, Mina can use her team or guiding coalition to infuse and link sustainability activity throughout Metro. Such activity is not limited to recycling that Mina initially considered, or reduced carbon footprint, or green building design that the CEO cautioned against. It includes maximizing natural resources, resource efficient transportation, and sustainable design.

A clear picture of why Metro is doing this now, an engaged and energized team, and a series of linked projects touching all parts of Metro are three keys to helping Mina get Metro's sustainability initiative up and running!

Carol Silk

Grassroots is the key strategy for success here! Jen is pointing Mina in the right direction for her to build a model that will work at Metro. Given the limited capital available and the staff's desire to develop meaningful sustainability projects, now is the right time to engage the front line in the development and implementation of this new "sustainable" initiative.

While sustainability is critical in terms of Metro's accreditation, Mina has the opportunity of creating a clear strategic link between sustainability and the hospital's overall vision and mission. Sustainability can be introduced as yet another driver in providing patients and their families with the safest, healthiest environment that they deserve. Such environments help ensure that patients get the care they need. Aligning these two messages of sustainability and patient care will have a better chance of appealing to and engaging healthcare workers whose primary value is putting patient care first.

Mina's commitment is clear and her first challenge is to create an infrastructure to engage other committed people with clear purpose. At the same time she is developing an approach to a grassroots structure, she will need to develop a role for hospital leadership to ensure that the sustainability projects are aligned with senior leadership's priorities.

A multiple-tiered approach would best serve Mina's needs. By developing a sustainability executive steering committee, Mina will be able to charge the group with creating an environmental vision statement for Metro and to begin identifying policies and practices that are already in place to achieve sustainability goals as well as any new policies they want to implement. Members of this group will also be responsible for framing and delivering key leadership messages around sustainability. As ideas begin to come from the front lines, this group will be critical in driving any appropriate policy changes.

Mina has a number of options around developing a sustainability network within Metro. One approach would be to establish *sustainability champions* throughout Metro. These people can help generate new program ideas and prioritize them. There should be representation from every major department, including off-shifts. These *champions* can explore a wide range of sustainability efforts in areas such as: energy, waste, food and nutrition, transportation, procurement, and so forth. Mina can deploy this group of champions not only as idea generators and implementers, but also as department communicators. Once ideas have been approved and implementation plans are in place, these champions can create enthusiasm for the new programs by speaking at monthly staff meetings and at daily unit huddles. They can help, on the local level, to drive such programs as recycling projects, carpool programs, energy conservation initiatives, and so forth.

Mina can engage the communications department in identifying forums where progress can be communicated throughout the hospital. Keeping sustainability targets and progress against those targets will be critical in keeping the initiative fresh and not appearing as simply a flavor of the month. Identifying opportunities to apply for local and state energy recognition awards can help to further build pride in the staff's accomplishments. Also, participating in national efforts such as Earth Day will even further appeal to hospital employees that they are not only helping local patients and their families, but are also participating in efforts that make a difference across the country.

Sharon Fletcher

The advice from Jen certainly offers a good, sound start for a sustainability campaign. In any sustainability process, an organization needs to link its objectives to that of the mission of the organization. Jen has offered Mina some good advice as to the need to seek simple projects that could build some excitement and collaboration around the goal of sustainability. Health care organizations are in a distinctive situation today to embrace initiatives that have cost containing measures, especially with the competing nature of the industry. Additionally, health care reform has brought a new paradigm to the industry, forcing organizations to think and act differently.

Defining a reliable structure for sustainability should be directly related to the type of initiative being explored. Any cost-saving initiative will most likely be palatable in an organization that already is suffering from lack of resources. Mina's organization of a sustainability initiative should start with identifying key stakeholders within the organization that share the financial concerns of Metro. Mina will need to involve the board of directors, CEO, and other key senior leaders initially to demonstrate the financial gains that will be achieved through deliberate focus on specific initiatives.

Gaining the voice of the internal customer, the employees, will also help to gain engagement. Mina should conduct an internal needs assessment to seek feedback from employees on operational opportunities to see where gaps may be found. Mina should narrow the operational concerns to find an opportunity that offers the best return on investment and focus on developing a task force of interested employees and key stakeholders to assist in the initiative. If Mina organizes the feedback from the assessments well, she should be able to create a compelling case of cost savings to get stakeholders engaged in the opportunity. Mina needs to keep in mind that Jen offered some good suggestions on ideas of projects for Mina to focus on initially. Mina needs to find a process to confirm Jen's suggestions and seek other opportunities that were uncovered in the needs assessment.

Once Mina has listed all the obvious opportunities, she should narrow her list and develop a strategy to present to senior leadership along with a few board members. Once agreement has been determined on which project to focus on initially, Mina should comprise a task force of subject matter experts (SMEs) from the operational areas that will be involved in the initiative. These members should also be role models in their areas and individuals that can offer input in processes and work flow. The team should meet to create a plan of action outlining the objectives to accomplish. Data needs to be collected on current state to establish a benchmark. System design and behavior will both have an impact in any change that occurs. The team will need to be proactive in recognizing change management techniques that may need to be deployed in order to assist the team and the new process.

Homer Johnson Responds

Great job panel! You have given Mina a nice blueprint for success. While I will not try to summarize the excellent advice offered by the panel, their responses triggered a couple of thoughts. For example, Tony raised the question as to why Metro is getting involved in a sustainability initiative. Is it because they are being forced into it by accreditation pressures? If so, this is probably not a good reason to start any initiative. It is hard to generate any enthusiasm for something you are forced to do. So, how serious are they this time around, and what commitment of resources can be expected? This is certainly an issue that Mina and the board have to seriously explore.

Following up on Tony's comment, both Carol and Sharon mentioned tying sustainability to Metro's vision and mission. Great idea! That would give sustainability both a purpose and a focus that seem to be missing in the case. People need a higher goal than "just doing it because we have to." I am not sure what this would look like, but tying the initiative with vision and mission, particularly as it pertains to improved patient care in critical areas, should be something people really could get excited about.

Finally, all three of our panel pointed out that if sustainability was going to be meaningful at Metro it had to be a broad, system-wide effort. It cannot be a one-shot, one-event effort. And further, the panel provided some excellent change guidelines, some ideas for an organizational structure, as well as strategies for high levels of participation and involvement, coordination, communication, supportive activities, and so on. Very impressive strategy!

Thank you Tony, Carol, and Sharon for your wisdom and provocative ideas.

ACKNOWLEDGMENT

An earlier version of this article was published in *The OD Practitioner*, *43*(4), 40-43.

SECTION III

POWER AND ETHICS

CASE STUDY 13

POWER AND ETHICS

Unethical Use of Power?

Therese F. Yaeger and Peter F. Sorensen

Jane is an experienced organization development (OD) consultant with a PhD in OD and 20 years of experience in OD consulting. She has just taken on a consulting contract for a large manufacturing company which has been rapidly expanding over the 5 years.

The president of the company has built the company over a 25-year period with a strong, decisive, almost authoritarian, style. He has a reputation for being bright, well-educated, hard-driving, and decisive with little tolerance for error on the part of his employees. As a consequence, the organization has taken on a number of his characteristics and is characterized in general as a power-oriented, authoritarian-style organization.

The company has moved from a U.S.-only company to a growth-oriented international company that now includes sales, marketing and manufacturing in Europe, the Middle East, and China. But as the company attempts to incorporate employees from different parts of the world, they are increasingly experiencing interpersonal problems, ethical issues, and as a result, increasing conflict across executives and employees at the various geographical sites.

Critical Issues in Organization Development:
Case Studies for Analysis and Discussion, pp. 123–130
Copyright © 2013 by Information Age Publishing
All rights of reproduction in any form reserved.

The president is anxious to resolve the growing incidents of interpersonal difficulties and increased conflicts. Jane has been trained in, and has used, laboratory training and t-group interventions, and is considering this type of intervention as a way of dealing with the organizational problems. She has had numerous conversations with the president, and he quickly agreed that these would be appropriate interventions, and he is ready to move ahead on these techniques.

Jane is surprised when he commands that he also intends to make this an all-inclusive activity and that all employees in every country will be required to participate in these t-group sessions. In his usual decisive manner, the president calls together his executive team, which is comprised of representatives from the major functions and members from each country, and makes the announcement of the training and that "all members will be required to participate." However, Jane senses reluctance on the part of some of the organizational members—reluctance which they are afraid to voice to the president. Although Jane is a highly experienced consultant, she has had little experience with such highly power-oriented individuals and groups, let alone an organization which is international and growing rapidly. Jane is beginning to second guess her t-group interventions, but the hard-driving president won't change his mind. Suddenly Jane feels coerced into doing something that might not be appropriate at all levels in all countries.

Are there ethical dilemmas when she attempts to practice certain techniques in other regions? What are the implications of going international without an appreciation of a global perspective? Are there alternative interventions that might be more appropriate? We have asked three OD consultants—Kathleen, Sarah, and Jerry—to assist with Jane and her dilemmas.

Kathleen O'Donnell

Jane has several ethical issues to consider before continuing with this potentially messy project. It has been made very clear that the president of this company has little tolerance for failure. Jane must find a suitable solution, and quickly. First and foremost, Jane must consider the impact of these ethical issues on the OD effort and the organization in the long run.

1. **Coercion**. What consequences would a forceful implementation of an OD intervention have on an organization? Will Jane or the president reach their desired results if many of the participants are participating against their will? It is unlikely. Coercion comes into direct conflict with a number of the values of OD professionals, such as freedom and responsibility (the participants are NOT free to choose how they will participate at work) and authenticity and openness in relationships. Jane needs to determine *why* this dissonance towards the OD intervention exists. With several diverse cultures represented, it is very possible that the interventions chosen by Jane and the president are not in harmony with the cultures and work styles of many of the employees.

2. **Cultural Competence**. Is a t-group suitable for every country/region of the company, or is there a more globally appropriate intervention? In hierarchical cultures like France, for example, a random, representative sample of employees would be nearly impossible to assemble; you will not get top-tier executives in the same focus groups as entry-level employees. The manufacturing company has experienced a large amount of growth in a very short period of time. The president and Jane both have plenty of work experience in the United States. Jane, then, must "know what she doesn't know." She has an ethical responsibility to herself and the organization to both understand the limits of her own competence, and involve one or more consultants with more international experience than she has. Jane cannot properly serve the organization without a stronger understanding of *who* she is working with.

3. **Conflicting Values**. While the other members of the board have not yet been interviewed (formally or informally), it seems as though there are conflicting values and goals present. Perhaps more apparently, there are some serious conflicts between the president's work style and the values of OD. Jane must make a decision—does she forego her personal values to please the main client (the president)? Or, does Jane stay true to her OD discipline? Does

she determine what the rest of the organization values, and side with the employees? Does she take the case at all?

Jane must decide if she is willing to work within this authoritarian culture. If she is prepared to do this, then she must first work towards finding and capitalizing on compatible goals and values. For instance, it is safe to assume that everyone involved would value a decrease in interpersonal conflict. In order to accomplish this, there must be more communication. Jane determined her course of action before fully understanding the company and its issues. Perhaps Jane needs to sit down with the president and discuss options that (a) involve and appeal to those uncomfortable with the initial suggestions, or (b) are more malleable to different cultures, thus allowing each region/country to work towards the organization's new goals while preventing the violation of cultural norms.

Sarah Peacey

If the president wants to mitigate the interpersonal problems that his employees are experiencing, there are several implications to consider regarding power and ethics now that the organization is international and multicultural. A new set of assumptions and expectations must be established that takes factors such as cultural context, power distance, local laws and customs, and institutional barriers into consideration.

Cultural Context

Culture is the collective programming of the mind distinguishing the members of one group or category of people from others (Hofstede, 2005). Culture exists at various layers. These layers can include national, regional, religious, linguistic affiliation, generational, social class, organizational, and departmental to name a few. All of these cultures contribute to the values, beliefs, and behaviors of individuals which have implications for interpersonal and team dynamics. Now that the company has operations that cross national borders, conflicts between national cultural dimensions such as power distance could be causing interpersonal conflicts.

Power Distance

Power distance is defined as the extent to which the less powerful members of institutions and organizations within a country expect and accept that power is distributed unequally (Hofstede, 2005). In countries with high power distance orientation like China and France, the authoritarian management style of the president is likely to be more accepted by employees compared to Scandinavian countries like Sweden, Norway, and Denmark where low power distance orientation is characterized by a preference for decentralized power, participative and consensus oriented management styles, and autonomy. This dichotomy can be another cause of the interpersonal conflict.

Jane needs to assess whether the root cause of the conflict is a result of cultural differences before selecting an intervention. The selection and design of the intervention is also impacted by culture. Intervention design must account for the cultural values and assumptions held by organization members. Interventions may have to be modified to fit the local culture, particularly when OD practices developed in one culture are applied to organizations in another culture (Cummings & Worley, 2009).

Local Laws and Customs

Knowing how local laws and customs can impact interpersonal relationships is also important for multinational organizations. The laws applying to global businesses are as diverse as the countries in which the firms operate (Sorensen, Head, Cooperrider, & Yeager, 2004). Local laws can also impact ethical perspectives of individuals within an organization. For example, in the United States we may believe that discrimination is an unethical business practice and we have laws that enforce those values. In countries such as Iraq and Qatar which do not maintain laws pertaining to certain groups, those same practices would be considered acceptable business practice.

Other considerations that Jane should make include accommodating regular business hours, local holidays and time zone differences of different countries when scheduling meetings and conference calls and anticipating translation and comprehension errors when English as a lingua franca (ELF), or communication in English between speakers with different first languages (Seidlhofer, 2005) is adopted.

Breaking Through Institutional Barriers

The president's natural intuition could be to maintain the current management style and culture of the organization which has become institutionalized over the past 25 years. After all, the power oriented, authoritarian culture helped them grow and achieve their current level of success, so why would he want to change it?

The president needs to understand that a new paradigm for the corporate culture and management style may be required to mitigate the current issues. Commitment, support and readiness of the leadership team will also be required for the success of any OD intervention. This could mean breaking down any barriers created by the institutionalized policies, practices and beliefs of the current organization members and building a new corporate culture that better supports their growth rate and global orientation. Perhaps Jane can continue to discuss the possibility of other interventions with the president before the t-group plan is rolled out.

Jerry Bell

Jane needs to slow down and take a step back before jumping into her planned intervention. At this point, she does not yet have a strong understanding of the power and organizational issues at play; she must take the time to understand the organization's changing dynamics before choosing an appropriate intervention.

The consultant in this scenario has to be aware of the numerous power concerns that can help or hinder the outcome of this intervention. Greiner and Schein (1988) explain, for instance, that it is critical for a consultant to define the political model of the organization. Jane should consider three types of power: downward power, upward power, and sideways power. Additionally, she will need to be aware of differing interest groups. Understanding the three directions of power and the importance of choosing the right model of power will help the consultant to properly diagnose the organization. What kind of power is the president wielding? Who else has significant power within the organization, and how do they exert their influence? Are there several powerful people/groups with conflicting goals?

The second characteristic of power that Jane will need to assess is the different power bases of the organization, giving consideration to both individual and departmental power bases. Jane should start by observing individuals in positions of power. What aspects of their personality and intellect have aided in their "rise to power," so to speak? Whose support do they have? Is this support stable? Additionally, the consultant needs to be aware of the departmental power bases, such as the ability to cope with uncertainty, substitutability, and centrality. How do these factors differ from department to department, or country to country? As a result, the consultant will need to assess each power base and then create strategies either to further develop and maintain or redirect certain power bases. By identifying these key power issues, Jane can better develop an appropriate intervention.

Finally, Jane needs to understand how she can use successful power strategies to gain support. The key idea behind successful strategies is to connect the strategies with the appropriate power base. First, Jane can use the power strategy of "playing it straight," and use data to influence individuals or focus groups. She could, for instance, provide the executive team with case studies of highly successful OD interventions. She could also use social networks (building alliances and coalitions, for example) to appeal to other's support power base. Jane will need to become familiar with the different types of strategies and then accurately access the current and evolving power bases in order to exert influence in the most appropriate manner.

Once Jane has a better handle on the power dynamics of the rapidly changing company, she should go to the president with a much more specific set of questions that need to be addressed. After these details have been sufficiently addressed, Jane will be better prepared to choose the most suitable intervention for the organization.

REFERENCES

Cummings, T., Worley, C. (2008). *Organization development and change.* Mason, OH: South-Western College.

Greiner, L. E., & Schein, V. E. (1988). *Power and organization development: Mobilizing power to implement change.* Reading, MA: Addison-Wesley.

Hofstede, G., & Hofstede, G. J. (2005). *Cultures and organizations: Software of the mind.* New York, NY: McGraw-Hill.

Seidlhofer, B. (2005). Key concepts in ELT: English as a lingua franca. *ELT Journal.* 59 (4) pages 399-341.

Sorensen, P. F., Head, T. C., Cooperrider, D. C., Yeager, T. (2004) *Global and International organization development.* Champaign, IL: Stipes.

CASE STUDY 14

SOME QUESTIONABLE PRACTICES AT COUNTY GENERAL

Homer H. Johnson

"This has got to be the highlight of my career, this is why I went into OD [organization development]," Darlene thought as she watched the Excellence Award presentations at County General Hospital. She was called to the stage twice that afternoon, once as part of a team that received the Most Improved Unit Award, and second, to receive an Outstanding Contributor Award for her efforts as an internal OD consultant in turning around a beleaguered patient transport unit. "It doesn't get any better than this," she shouted to the audience as she received her second award.

The story started some 18 months prior to the award ceremony when she received a frantic call from the CEO of County General saying that he had to see her immediately. In response to numerous complaints regarding the patient transport unit, the state regulators paid County General a surprise visit. And to no one's surprise they uncovered a myriad of problems and several violations of state hospital regulations.

County's patient transport unit had long been a source of complaints from both patients and hospital staff. The unit was a very important and busy 24-hour operation, averaging 3,000 internal transports per 24 hour

Critical Issues in Organization Development:
Case Studies for Analysis and Discussion, pp. 131–141
Copyright © 2013 by Information Age Publishing
All rights of reproduction in any form reserved.

period. Unfortunately the unit had been plagued with ineffective and ever-changing leadership, poor organization, high turnover of transport workers, and poor service.

The state regulators singled out the lack of training of transport workers as being a root cause of many of the problems. Before they are allowed to transport a patient, all workers must complete a training program on proper care of patients, and, in addition, must partner with an experienced transport employee for 2 weeks. However, because of the high turnover of employees and the high work demands, new employees were being pressed into service immediately. Only about half of the current transport employees had received the necessary training and supervised experience.

Moreover, less than 10% of the transport employees had been given instruction on emergency evacuation procedures. This training was typically given after the employee had been on the job for 6 months.

The CEO said that Darlene's assignment was to work with the new manager of the unit, Danny, to "get that unit running smoothly and in compliance as quickly as possible."

Darlene bonded with Danny almost immediately. He was very motivated to improve the performance of the unit and very open to her suggestions. Much of her work initially was basic OD—helping Danny's management team develop a mission for the unit, setting standards of excellence, and setting both long-term and short-term goals to achieve the standards of excellence.

However, Darlene's OD background did not prepare her for some of the tasks in which she became involved. For example, she facilitated and acted as a resource person in developing performance management criteria and procedures for the transport workers, and she was part of a team that implemented a new computer-based patient tracking system.

The assignment took almost 100% of her time for about 6 months. After that initial period, she gradually reduced her time commitment to the unit such that she had completely disengaged after an additional 6 months.

As noted in the awards ceremony, the unit quickly became a model of excellence. Patient and staff complaints went down dramatically, employee turnover was cut in half, 100% of the transport workers had received the basic patient care training, and almost 80% had received training on evacuation procedures.

Darlene was very proud of her work with the unit. She displayed her award on her desk, and frequently used the unit as an example of how struggling units can rise to the level of excellence.

About 7 months after the award ceremony, Darlene saw three of the transport workers she knew eating lunch in the cafeteria and asked to join them. In the course of the conversation, they discussed the award cere-mony and Darlene told them that she was very impressed with the fact that the unit had gone from about 50% trained workers to 100% in a very short time, and how most transport workers were additionally trained on emergency evacuation procedures.

The group suddenly went silent. "Did I say something wrong?" Dar-lene asked.

More silence.

Finally, one of the workers at the table, Rosa, said, "Well, I suppose we can tell you now, but actually a lot of the training certificates were forged. We were understaffed and couldn't afford to send people to training. So, the new employees just worked with an experienced employee for a cou-ple of days and then they were on their own." Rosa went on to explain that since they were under pressure to comply with the state regulations for 100% trained personnel, Danny forged a lot of the training certificates and told the workers that they would get their training when the unit was less busy.

"But," Rosa quickly added, "Now every new employee gets trained properly, so we are probably getting close to the 100% we got the award for. So, everything's okay now."

Darlene was shocked. "Are you saying that many of the new transport workers did not receive the basic training as required by the hospital and the state?"

All three employees nodded yes. "There was no time to train people. We were too busy! We were short people and had to move patients."

"How about the evacuation training?" Darlene followed.

"Same problem, no time," they replied. But they hastened to add that many of the workers were starting to take the evac training now.

Darlene left the lunchroom very upset and very angry. She had no doubts that Rosa and the other workers were telling the truth. She had known them to be three of the best transport employees—very honest and very hard working.

She started to think about what she should do now. Maybe just forget about it? While it might be true that some lies were told to satisfy the reg-ulators, no harm was done as far as she could tell. No patient died because of the lack of training, and Rosa assured her that the unit was close to 100% trained now. So it's over; it's history, and it's not Darlene's problem, so why stir things up now?

On the other hand, Darlene felt that she had been hoodwinked. She and the unit had been given all sorts of accolades and awards that were based partially on lies. She had been lied to, the hospital administration had been lied to, and the state regulators had been lied to. And patients' lives had been endangered. That is not only unethical, but it is illegal!

Maybe she should go immediately to the CEO, or to the hospital compliance officer, or to the state regulators and blow the whistle on what had occurred.

But she also realized that if this information got out it could cause a lot of trouble. Danny could get fired, and so could those employees whose training certificates were forged. Moreover, the hospital would get into a pack of trouble with the state regulators and heads could roll because of that. And since she could be seen as the cause of the problems, she would end up on everyone's hate list. Maybe it's best to keep her mouth shut.

Assuming that Rosa's information is correct, what would you advise Darlene to do? Why?

Looking at the broader issue of ethical behavior, what advice do you have for OD consultants who face ethical issues? Are there any general guidelines that can be followed?

We asked three expert consultants, Ginny Storjohann, Tammy Seibert, and Kit Tennis to tell us what advice they would give Darlene, as well as how to handle tricky ethical situations.

Ginny Storjohann

I just hate how often the root causes of my consulting issues seem to turn up in my own mirror. Way before directing her sense of betrayal toward the client, who obviously made some poor choices, let's reflect on how she likely helped create this. With that perspective in place we'll be better prepared to consider next steps.

For starters, I'd like to begin with some entry and contracting curiosities:

Beyond "getting that unit running smoothly and in compliance," what clarifying discussions did she have with the CEO in framing this project for success? How did the CEO and others collude in making the Patient Transport system a "long source of complaints"—turnover? More importantly, what ownership and support are they providing now to turn it around?

Who was the client? The CEO? Danny? Danny and his management team? Was she clear in letting each of them know what was needed from them?

What data gathering did she use to get a handle on current realities and essential changes beyond that which the state regulators described?

"Darlene bonded with Danny almost immediately ... very motivated to improve ... open to suggestions." What is confluence? She may have failed to develop understanding around a variety of expectations that needed to be clarified with Danny. Was she taken in innocently by his willingness to agree with her and the direction she wanted to go? This is often a learned survival behavior, especially for those bottoms of an organization. How did she delve beneath?

"Darlene's background did not prepare her ... part of the team ... 100% of her time." How were roles, responsibilities, work norms, mutual expectations and avenues for redress of disagreements defined? Her positive intention, enthusiasm and willingness to pitch in to get the job done are both respectable, and likely to have affected her ability to hold perspective and influence direction.

Next question: So, what now?

I'd cue up these guidelines for consideration as she persists through the difficulties and sets out to transform these events into a more positive learning opportunity: First, set her goals and define her own minimum ethical requirements. For example, her intention could be to create openness and honesty wherever she feels she:

1. Has had any kind of role, albeit unknowing, in what became a deception; and

2. Anywhere that her role in the organization may have implicit or explicit responsibility to model a higher standard of accountability in such matters.

Second, consider the working hypothesis that problems are usually best identified and solved at the level they were created and by those most involved and affected by them. Seems like a heart-to-heart with Danny and other key management members of the hospital transport system is where to begin addressing relationship issues, sorting data from interpretation and addressing legitimate system responsibilities and implications. Necessary steps and next contacts are likely to emerge.

Third, without compromising her ethical boundaries, I'd recommend she create a polarity map to supplement her thinking and balance some of the forces at play here. For example, there are likely to be interdependent needs to be both candid and diplomatic as matters become more public. My hope would be that by inviting this broader view, she'll be able to consider the best interests of all parties.

It's what makes OD consulting distinct from other disciplines that needs to show up now. She's obviously connected with some system dysfunctions that probably preceded and now belong to her. It's who she is and how she attends to these difficulties that will give new meaning to her comment "this is why I went into OD."

Tammy Seibert

Darlene has two options: She can go directly to the CEO of County General and report the information which she has acquired, or she can meet with Danny about what she has learned. "Keeping her mouth shut" is not an option because Danny's actions have subjected County General to significant legal exposure, and his team and hospital leadership to trust and integrity issues. Darlene cannot make the assumption that Danny, his group and she are the only people aware of Danny forging the signatures on the training documentation.

How Should Darlene Approach Danny?

- Make the decision to work with Danny in understanding his actions versus going around Danny to the CEO with her discovery.
- Immediately set up a meeting with Danny.
- Prepare for the meeting by, first and foremost, setting aside any personal feelings of being "hoodwinked." The focus needs to be on

the organization and Danny. Darlene needs to keep in mind that turnover rate has improved for the group as well as a decline in number of patient and staff complaints. By no means are the other improvements justification for Danny's actions but it could help his case if he were to come forward with his actions. She needs to gather all sides of the "story" in a non-threatening way. Devise a plan on how to approach Danny and be prepared for a range of emotional responses or lack of response as well as lack of ownership of the problem.

- Keep the meeting focused on the issue at hand and its implications on team members and the organization.
- If, during the meeting, Danny is open about his actions and wants to set things right, Darlene could offer to brainstorm with him to come up with a plan for him to approach County General's leadership with what he has done and how he plans to rectify the situation. If during the meeting Danny is not cooperative or responsive and Darlene has exhausted all means of sharing with him the implications of his actions, she then should escalate the discovery of forged training certificates to the appropriate leaders.

Darlene is in a difficult and likely an emotionally charged situation. Ethically, with or without Danny's cooperation, Darlene is obligated to be open with County General's leadership on the information she has learned from hospital staff. She cannot internally justify that, because patients did not die due to a lack of training, doesn't mean it cannot happen in the future.

I would hope that Darlene would have the following learnings from this assignment:

- At the start of the project be clear on contracting individual roles and accountabilities and stick to it. It appears that partway into the project Darlene was doing work that Danny or his managers should have been leading.
- As an internal OD consultant, it is Darlene's role to facilitate and promote Danny's ownership of the project and support his ability to sustain change after the project ends. Darlene probably should have not become completely disengaged from the project until all short-term and long-term goals were met. Instead, she should have set up check-in points or evaluation points with Danny and his team to ensure that they were on track.

Christopher "Kit" Tennis

Darlene's challenge is to do the right thing for the hospital, their patients, and her career at the same time. Here's what I would tell her:

E-mail yourself a memo that details what you have learned. This will establish a dateline in case you are confronted with someone claiming you were in on the deception, or any other malfeasance.

Meet with Danny. Tell him what a terrible position he put everyone in—you, him, hospital leadership, his employees, and especially the patients. Tell him you will have to take action, but the action you will take may be affected by what you discover about what has happened.

- Learn from him who knows of the forgeries—and whether this list includes anyone from hospital administration.
- Ascertain the actual compliance rates for training.

If the hospital administration does not know what transpired, and nearly 100% of transport employees have received the required training as Rosa and other transport workers reported, advise Danny that you are going to carry this information to the CEO in one week, unless Danny does so himself in that time. This gives him a week to gather his numbers and "arrange his affairs." Require Danny to sign a memorandum of today's conversation between you and him as a good faith assurance of each other's actions—you will sign it as well. Begin an analysis of the entire situation—systemic pressures, outcomes, feelings, and so on, and potential lessons the organization could learn from this event.

If the numbers are still miserable, give Danny one day to act before you tell the administration what you have learned. Get Danny to sign the memo of today's conversation, or lacking that, immediately e-mail yourself an update on what transpired.

If numbers are good but the hospital administrators knew what was going on, get ready to confront them and prepare your résumé. They all played you for a dupe.

If the numbers are bad and hospital administration is complicit in the fraud, immediately contact a good employment attorney experienced with whistle-blowing, get ready to go to the state regulators, and prepare your résumé.

General Guide

When you are faced with ethical issues, back away from dichotomous thinking (e.g., collude or quit) to get some broader understanding of the entire situation and the people involved—their perceptions, their constraints, their aims, and their values.

- Consider what best serves the client system, the system customers, other public and private stakeholders, your own conscience, and career.
- Consider what personal, positional, and moral leverage you have for correcting the ethical breach and for teaching the system.
- Consider the magnitude of the breach and the appropriate intensity of your response.
- If you see any possibility that you could be dragged down with the ethics breach, create a dated paper trail to corroborate your story.
- Finally, always be prepared to walk away. When you are perfectly clear that you have other job and career options, you are fully empowered to speak the truth and act ethically, which makes you a powerful OD partner to any organization.

Homer Johnson Responds

Great advice from our panel on a very sticky question.

I thought it interesting that all panel members advised Darlene to face the issue—ignoring the problem would probably be the easiest response in this situation but for the panel that was not an option! And all advised Darlene to first meet with Danny and get his version of the story—Danny has to take responsibility for his actions. If that meeting did not provide any action, the next step would be to go to the hospital administrators. Each member of the panel had a slightly different approach for dealing with Danny, and I urge the reader to compare approaches.

Also worth noting is the panel's advice to use the experience as a learning experience. Both Darlene and the organization can learn much from what happened at County General. And the panel pointed to several ways that Darlene needed to reexamine her behavior, particularly in the contracting phase of the consulting process. Again, the reader is urged to consider the approaches outlined by the panel members.

Finally, I liked Kit's advice to "always be prepared to walk away." Or, as Larry Anders once told me, "Always keep your résumé current!" Implausible as it may seem, consultants (and employees) sometimes find themselves perceived as troublemakers and bad guys simply because they raised an ethical issue. Those who were trying to do the "right thing" often end up on the company blacklist. If you find yourself in such a situation it is time to walk and to walk quickly. You might also get a good attorney; your days of helping that organization are over.

Thank you Ginny, Tammy and Kit—nice job!

Many thanks to Cecily Crowther for information related to this case.

ACKNOWLEDGMENT

An earlier version of this article was published in *The OD Practitioner,* *38*(1), 50-54.

CASE STUDY 15

THE CASE OF 360 DEGREE REVIEWS AT ELECTRONICS DIVISION

Homer H. Johnson

James Talltree was very pleased when Cindy Walsh, the Associate Vice President of human resources (HR) of the electronics division of CarCorp, informed him that he had been chosen to lead a new 360 degree review initiative for the division. CarCorp was a large corporation that manufactured a variety of auto parts both for the major auto companies as well as for the auto aftermarket. The electronics division was the largest and most profitable of the four CarCorp divisions. James had only been with the division for about 3 years as a member of a small, four-person, internal OD unit that reported to Cindy (who, in turn, reported to the division vice president of human resources). This was the first time he had been asked to lead a project, and as Cindy indicated, this was a "dream assignment" and a great opportunity to show the top people what he could do.

As Cindy explained, electronics was embarking on a major leadership initiative of which 360 degree reviews would be an important part. In this review process, managers are rated on their behavior and performance by their employees, peers, as well as the persons to whom they report. The ratings are then given to the manager in the form of a feedback report.

Critical Issues in Organization Development:
Case Studies for Analysis and Discussion, pp. 143–152
Copyright © 2013 by Information Age Publishing
All rights of reproduction in any form reserved.

Over the next 2 years all 400 senior and middle managers in electronics would receive 360 degree reviews. Just how to do this was James' assignment.

Over the next 4 months, James interviewed the division executives to better understand their expectations for the project. He also conducted focus groups of middle and upper managers to determine how they thought the project should run and what they would need from the process to help them develop as managers and leaders. He also benchmarked several corporations who were noted for their 360 process, and interviewed four vendors who could customize the 360 questionnaire and the feedback report to electronics' specifications.

At the end of the four months James submitted a proposal to Cindy that outlined a recommended process. He was particularly proud of several points contained in the proposal that he thought would make the process particularly effective. First, there were assurances that the persons who rated a given manager would remain anonymous. This should provide managers with honest feedback about their performance. Second, no one would see an individual manager's feedback report other than that manager. The reports were to be confidential. The 360 process was for developmental purposes only, not for assessment or evaluation. Finally, all managers would be provided with follow-up support, either through the use of executive coaches or a series of half-day workshops. These conditions would be spelled out in a "contract" that would be sent to both raters and managers.

The proposal was widely distributed and all top managers and all human resource executives had an opportunity to comment on it. James was pleased that almost all were very complimentary and the changes suggested were minor.

The project started on schedule and by all accounts it was very successful. Post project evaluations conducted by Cindy found that over 90% of the scores were either 4 or 5 (with 5 being the highest score). James received numerous personal thank you notes from individual managers, and the president of the electronics division sent James a note congratulating him for a very successful initiative. The president added that he thought James' efforts had made a substantial contribution to improving the effectiveness of the division.

About 3 months after the managers in electronics had received their feedback reports, James was called into Cindy's office and was told that the vice president of manufacturing for electronics had requested the ratings and the feedback reports on seven managers. The vice president explained that these managers, listed by name, were going through a "management review," and the 360 data would be helpful in that review.

He made it clear that he was acting on order of the president and top management team at electronics who were conducting the reviews.

James had assumed that everyone in the division understood that feedback reports were confidential and only to be seen by the individual manager. That was critical for the developmental nature of the process. That was the "contract" with the managers. He was further concerned that the reports would be used as a part of a "management review." While the purpose of this review process was purported to assess a manager for "promotion and other assignments," it was common knowledge that the reviews were used to provide documentation for managers who were being considered for termination. Using the reports for this purpose was a violation of the "contract" because managers were assured that the 360s would be used for their individual development, not for assessment or evaluation.

James explained this to Cindy and they decided that James would write a response to the manufacturing vice president explaining why he could not comply with his request. The response outlined the points noted above, and also attached was a copy of the original proposal as well as the "contract" information that was sent to all participants.

When James did not hear back on his memo he assumed the issue was settled. However, three weeks, later, Cindy called him into her office and showed him another memo from the same vice president. Once again, he requested the information on the seven managers, specified a date by which compliance was expected, and also asked for the name of the contact person of the vendor who was providing the feedback reports. The memo also indicated that this request did not violate the spirit of the "contract" with the managers because the management review is used for developmental purposes in that it looks at where best to place a manager. With regard to the confidentiality issue, the vice president stated that any information collected by the division on an individual manager could and should be used in making a personnel decision.

James became very angry and told Cindy he thought this was an ethics issue. The "contract" with the managers could not be violated. Further, since the 360 information would probably be used to terminate these seven managers, how could someone say it was developmental?

Cindy was less concerned with the request. While she acknowledged that the management review was primarily used to terminate managers, she asked how the release of this information could hurt? Assuming that there was a high likelihood that these managers would be terminated anyway, if the 360 was negative it wouldn't make much difference. The managers were on their way out and given a negative 360 report they probably should go. But if the 360 information was very positive maybe the reviewers would have second thoughts and retain the manager. So, the release of the 360 information might actually save the careers of some of the managers. However, she also indicated that she could understand and was sympathetic with the point that James was making.

The meeting ended with Cindy saying it was James' call. He was the project leader and had to make the decision. For the next 2 days James pondered his decision. Did Cindy have a valid point and maybe he should release the information? Or, maybe not release the information but tell the vice president to get it from the vendor, given that the vendor was under no "contract" to withhold the information? In this way, the vice president would get the information and James' conscience would be clear (sort of). Maybe he should appeal the request, but to whom? Or maybe he should simply say "no" again. In the back of his mind he was also thinking about how his decision would affect his career at electronics. This "dream assignment" was turning into a nightmare.

What do you see as James' options? Assuming you are James, what would you do? Why?

Paul Cadario

The manufacturing vice president (VP) for the electronics division is on the verge of breaking many of the basic tenets of 360 degree feedback, and may have already exposed the organization to significant morale, trust, and legal exposure.

James has behaved very professionally in developing and implementing the 360 degree program, benchmarking it, all with the support of senior management before starting out. It was clear from the outset that the business case for the pilot was based on the managers using their own feedback for developmental purposes, that it was anonymous and confidential, and that it would not be shared. This was spelled out in a written contract with the participants, and presumably the providers of feedback understood this as well.

The manufacturing VP for electronics now wants to break that contract with staff and use the feedback results for both assessment and evaluation. If allowed, this would put James and his HR colleagues, particularly Cindy, in an untenable position. Future communications from HR about other initiatives, and even the possible roll-out of a very successful 360 degree program pilot throughout CarCorp, are jeopardized. James' fall-back position, to direct the manufacturing VP to the vendor, will have much the same consequences for electronics as if James had handed over the data himself or provided it to Cindy or to the HR VP for the business unit. More than the credibility of HR is at stake; staff and manager trust in senior management is now on the line.

To use data for "management review" purposes, and by implication remove some of the seven managers, may expose the company to legal liability. In addition to the broken written undertaking not to use the feedback results for anything but development, the company may be liable should a manager who was dismissed argue that the action was taken unfairly, using data that were to be used for something else. In subsequent litigation, Electronics may find its full scheme of HR practices open to challenge, particularly if the opaque management review process is discovered to have other features that might expose it to EEOC scrutiny and legal challenge.

In fact, the very request for the data may have already exposed electronics to legal problems. It appears that Cindy, and perhaps others in HR, see the management review process as primarily to terminate those it reviews: the negative 360 degree results may well confirm what the meetings would have concluded anyway. But in the context of the potential negative consequences: questions raised by a disgruntled ex-manager and her or his lawyer, in legal proceedings that would inevitably cast doubt more broadly on management's behavior in the placement and promotion of managers, and the damage done to internal morale, such confirmation comes at too dear a price. If the case could be settled outside of court as electronics' general counsel and outside employment counsel might well advise, the damage could be less rather than more, but that determination would not be made until a future time.

As James's manager, Cindy has an obligation to see that this promising and apparently very talented young OD professional is not made a scapegoat for the manufacturing VP's improper behavior. At this point, as a corporate officer, she should work with other HR peers, including her superior, as well as electronics' lawyers, to frame their refusal to hand over the feedback results in the context of the broader legal and reputation consequences to electronics. The general counsel should present these arguments to the management team: it is no longer just an HR or OD matter.

Sherry Camden-Anders

As consultants we can certainly find ourselves in situations where we have to make choice decisions—decisions that sometimes challenge ethics and morals. Such is the case for James Talltree who must answer two questions for himself: What shall I do? And who shall I be?

James has done all the things necessary to make the 360-degree feedback process a useful tool in the electronics division for the 400 managers. It has been contracted as a developmental process, confidentiality granted to participants, and reports given only to the individual manager with coaches available for follow-up. He is faced with an ethical dilemma when the VP of manufacturing asks for the reports of seven managers. We might question whether the executive team initially understood the contract and the ethical issues involved!

What should James do? The following are options I would choose in order to maintain my integrity and my ethical responsibility in practicing OD:

- Request a face-to-face meeting with the VP of manufacturing and the president (willing to meet with each individually or together) explaining that I would like to discuss the ramifications the request would have on the division/organization as a whole.
- If a meeting is accepted, then I would prepare my remarks to focus on the positive impact of the 360 for developmental purposes, the consequences and impact of sharing confidential information, and be prepared to discuss the current process for management reviews, including how they are perceived in the organization.

- If a meeting was refused, then I would write a response and refuse to provide the information, once again explaining the agreed upon contracts and the consequences of breaking those agreements.
- Share what I plan to do with Cindy and why.
- Prepare to resign gracefully depending on the outcome.

I believe I have to understand my vulnerability as a consultant (ethical dilemmas can occur at any time in my work with organizations) and anticipate that I might find myself in situations where my job, money, or career cannot take precedence over my integrity and character. I need to be familiar with and live the OD code of ethics. In anticipating how an intervention may impact an organization and its people, I have a responsibility to be clear in the initial stages regarding what is or is not ethical and to build a relationship and understanding with the executives involved in the project. James, in his dilemma, needs to let go of his career with this company and take a stand—refusing to give the reports to the VP of manufacturing. At jeopardy (should he choose to go along with the VP) is the trust of individuals in the organization towards management, the units represented, such as HR and OD, and the individuals involved. The project would fail—the individuals and the organization would ultimately suffer.

Chris Pett

While a difficult situation, James has the opportunity to emerge as a solution-builder, engaging the leaders involved—both line and HR—in a way that could model the leadership qualities embodied in the 360 survey. Or he will have modeled those qualities in his own behavior in support of his personal and professional integrity.

Here is a proposed course of action for James and the involved parties:

James meets with the manufacturing VP one-on-one to clarify his immediate needs and concerns; James works with his manager and division HR VP to craft a short-term solution that helps the manufacturing VP to conduct a review exclusive of the 360 feedback data. An alternative suggestion might be to generate new data in a process agreeable to the seven managers. After having met the immediate need of the manufacturing VP, bring together the appropriate leaders and line managers to review the 360 process and its goals to reach a decision about whether this will remain a solely developmental tool or also be used in an evaluative manner. Perhaps the organization needs to take a look at how manager reviews have been conducted in the past and consider creating an updated process that uses alternative data.

If the group cannot agree to a mutually supported solution, the senior HR and OD leaders would escalate the issue to the division's senior leader or beyond.

Learnings: James should have met with the manufacturing VP immediately when the first request for data was made to clarify the needs and issues of both sides of the situation and not rely on sending a response via memo. Also, he should have quickly involved senior HR leaders in supporting a response that everyone was willing to stand by.

In any case, James should stand his ground and not agree to release the 360 data. Ideally, he will have built support from the senior HR leadership and if necessary worked with them to escalate the case to the senior divisional leader. If James does not get this support, he should document the process to protect himself and ensure the facts of the situation are captured. I would like to think that if I were James and experienced personal repercussions, I would seek the appropriate redress and if necessary, negotiate a respectful process for leaving the organization.

Homer Johnson Responds

The broader issue raised by this case deals with the confidentiality of data collected by OD consultants. I am aware of a couple of 360 cases similar to that described in the electronics division case. in addition, there have been cases involving survey feedback, and action research, in which the feedback reports that were to be seen only by the members of the unit involved were requested by other members of the organization. OD consultants, both internal and external, often collect data that could be considered very sensitive to individuals and organizations. Who sees this data, or who doesn't see this data, sometimes can provide an interesting dilemma for the consultant, particularly the internal consultant whose job is on the line.

There are several interesting variations of the electronics division case. For example, one company requested the services of an external OD consultant to assist with coaching their midlevel managers who were receiving 360 feedback, and made it clear to the consultant (and managers) that, although this process was developmental, the feedback reports were to be shared with senior management. Or consider the company who wanted the coach to send periodic "progress reports" to senior management used to evaluate the progress being made with each of the managers she was coaching, with the implication that if the coach reported insufficient progress, the manager would be terminated or reassigned. Although neither of these cases involve a violation of a "contract" with the employee, as in the electronics division case, would you as an OD consultant feel comfortable in accepting such an assignment?

In the electronics division case all members for our expert panel saw a clear violation of the company's contract with the managers in question, and all were in agreement that they would not provide the manufacturing VP with the feedback report. Each panel member had a slightly different way of addressing the problem. I will not repeat these here except to note a couple of points that stood out.

Paul Cadario makes a very important point in noting that there is a lot at stake in that the release of this information would seriously jeopardize the credibility of HR as well as any future initiatives coming from that function. Moreover, as Paul points out, there may be legal consequences if the information is given to the VP of manufacturing, no matter who provides that information. Certainly these points should be central in any discussions with the manufacturing VP.

All panel members suggested a meeting with the VP of manufacturing (no more memo writing). And there was some consensus that this is not something that James should do alone. Given the potential risks to HR and electronics, Cindy needs to be involved as does her boss, the division VP of HR, and possibly the legal counsel. James' top priority now is building support with these other parties.

Chris Pett offers an interesting and constructive approach to this dilemma by suggesting that James and HR take a problem solving focus in their meeting with the VP of manufacturing. How can they help him/her conduct the management reviews, exclusive of the 360 reports? Perhaps they can assist in the development of a better and more valid process for what is usually a very difficult decision. This would meet the needs of the manufacturing VP and also preserve the integrity of the 360 process, thus creating a win-win situation for all parties. Moreover, this would enhance the credibility of HR and OD as people who can be called upon as company problem solvers.

Finally, as Sherry Camden-Anders points out, we do have an OD code of ethics that provides valuable guidelines for a variety of dilemmas that arise in professional practice. She further suggests we need to anticipate how an intervention may impact the organization and its people, and to develop an understanding with the client in the initial stages as to what is or is not ethical.

ACKNOWLEDGMENT

An earler version of this article was published in *The OD Practitioner*, *35*(1), 38-42.

CASE STUDY 16

YOU WALKED INTO A POLITICAL MINEFIELD, AND I HOPE YOU SURVIVE

Homer H. Johnson

The new job at MajorCorp was exactly the type of organization development (OD) position that Charlie had been looking for. Not only was the salary great but he would be involved in some very big change projects. He reported directly to Joan Dary, who had also recently joined the corporation as the Corporate Vice President for Human Resources. Joan had told him that he was to be their "expert on change."

About a month after he joined the organization he received his first assignment, which was to help install a new managerial performance appraisal system corporate-wide. The new system was quite similar to that developed at General Electric (GE). Each year, all managers would be rated on a variety of "leadership competencies" as well as on the performance of their work unit. These ratings would be converted to a ranking, such that all managers in a facility or division would be ranked from high to low. Furthermore, the new system would follow the GE 20-70-10 policy. The top ranked 20% of the managers would receive substantial salary increases and stock options; the middle 70% would receive solid salary increases; and the lower 10% would be transitioned out of the corporation regardless of how well they had performed. This latter group would be given nine months to find another job, and would be given ample outplacement support.

Critical Issues in Organization Development:
Case Studies for Analysis and Discussion, pp. 153–161
Copyright © 2013 by Information Age Publishing
All rights of reproduction in any form reserved.

Much of the new system was not too different from the performance management system now in use, although it added some new "performance-related" competencies. What was quite different was the 20-70-10 policy. Joan acknowledged that the MajorCorp managers would find this policy difficult at first, and stated that the system would be phased in—the managers would be only ranked the first year of the new system to work out the bugs of the ranking process. Once the managers understood the process, the 20-70-10 policy would be introduced in the second year.

Charlie's assignment would be to design the change process and help facilitate the change. While key managers would have the responsibility of implementing the change, they would need a lot of help in mapping out the change process and in working through some of the sticky issues. That was where Charlie's expertise would be valuable.

In the next month and a half, Charlie kept busy learning as much as he could about the new system. He read the initial proposal on the system that had been presented to the executive committee at MajorCorp, as well as several articles that Joan had given him. He also flew to Boston to review the materials offered by the vendor that Joan had recommended, and visited another corporation that had installed a similar system about a year ago.

After getting a good idea as to what the new system would look like, Charlie decided to turn his attention to thinking about how it might be implemented at MajorCorp. He had been told that a great resource would be Terri Kraemer. Terri reported directly to the chief operating officer (COO) and was in charge of "special projects" for the COO. Much of her job involved implementing change and she seemed to be the ideal person to give him some advice about implementing the new system. So, he set up a lunch meeting with her.

Approaching her table, and before he could even say hello to her, she said rather jokingly, "I understand that you are the one that has been chosen to ram the new performance system down our throats!" Charlie was a bit shocked by her greeting, and could only respond by saying, "I don't understand what you are saying. What do you mean?"

Terri went on to explain that MajorCorp had hired a new CEO about three years ago who committed to making some rather dramatic changes, the performance system being one of them. However, the proposed performance management system proved rather controversial and was opposed by most of the top managers in the corporation.

"Didn't the executive committee approve this?" Charlie asked.

"Not really," Terri said, "The CEO made the proposal at one of their meetings. The group objected, and the Big Guy said, well, tough, we are doing it anyway. So, not only don't the top managers like the idea, they also don't like how it is being shoved down their throats!"

Terri went on to talk about how MajorCorp had enjoyed much success over the years by using a very team-based and collaborative culture. There is a great deal of fear that the new performance management system would destroy that culture by introducing a strong competitive element among managers. She added, "The former corporate VP for HR led the opposition to the proposal. As a result, he was let go. Joan was then brought aboard. Then she hired you to ram it through."

"There is an interesting political dynamic going on in the corporation now," she observed. Her analysis was that when the new CEO was hired 3 years ago, he made a lot of glowing promises to the board of directors which haven't materialized. "All he has done is create a lot of dissention," she said, "and very few results. I think this is his, probably final, attempt to move the corporation." "But," she added, "Rumor is that the top managers will either block or sabotage the new system, which will make him look bad. I don't really think he will be here much longer."

As they left Terri said, "I'm glad I am not in your shoes. I think you just walked into a political minefield, and I hope you get out alive. You seem like a nice guy!"

As he walked to his office, two questions seemed to keep popping up:

First, he was starting to think that maybe the change he was supposed to be implementing was not good for the corporation. But then again, should he be deciding what is good for the corporation? Isn't it his job as an internal OD specialist just to help implement the programs decided upon by others, regardless of what he thinks about them—good or bad? Just what are the internal consultant's obligations?

Second, assuming that Terri is correct—that the key managers will not implement the new system, or they purposely are going to sabotage it— what should he do now? Just go through the motions and hope for the best? Or tell Joan to cancel the project? Or stall for time to see how the politics play out? Or what?

What is your advice to Charlie regarding these two questions? What should Charlie do?

Moreover, what advice would you give OD consultants who find themselves in the middle of a political minefield? What's a good overall strategy?

We asked three expert consultants, Ross Tartell, Rose Hollister, and Lola Wilcox to tell us what advice they would give Charlie, as well as how best to handle tricky political situations.

Ross Tartell

Charlie should make a good faith effort to implement the new performance management system because that is what he agreed to do when he took the job. There is no question that Charlie is in a tough spot; however, he will have a chance at working through the issues if he follows these OD principles: Focus on the business case for the change, clearly understand the client, and do a thorough analysis of the key stakeholders and constituencies.

Charlie's first instincts are correct. He needs to understand the new performance management system. This need extends to the definition of the business case. Why did the system work for other corporations? What was the business case presented to the board? How does that apply within the MajorCorp environment?

Because of the extraordinary level of dissension in MajorCorp, a two-pronged approach may work: engagement and influence, coupled with exercising of position power. Charlie can take a "please orient me" approach to enable him to have candid conversations. During these dialogues he will be able to explore the business case, how the process might work, and, unlike an external consultant, build rapport by taking a "we are all in this together" approach. As he works through the key players, he will be able to define people's objections, do a stakeholder analysis to pinpoint areas of support and resources, and to keep Joan involved. Joan can be invaluable not only for her "intelligence" but for her position power, which can be deployed in response to threats to the process. Charlie also needs to identify the client (i.e., the CEO, line management?) and clarify his role in order to understand how to respond to the political minefield. Charlie will need to reinforce his role of designing the change process and helping key managers with the responsibility of implementing the change. If he is seen as the person "ramming this down their throats," the project will probably fail and he will not likely survive.

What does this case delineate for the OD professional? First, know the client. Second, use engagement and listening as a way to build understanding and a foundation for conflict resolution and common goals. Third, define the business case in order to keep objectivity and motivation for change. Finally, participate fully in the debate and dialogue before the decision is made. Then, assuming the decision is ethical, do your professional best to support/implement it.

Rose Hollister

Charlie has spent 6 weeks learning about the performance system. Now it is time to shift his attention to the MajorCorp system and the factors that could support or derail this change project.

Push Ahead?

No! Charlie needs to use this information and begin the change process with the CEO.

Question One: Where is Joan and what role will she play? Charlie needs to strategize with Joan Dary. Will she or Charlie work with the CEO and the senior team? What does Charlie need from her? How will the two of them work together? Charlie needs her direct and visible support.

Question Two: Does the change have a viable sponsor? Charlie needs to contract with the sponsor, the CEO. Having a contracting conversation that clarifies goals, relationships, and needed outcomes can begin to provide the framework to discuss the many questions above.

Can Charlie get him to see the need to build ownership organizationally? Will he own the change? Is the CEO willing to be the face of the change? The CEO's role is to talk about it, answer questions, hear people's concerns, work with the senior team until they can support him, and make appropriate modifications. If the CEO is not willing, Charlie does not really have a sponsor; and, a change process without a sponsor should stop.

Question Three: Why are we doing this? Good change initiatives must support the business in accomplishing its goals. Joan and Charlie need to understand the business case from the CEO's eyes and help him see the dangers of pushing. Use the senior team's wisdom to ascertain the change issues. Their issues are indicative of the questions and fears of the whole organization.

If the CEO is willing to change, Charlie and Joan help him to lead a senior team discussion that asks:

1. What is the business need for implementing this system?
2. What are the benefits to implementing the system?
3. What are the barriers at MajorCorp in implementing this?
4. What are people afraid of?
5. Who are the key stakeholders?
6. What impact will the system have on current values and culture?
7. What would it take to be accepted at MajorCorp?

Question Four: What do we know about why this may fail? Charlie needs to also do research on companies that have abandoned using this type of system. Charlie needs to know the problems with forced distribution systems. He needs the CEO to know these issues and be ready with answers.

Question Five: Can Charlie and Joan fight the urge to implement for the wrong reasons? People in new roles want to show results quickly. However, jumping into a political firepot could get them killed. Often, the best role of the OD consultant is to hold up the mirror and ask the questions. If the senior team does not buy this, why will others?

In summary, change projects often have a political aspect. As change consultants, we need to understand, embrace, and assist our clients in addressing and resolving the politics. Then we equip the organization to embrace a new change.

Lola Wilcox

In order to frame my response, I am going to assume that new competitors are entering MajorCorp's traditional market because it is expanding. I assume further that the board understands there is a short window to compete or be acquisitioned or destroyed, and they hired a highly competitive CEO to lead MajorCorp's critical growth.

Using the performance management changes to gain entry, Charlie interviews the top leadership, not only about performance management, but also the needed cultural change to a more competitive culture. From these visits he creates a network map of the core leaders. Charlie and Joan develop a "change plan" based on the discovery of the strength of MajorCorp's collaborative, networked culture, incorporating the leaders' ideas, and take the plan to the CEO. The first step is to connect the CEO with MajorCorp's natural leaders to convince them of the competitive situation, and the necessity of change. The CEO and the top leaders work together to map a change strategy, with different network leaders taking responsibility for winning in various market spaces. The executive team sponsors various aspects of cross-cultural work. Joan and Charlie's list includes:

- Train the corporation on the changing markets and the competitive strategy, helping identify both competitors and potential partners.
- Help network leaders identify and contract employees they must keep.
- Design a rich, early retirement option, honoring years of service.
- Create a Six Sigma type program to meet the market needs for quality, speed to market and, if possible, to create a pricing margin for the sales force with a new quality VP, hired from outside.

- Implement the performance management plan, incorporating a sales bonus program for competitive wins.

As an experienced change agent, Charlie knows it's possible that the CEO's competitive personality will keep him from understanding and utilizing the network leaders. The CEO may continue to believe the old culture must be destroyed. Joan and Charlie may be directed to restructure or to break up the "old culture" networks, and get rid of "dead wood." Charlie must simultaneously institute a fast process for hiring competitive replacements.

Charlie defuses the suggestion of an early-out program that could shift top talent towards joining the competitors. Charlie manages damage control by implementing a fast start-up transition process that helps newly restructured organizations quickly reform, defining roles and responsibilities for both new and traditional employees. The performance management plan is introduced as part of the transition. As the restructuring may cost the company its competitive window, Charlie is ready to prepare the company for acquisition by getting and staying as lean as possible.

Advice: Whenever possible, use the natural strengths of a corporation to help it turn in the direction it must go to survive. If you can't use the natural strengths, do what you must as well as possible, and mitigate as much of the damage as quickly as you can.

Homer Johnson Responds

Great advice from our panel of expert consultants! I don't want to repeat the panel's response (as they did a much better job of explaining it than I ever could). However, I was struck by their unanimous opinion that Charlie has the responsibility to see this out. No one said that change is easy.

The panel was also unanimous in their opinion that Charlie is not ready to implement anything, and that his preliminary work has only just begun. He is off to a good start, in that he has developed an understanding of that which he is called upon to implement, but there is a lot more to be done. For example, as the panel points out, Charlie needs to develop the business case for the new system ("Why are we doing this?") and certainly some key people will have to be convinced that this is going to be good for the corporation.

And, as the panel also clearly points out, Charlie is going to need a lot of help. In some sense, this is not Charlie's project and he should not have the burden of selling it to the rest of the corporation. Charlie needs to get the CEO involved, as well as Joan, and needs to help them get a good understanding of the issues that they will face as they try to implement this new system. Charlie can be a valuable resource to them (as well as other key people) in helping them understand the dynamics of change. Change is always about "politics," in the sense that it is loaded with issues of power, position, and personal preferences. Part of Charlie's job is to help the CEO and others understand the constructive use of the politics of change, particularly as they apply to MajorCorp.

Lola's response was very interesting in that it put the change in the performance management system in a broader context. If we assume that MajorCorp is in financial trouble and needs a major restructuring, the performance management system is only one of several major changes that will be needed to bring MajorCorp back to financial health. No single, one-shot intervention will have much of an effect on the competitive position of MajorCorp. And here again, Charlie's OD expertise on changing cultures will be a valuable resource to the corporation.

Thank you Ross, Rose, and Lola—Great Job!

ACKNOWLEDGMENT

An earlier version of this article was published in *The OD Practitioner,* *37*(4), 48-51,

CASE STUDY 17

THE TRANSITION
ISN'T WORKING!

Homer H. Johnson and Anthony Colantoni

When Rena Salazar was first contacted about the Marchon assignment she was very excited. After 12 years as an internal consultant, she had recently hung out her shingle as an independent organization development (OD) consultant, and had hoped to capitalize on her past experience in working with executive teams and in coaching executives. Although she had acquired a broad base of OD experience in previous companies, in the last couple of years her focus had been working with upper level management.

Marchon turned out to be an interesting company. They were a coffee cooperative that bought coffee on the open market and made special arrangements with groups of growers, and then distributed the coffee to the coop members. The members varied considerably in size and the amount they purchased; however, probably 30% of the coffee sold in the United States was purchased through Marchon. The advantage of the coop was that by purchasing large amounts of coffee, the cost to the coop members was much lower than if they purchased on their own.

The cooperative was run by a board of directors made up of coop members, who made it clear up front that they were the client and that Rena reported to them. They also made it clear that her primary assign-

Critical Issues in Organization Development:
Case Studies for Analysis and Discussion, pp. 163–172
Copyright © 2013 by Information Age Publishing
All rights of reproduction in any form reserved.

ment was to facilitate a smooth transition in upper management. The current CEO, who was in his 70s, was being gently pushed into retirement and the current general manager was set to move into the CEO position. Both had been informed about the changes. The board gave Rena two years to accomplish the transition.

The CEO, Luis, had founded the coop 20 years ago. However, the board members thought that the industry was changing quickly and the coop had to change also, and Luis was not the person who could lead this change. They were very respectful of his past leadership in the coop, which apparently was the reason that the transition period was to occur gradually over the next 2 years.

The current general manager and CEO apparent, Bob, had worked for Luis for about 15 years and was considered by the board as the ideal replacement for Luis. Bob knew the business, was well-liked, and had been the initiator of several significant operational changes that impressed the board.

Although this looked to be a fairly easy assignment, Rena quickly learned that it was a bit more complicated than it initially appeared. Her first contact with Luis and Bob was during the quarterly board meeting at which she was introduced. During the meeting it was obvious that there was considerable tension between the two men. Rena noted an interesting dynamic in the board meeting in that they never spoke to each other, but instead spoke about each other in a manner such that it appeared that they didn't acknowledge that the other was in the room.

After the board meeting she interviewed each man, and in her interview with Bob, she confirmed her suspicion that the relationship between the two was strained. Bob thought that Luis was out-of-touch with recent trends in the industry, but insisted on calling the shots. Luis was a "micromanager," according to Bob, who wanted to be involved in all decisions. Apparently Bob had given the board an ultimatum that either he became the CEO or he was leaving. The board recognized his value, he said, and assured him that he would become the CEO shortly. Although the board had not related this information to Rena, this apparently had much to do with Rena's hiring.

Luis was less informative in his initial interview with Rena. He talked mostly about how he founded the company and led it to become the number one coffee coop in the United States. When Rena asked him directly about his relationship with Bob, he said it was "ok," that he had taught Bob the business, but Bob still needed a lot of his (Luis') advice and direction. "He's not ready to take over yet," was his analysis of the situation.

Rena's approach to the transition was to work with Bob individually to ready him for the CEO position. With Bob's consent she conducted a 360-degree assessment, received feedback about Bob from the board, and then followed up with executive coaching. Bob responded very positively to these efforts. Working individually with Luis was a bit more difficult. He lived and breathed the coffee business. He told Rena that "I have more contacts across the world than the CIA has. I am on top of anything that has to do with coffee." He was loaded with energy, had no hobbies, and had never expected to retire. Rena worked with him on his feelings towards retirement, what he might do if he retired, as well as alternatives to retirement.

To facilitate the transition Rena developed a strategy whereby there would be a gradual handoff of Luis' responsibilities to Bob, with Luis mentoring Bob as Bob took over that responsibility, and Bob would do the same for his replacement. While she had some concerns about this strategy after she had interviewed both parties, both Luis and Bob agreed that this seemed to be a good way to go. With some difficulty the three of them charted the responsibilities of both Bob and Luis, and set up a time table for transitioning Luis' responsibilities to Bob, and Bob's to Bob's successor.

It has been a year and a half into the "transition" and there has been little to show for it. Bob has taken over a couple of Luis' responsibilities (with no help from Luis). However, Luis still sees himself as calling most of the shots and is quite outspoken in saying that Bob is not ready for the CEO spot. And Bob seems unwilling to accept Luis' advice or input. The relationship is still quite strained. In fact, they rarely talk to each other.

Rena is now wondering what went wrong. She had seen herself as a person who could easily handle difficult situations, but this one seemed to get away from her. She wondered if she had approached this assignment in a different way, would things have worked out better? Maybe she is the problem, not the solution? Maybe she was not confrontational enough once she observed the dysfunctional behavior, and didn't force both Luis and Bob to examine their behavior and resolve their issues. Or maybe she should have involved the board of directors. However, they seemed to not want to get involved. They seemed to want to maintain good relations with both Luis and Bob. She is very discouraged and not sure in what direction to go.

What advice would you give Rena at this point? What should be her next steps?

Could Rena have designed a better strategy for working with Luis and Bob, a strategy that would have been more successful? What strategy would you have tried?

What are some tips for dealing with client resistance? What general rules do you recommend a consultant follow when faced with a client or clients that don't seem to want to move in the direction in which you are expected to move them?

We asked three expert OD consultants to assist us with this case and to give us their analysis and suggestions as to how Rena might resolve her dilemma. Sherry Camden-Anders has been both an internal and external consultant, and more recently on the faculty of Goldsmith School of Management at Alliant University. Ross Tartell is a Director Team Leader for Pfizer Inc. Tracy Lenzen has considerable experience coaching executives, and recently joined United Airlines as an organizational change consultant.

Sherry Camden-Anders

This case study is complex because it is unclear as to who is really the client. A consultant who has worked with executive-level managers and is then hired by a board of directors must also understand the purpose, authority, structure, and responsibility of the board of directors for that particular company (the board's operations). It would be safe to say that, in this case, it appeared that the board of directors in this company shifted their responsibility to an outside consultant, Rena. She was being asked to handle a situation that the board had chosen to avoid.

How could Rena be successful in a situation where board accountability was missing and where the power structure was unknown? As a strategy, it is important to be clear about the responsibility and roles of a board. Then as a consultant, a clear contract can be proposed that would include working with the board to fulfill their responsibility to the corporation. For example, in most cases, a board's responsibilities include reviewing and evaluating the CEO performance regularly, offering the CEO administrative guidance, and determining whether to retain or dismiss him/her. In this case, a contract and strategy with the board needed to happen at the very beginning of the client relationship. The contract would have defined the work she would perform with the board, who she reported to on the board, and how they would work together—making it clear they were the client.

As a first phase of this contract, Rena could have interviewed all the board members individually to gather their input, for example, on where they saw their responsibility, what interactions had taken place, had they discussed it individually and as a group, what impact would the decision to change leadership have on the organization, how did they arrive at the decision to hire a consultant and take the action they were proposing, and how had the decision to change leadership impacted them personally (in addition to gathering information on the operations of the board). Then, she could have determined her next steps and followed with a second phase of the contract, reporting back to the board on her recommendations for moving forward, if she decided to pursue it. board involvement would be part of the contract; otherwise, it becomes one of those situations where the consultant decides they are not the person for the job.

As it turned out, Rena was placed in a difficult situation. As for the next step for her, perhaps she could renegotiate her contract with the board as the real client, and work on their resistance in dealing with the situation. If she succeeded she could then assist the board in taking ownership and accountability for changing the leadership of the corporation.

Ross Tartell

So what is going on? Marchon is "an interesting" company. After 18 months of a 2-year transition process, Bob is making little progress. Luis, the founder, has handed off few responsibilities and believes that Bob is "not ready for the CEO spot." Finally, where is the board that was so clear that they were Rena's client?

Some of the diagnostic clues can be found in the history of Marchon. Luis founded the cooperative 20 years ago, and then built a company that has a significant presence in the coffee market. The board of directors, made up of coop members enrolled by Luis, has followed his lead for years—a difficult habit to break. They may want change, but they are avoiding making the hard decisions necessary to move the business forward.

The board may want a change in direction, but Luis believes his vision is the right one. His lack of hobbies, never expecting to retire and his total engagement in the business, regardless of the steps in the transition plan, indicate that transition is the last thing Luis wants.

Bob has worked at Marchon for the last 15 years and is ready to be CEO. Now, 18 months into the transition, he is frustrated and is likely making other career plans.

If the current trends continue, Marchon's future is bleak. This will be a classic case of a failed founder's transition. The change Marchon needs for survival will never occur. Bob will leave and Luis will remain CEO until he can no longer physically function.

For Rena, this is the consultant's moment of truth when you realize that the original course of action is failing. Here is what I think she can do.

The potential answer lies in working with the board to create the future they originally outlined. The board must assume its responsibility and move Luis respectfully into retirement to make the transition successful. Effectively moving this change forward requires three fundamental actions.

First, dealing with Luis will not be easy—he is resistant, savvy and politically astute. To manage this, the board must have a single representative who will be the primary contact between the board and Luis for the transition plan. The person chosen must be tough, focused, and respected by the board.

Second is the development of a series of celebrations and milestones that publicly announce the transition and build momentum. Examples are a retirement party, announcements of key retirement milestones, and the creation of a severance and retirement pay plan.

Finally, structural and process changes will need to be implemented to prevent Luis from attempting to reassume control. After retirement he will need to give up his office and all his mail will need to be forwarded to his new address.

Transitions like these are not easy, and can only succeed if the board is aligned and focused on making the transition happen. Rena needs to re-contract with the board to align their support, and then provide the consultation to ensure success.

Tracy Lenzen

Start with the assumption that both leaders' perceptions are valid. These leaders have worked together for 15 years and know a great deal about each other's strengths and weaknesses. Luis believes Bob is not ready to take over (although he has not provided details on the competencies Bob needs). While the board believes Bob is the right choice, they do not have the opportunity to evaluate Bob's day-to-day leadership skills. Rena should help Luis articulate his perceptions about Bob using scales found in an executive-level leadership assessment. I would also pay attention to Luis' participation in this exercise. If Luis is using Bob's readiness as the justification to resist his life changes, Rena will likely experience difficulties in getting specifics from Luis. She can then leverage Luis' significant emotional investment in the coop to help him realize the long-term implications of delaying development of an effective successor. If Luis has accurately assessed Bob's readiness, his concerns about turning over his life's work must be addressed for him to willingly step down. Administering a second assessment to Bob (in addition to the 360), one that assesses the scales most important to Luis, will provide objective information that can be shared with the board and turned into tangible action steps for both Luis and Bob.

Second, Bob's choices of "micromanager" and "out of touch" paint a picture of frustration for Bob, yet he has not initiated a dialogue with Luis about issues that concern him. Bob's ultimatum to the board further suggests frustration, and self-limiting thinking about alternatives for achieving his goal. Rena should continue coaching Bob to help him increase his understanding of his frustration triggers and to develop his capacity to generate alternative strategies for achieving goals.

Finally, Bob and Luis have developed a pattern over the years of avoiding their conflicts. If transition discussions are to take place, Rena must help the parties prepare for dialogue. She may need to leverage their specific dissatisfactions to create a productive level of tension and increased motivation to talk to each other. She should also assume that directly confronting conflict creates anxiety for both parties. She should therefore plan for tightly structured dialogue sessions, including accounting for power differences, to provide emotional safety for both men. One approach that addresses their perception, structure, and power issues is for Luis and Bob to both complete the second leadership assessment and share results with each other in sessions facilitated by Rena.

Homer Johnson and Tony Colantoni Respond

Great insights panel! As the panel notes, Rena may benefit from a dual approach: recontracting with the board as well as refocusing her efforts to work more intensely with Bob and Luis to resolve their differences as they manage the transition.

Sherry Camden-Anders pretty much nailed a key part of the problem when she points out that, like many consulting problems, much of the current difficulty can be traced back to the initial contract between the board and Rena. The board abdicated their responsibilities and laid the problem solely in Rena's hands. Sherry explains how the initial contract might have been negotiated, and further makes a very important point in noting that contracts can be renegotiated, particularly when it becomes obvious that the initial contract was not adequate to resolve the problem posed in the assignment. And, in this case, a renegotiated contract would seem to be Rena's next step.

Given that this is, to a great extent, a board problem, what do we expect the board to do? Ross Tartell does a great job in explaining some of the dynamics going on in this "interesting" company, and points out that this seems to be a classic case of a failed founder's transition. He also portents a bleak future for Marchon if something is not done, particularly by the board, to control the process. The three actions he suggests are clear signals to the board that they are in charge of this transition process, and the transition is going to occur.

Tracy Lenzen follows nicely by offering some suggestions as to how Rena might deal with the current issues. Importantly, she notes that both Luis and Bob may have valid information that might provide assistance to each other. After all, they have worked together for some 15 years and probably know each other's strengths and weaknesses. Using Luis' insights may move Bob ahead more quickly. She also points out that Bob and Luis have a history of avoiding conflict (indeed, avoiding each other, period) and some tightly structured dialogue sessions might prove valuable. However, this would seem to be a delicate process, and her suggestion of structuring it around the second leadership assessment might provide a focus and structure to enable the dialogue to be constructive.

Nice insights and advice for a complicated case! Thank you Sherry, Ross, and Tracy!

ACKNOWLEDGMENT

An earlier version of this article was published in *The OD Practitioner,* *41*(3), 50-53.

SECTION IV

CONFLICT

CASE STUDY 18

THE CASE OF FOOD SERVICE

Homer H. Johnson

I received a call from a vice president (VP) of a large organization who wanted to hire an organization development consultant who spoke Spanish and wondered if I could recommend someone. The VP said that they were having a problem in their food service area. There seemed to be some conflict between the supervisors and the cooks and kitchen staff. A key piece of information he wanted me to know was that the cooks and kitchen staff were all male and recent arrivals from Mexico who had a limited use of English. The supervisors were all female, White Americans, with limited use of Spanish. It was the supervisors who brought the problem to the VP's attention. Beyond that he couldn't tell me much more about the issues involved.

A consultant in our graduate organization developement (OD) program seemed to be ideal for this consulting assignment. She was born in the United States; however, her parents were from Mexico and spoke Spanish in the home. Thus she was fluent in both English and Spanish.

I forwarded the consultant's name to the VP, who, in turn, called her and discussed the assignment with her. She apparently passed his scrutiny, because he asked her to call the lead supervisor who would handle the assignment from then on.

Critical Issues in Organization Development:
Case Studies for Analysis and Discussion, pp. 175–185
Copyright © 2013 by Information Age Publishing
All rights of reproduction in any form reserved.

About 3 weeks later I received a call from the consultant saying that she had an initial meeting with two of the supervisors earlier that day. The supervisors had given her their side of the story regarding the problems they were having with the cooks and the kitchen staff. The supervisors also emphasized that they wanted some outside help.

After hearing the two supervisors describe the situation, the consultant said she then suggested how she might handle the consulting assignment. The consultant proposed that she first conduct several interviews with both the supervisors and the cooks and other kitchen staff. These interviews would give the consultant a good indication as to what major issues were at the heart of the conflict. The consultant also said that at some point, after the interviews had been conducted, there would be a need for some (perhaps all) of the cooks, kitchen staff and supervisors to meet together and talk over (hopefully resolve) the major issues that the consultant had identified as central to the conflict. The consultant further explained to the supervisors that she could not be specific as to what this latter meeting might entail as she wanted to better understand the issues first, and also wanted to solicit the opinions of all parties involved as to how best to proceed.

The supervisors responded very negatively to the proposed process. They told the consultant that they did not want her talking to the cooks or kitchen staff. The consultant was to work only with the supervisors and assist them in better dealing with the cooks and the kitchen staff. The consultant, in turn, attempted to explain the logic of her proposed strategy. She explained that she could be most helpful if she understood the concerns of the supervisors, as well as the cooks and the kitchen staff. It would be difficult to advise the supervisors on how to better work with the cooks and others, if neither consultant nor supervisors were really sure what the issues were. And the consultant also indicated that getting both sides involved in the solution would lead to a more lasting resolution.

The supervisors were not swayed by the consultant's arguments. They emphasized that although they wanted some help in dealing with the cooks and kitchen staff, they did not want the consultant talking to the cooks and kitchen staff. The consultant's purpose in calling me was to ask my assistance in making a decision as to how to proceed.

So, What Would You Do?

Now that you have a brief overview of the situation faced by the consultant, what would you do if you were the consultant in this case? Would you agree to work with the supervisors under their terms? Or would you decline the consulting assignment if the cooks and kitchen staff were not involved? Would you go back to the VP for a discussion of the situation? Or would you use another approach?

We asked seven OD practitioners to be our expert panel and to tell us what they would advise the consultant in this case. Because of space limitations, we give you the offerings from three of them.

Chris Worley

The new OD practitioner in this case is facing a classic dilemma: meet the client where they are at or refuse to perform the work because the conditions for success are not present. The first few options seek to find a way to continue the relationship. Most of these seem reasonable to me but I'm against going to the VP without first communicating with the supervisors. Going around the supervisors would alienate them and doom any future efforts at improvement.

When choosing between continuing the relationship vs. not taking the work, I lean toward continuing the relationship. The supervisors have asked for help but are unsure about the process the consultant has proposed. That is the area where the work should begin. In doing so, I believe the supervisors will eventually see the untenable stance they have taken. That is, the practitioner will be able to ask, "How do you know what the conflict is?" They will have opinions, to be sure, but the consultant can ask, "How do you know that?" Eventually, I think the supervisors will see that their own limitations are the biggest problem to be solved.

The new OD practitioner has a great opportunity to improve the capacity and capability of these supervisors to lead people and manage change. I suspect that it is the supervisors' own perceived vulnerabilities that are creating the resistance to the proposed process. By working with the supervisors on their terms and then helping them to see their own role in the problem, the OD practitioner will have made an important contribution to the organization and gained valuable experience in OD.

Bev Scott

This case presents a conflicting dilemma between the value of informed choice, problem solving based on the data to be collected by the OD consultant, and the value of voluntary participation by the supervisors. Their resistance is potentially based in a lack of experience as well as a lack of trust of the consultant and perhaps an unspoken fear of reprisal from the organization. These issues would only be exacerbated by appealing to the VP, which would also undermine the supervisors' voluntary participation.

Fear and mistrust will be potentially overcome by demonstrating a willingness to meet the supervisors' terms, to build a relationship with them, to hold their information confidential and to stay neutral regarding their actions as supervisors. Once they begin to trust, their fear becomes minimized and they will see for themselves the value of the consultant talking with the staff.

So my advice would be: Start with where the client group is, follow the supervisors' wishes, and work with them without contacting the cooks and kitchen staff. In this agreement, the consultant would indicate that after they begin their work together, she would like to explore the option with them at a later time to see if they believe it would be helpful to learn more about the perspective of the cooks and kitchen staff. In the meantime, she should provide the help that is possible without the data, and build the trust and relationship with the group. When they are ready to explore the issue again, provide material for the supervisors to review, as well as talk with them about how the process works. It would be important to continue to reassure them about confidentiality, to support their roles as supervisors and to help them be open to explore the differing perspectives of the kitchen staff.

Ed Schein

The consultant has not figured out who her client is—the VP, the supervisors, the cooks, the whole system—so she trapped herself into making a recommendation. Since when do OD people recommend processes and persist in their recommendation even if the contact or primary client resists?

The consultant is enamored of a formal process that may have no relevance in this situation at all. On what grounds is it necessary to learn what the cooks have to say? It is much more interesting to find out why the supervisors are having these problems and help them to figure out some alternatives. The consultant seems to have felt the need to take charge even when her clients clearly indicated that they did not want her to do the so-called "data gathering."

I see this as a classic case of the consequences of models that advocate "data gathering" instead of starting from the perspective that the consultant is always intervening and that data result from observing the effects of one's interventions. Frankly I am appalled that the consultant is persisting in arguing her case instead of trying to build a helping relationship with the supervisors to learn more about what is going on from them and why they feel they cannot handle it.

The consultant seems completely oblivious to the possible consequences of interviewing the cooks. I would give this consultation a very low grade for gross insensitivity to the client and self-absorption with her own model.

Homer Johnson Responds

The Survey of Consultants: I find this case very revealing in bringing out consultant values and approaches. I have given this case to some one

hundred or more consultants from a variety of backgrounds and affilia-
tions and asked them what they would do. Would they accept the assignment by working only with the supervisors, would they decline the
assignment, or would they suggest another approach? Regardless of what
they would do, I ask them why they would do it that way?

The Management Consultant's Approach: Management consultants,
usually with MBA backgrounds, have absolutely no question as to what the
consultant should do here, and don't see why the consultant had any
questions about how to proceed. In their minds, the supervisors are the
client and the consultant should work with them as she is directed. No
issue here -what the client wants, the client gets. That is the role of any
consultant: to serve the wishes of the client. They also were uncomfortable
with the process originally suggested by the consultant, as this is really not
how management consultants typically operate. Soliciting the concerns of
the cooks and kitchen staff might be useful, but having them as part of a
problem-solving (and decision-making) effort would be questionable. The
consulting strategy for the management consultants would be first to do a
diagnosis of the situation and then, based on the diagnosis, recommend
specific actions to be taken by the supervisors. When asked what interventions they might employ in this situation, these consultants seemed most
comfortable with instituting more management control (rules and procedures) or changing work processes.

The OD "Idealist's" Approach: OD consultants who were given the
case were split about 60-40 on how to proceed. About 60% tended to side
with the management consultants cited above in that they agreed that the
supervisors were the client and the consultant should honor the client's
wishes. And about 40% of the OD consultants thought that the consultant
should decline the assignment unless the cooks and kitchen help were
involved in both the diagnosis and resolution of the problems.

The OD consultants who stated that they would have declined the
assignment, here labeled the "Idealists" (see below), usually invoked traditional OD values as the reason for declining the assignment. They argued
that in order to success fully manage this conflict; the whole system had to
be involved. For the Idealists, the client was not the supervisors; rather,
the client was the whole system. The Idealists' goal was to build an open,
honest and trusting environment in which all members of the system
could work collaboratively to deal with the problems facing the organization. Their preferred intervention strategy would be the action research
model, in which all members of the unit would collaboratively participate
both in the diagnosis of the problem, as well as the decisions as to how to
resolve the issues.

By excluding the cooks and the kitchen staff from consideration, the
consultant would be sending a strong message that the cooks and the

kitchen staff really didn't count and their opinions were not important. Many of the Idealists pointed out that it was the cooks and staff who did the "real work" in the food service and they were most aware of and most impacted by, the problems in the unit. They would have to be involved if there were to be any effective and lasting resolution of the problem.

The OD "Realist's" Approach: Those OD consultants who stated that they would take the assignment and work only with the supervisors typically were aware of OD values and the possible dilemma that accepting such an assignment could bring. However, this group, who tends to label themselves as "Realists," was quick to point out that "there is a reality out there that sometimes doesn't fit the perfect world that the Idealists sometimes look for." They argued that many, maybe most, consulting assignments do not easily conform to the techniques advocated in the OD textbooks. One has to start where the client is, not where the consultant would like the client to be. For the Realists the question seemed to be whether, by their involvement, the situation could improve for all parties involved.

The Realists agreed with the management consultants in that they would work with the supervisors even if they could not talk to the cooks and kitchen staff, and they also agreed that the first step was a good diagnosis of the situation. However, they disagreed with the management consultants on a couple of basic points. First, the management consultants were prone to play the expert role, and once they conducted the diagnosis, would give the supervisors their expert opinion as to what should be done in this situation. The OD Realists, on the other hand, were more prone to facilitate a process that would assist the supervisors themselves in analyzing and discovering how to improve the situation.

Second, and following from the first point, the actions that might be recommended would differ also. The management consultants were prone to focus their intervention on processes or rules or policies. The OD Realists, on the other hand, talked about helping the supervisors look critically at the situation, and to see if together they could determine what is causing the problems and what actions to take. While changes in work processes might be needed, they wanted the supervisors to discover that. They also indicated that their involvement might take a broader approach, for example: Some Realists suggested that they might help the supervisors understand the culture differences; or help the supervisors improve their use of Spanish; or teach them some collaborative problem-solving skills that they could use in working with the cooks and kitchen staff; or teach them conflict management skills; or help them work through some of their stereotypes or feelings about working with the cooks and the kitchen help.

For the Realists, just because the action research model wasn't accepted here, and just because one couldn't get the "whole system" working together towards a solution, did not mean OD values could not be invoked. They argued that building the competency of the supervisors to better understand the needs of the cooks and the kitchen staff, as well as to improve their conflict management skills, was certainly in line with OD values. They emphasized that their strategy was not to help the supervisors become better "bosses," but rather to help them manage people more effectively and humanely.

Advice from the Expert Panel: Let's return to our panel of seven experts to see where they fit in relation to the above discussion. Most were in agreement in advising the consultant to work with the supervisors. In that respect they fell in the category of the "realists" as described above. However, a couple of the experts advocated a more systems approach, and wanted to involve the cooks and the VP at some point in the process. For example, Hedley Dimock suggested using the intervention and collaboration model in this case, which would require that the powerful people in the system (certainly the VP and perhaps the president) be involved in the process. While the model does use action research (which the supervisors rejected), the process involves considerable buy-in prior to getting to that stage.

The members of the panel offered several interesting pieces of advice to the new consultant in this case, which should be of value to any consultant, new or experienced. These are:

1. Start Where the Client Is

Several of the experts pointed this out in different ways. Don Warrick talked about this as "starting where the energy is," and Bill Pasmore talked about "keeping alive," in that you can't change the system if you are not part of it. Given that the supervisors are the client (although there is some debate about this), the start point of this consultation probably should be in understanding their concerns and needs. And the hope is that as the consultation progresses, and the supervisors become more comfortable with the process, they will become more open to involving the cooks in the discussions.

2. Don't Get Fixated On Your Pet Model

Ed Schein was most forceful on this point and suggested that the consultant in the case seems to be "enamored with a formal process that may have no relevance to this situation at all." The consultation should be viewed as an opportunity to help clients with very difficult problems, and should not be seen as an opportunity for the consultant to use his/her favorite intervention. OD consultants, new and experienced, often are fixated on a couple of favorite tools and techniques, which they apply indiscriminately. What the experts were saying is to forget the techniques, and start with understanding the client's needs.

3. Set Realistic Expectations

Focus on what's doable given the situation, and set some realistic expectations both with the client and for yourself. Progress is sometimes measured in baby steps. As Chris Worley notes, by working with the supervisors on their own terms and helping them to see their own role in the problem, the consultant can make an important contribution to the organization. And maybe that's all you can do in this situation.

4. Work (Slowly) Through the Client's Fear and Resistance

Several of the experts focused much of their discussion on dealing with the supervisors' fear and resistance. This apparently was a key issue for some of our experts, and certainly appears to be a major barrier to change in that unit. For example, Bev Scott pointed out that a willingness to work with the supervisors on their terms is a start in gaining their trust. And Gibb Dyer suggested meeting with each of the supervisors one-on-one to get a better understanding of their concerns. However, the approach advocated was one based on understanding, trust and patience. You cannot force your way through fear and resistance. It's a slow process.

5. Hold Firm to Your Values

A couple of members of the panel, for example, Linne Bourget and Bill Pasmore, questioned whether racism might be an issue in this case, their point being that consultants should not be a party to racism in any organization. While the consultant may become involved in combating racism, the panel saw this as more of an issue that needed action at the vice president's level or above, and the consultant's duty would be to bring it to the attention of the proper authorities. The message was to know your values and hold to them.

6. Know When to End the Relationship

One of the experts noted that in some situations even the most experienced consultants will not be able to assist the client, and this may be one of them. If it's not working then the honest and ethical approach is to be open with the client and admit it isn't working, and it is time to move on. In Kenny Rogers' song "The Gambler," the chorus says something to the effect of "know when to hold, and know when to fold." Hold if you are making progress, and if it is going nowhere, it is time to fold. Finally, for those of you who were wondering what decision the consultant actually made in this case. She declined the assignment as she thought that at the very least she would have to interview some of the cooks and kitchen staff to get an accurate understanding of the problem.

ACKNOWLEDGMENTS

The author expresses his appreciation to Liz Serrano for providing information related to this case. The editor thanks the following OD practitioners for participating in this case exercise: Linne Bourget, Hedley G. Dimock, W. Gibb Dyer, Jr., Bill Pasmore, Beverly Scott, Ed Schein, and Chris Worley. An earlier version of this article was published in *The Practitioner, 34*(2), 7-11.

CASE STUDY 19

"DO YOU WANT TO WORK FOR A JERK?"

Homer H. Johnson

Jeanne Wong was extremely surprised, almost shocked, when Buddy Myers came up to her after the planning retreat and not only complimented her on "a very nice job," but also added that he would like her to facilitate a planning retreat for his company. And he quickly said, "Don't worry, I pay," as he handed her his business card.

Jeanne had volunteered to design and facilitate a 2-day planning retreat for the board of directors of a local chapter of Environmental Awareness, a nonprofit organization dedicated to the preservation of the natural environment. Donations to the organization had decreased by about 40% because of the recent decline in the economy and the board had called for an emergency planning session to plan how they would respond to the decreasing financial resources.

Of all the participants, Buddy and his wife Nina were clearly the most vocal participants in the retreat and had some strong opinions on almost all issues raised. And on a couple of occasions Buddy had questioned both the design of the retreat as well as Jeanne's skills at facilitating the process. So when Buddy handed her his business card, Jeanne was surprised, as well as somewhat flattered by the fact that she had converted a critic into a believer.

Critical Issues in Organization Development:
Case Studies for Analysis and Discussion, pp. 187–196
Copyright © 2013 by Information Age Publishing
All rights of reproduction in any form reserved.

While something in her gut told her that this might be a tough consulting assignment, she did follow-up with a call to Buddy. He seemed genuinely excited to hear from her and they set up an appointment for the next week for her to "meet the team." As she understood from the phone conversation and from researching the website, Buddy was the founder and owner of a market research company whose main services seemed to be customer needs and customer satisfaction surveys.

Jeanne's schedule for "meeting the team" first involved meeting with Buddy and his vice-president for sales, whose name was Walter. Then lunch with a group of project directors. The session with Buddy and Walter went fairly well. Buddy was quite eager to talk about the history of his company and his vision of its future. The company was about 10 years old. Buddy had been teaching at a community college when a relative asked him to conduct a customer satisfaction survey for his company. "That launched our career. Our first office was our kitchen table," he related, "and look at us now!"

As Jeanne understood the consulting assignment, Buddy wanted to do a 2 day retreat with all employees involved to review current operations (which he characterized as "raggedy"), and to plan for an expected business expansion. The company had 12 full-time employees, however, subcontracted much of its survey work to outside vendors. But Buddy anticipated a "breakthrough" which would expand the company considerably. Apparently he had developed a "sure fire" customer needs analysis that was so accurate he could guarantee the client a dramatic increase in sales. If sales didn't boom, the client owed Buddy's firm absolutely nothing—the service was free. "This is a new concept in market research—guaranteed results," Buddy stated, "And believe me the phone has been ringing off the hook with companies wanting to sign up for my new technique."

Jeanne's time with Buddy and Walter went quickly. Buddy was very charming, talked nonstop, Walter said nothing, nor was Jeanne able to ask many questions. Buddy ended the meeting abruptly at 11:45 as he and Walter had to go to a client meeting. Jeanne then was turned over to Stella who had organized a box lunch in the company conference room with three of the project directors.

Stella was the office manager as well as the person who handled the subcontractor relations. Since much of the work was outsourced to subcontractors, Stella apparently played a key role in the company. The other employees at the lunch were project directors, which meant that they worked with a specific client, designed a study or survey to meet the client's needs, made sure the subcontractor collected and analyzed the data properly, and wrote the final report to the client. All three were in their late twenties and had not been with the company long.

After getting to know each other, Jeanne explained why she was there. She related how Buddy wanted to have a planning retreat involving all employees to review how the company was performing currently and how they might improve, as well as to think about how they would handle the anticipated expansion in the future. She also explained that her style is to engage everyone in planning the retreat and she would be interviewing each of them for their ideas.

All seemed to agree that this sounded like a good idea. The consensus was that there was plenty of room for improvement in the company—things were not going very well. However, when Jeanne pressed them as to what issues particularly they would like to see addressed, she received a lot of very vague responses. Finally, as Jeanne continued to press, Stella blurted out, "Well there is one big problem around here and that is Buddy the Jerk! That's what we call him here—Buddy the Jerk."

Stella's comment opened a flood gate of complaints about Buddy. The behavior Jeanne witnessed at the Environmental Awareness retreat apparently was typical Buddy. He thought he had the answers to all questions, was hypercritical of everyone's work, had to control everything, and did not tolerate anyone disagreeing with him. As to Walter, he was known in the office as "Walt the Wimp," and his role in the company was to be Buddy's "yes man," a role that he apparently performed with utmost skill and dedication.

The group was not very eager about going to a planning retreat with Buddy. As one project director explained, every Monday morning they have a planning session to review the status of each project as well as to plan for new business. Buddy dominates these meeting and spends most of the time criticizing the directors' work.

As to the new customer needs technique that Buddy had developed, the project directors said they hadn't seen it and suspected it was a lot of smoke. Buddy, they said, often has rather grandiose ideas that don't amount to much. With respect to the expansion plans, Stella stated that the company has been in rocky financial shape for a couple of years, basically living from paycheck to paycheck. "If we don't get our act together," she offered, "we aren't going to be around much longer. The issue is making it through the next year, so let's not talk about expanding," she concluded.

As the meeting broke up and Stella walked Jeanne to the elevator she asked "So, what do you think. Are you going to work with us?" Jeanne said she didn't know, at this point she was just trying to find out about the company and how she could contribute. As the elevator door closed Stella said, "Well, I guess the question is—do you want to work for a jerk?"

As Jeanne rode down in the elevator she wondered if this was a no-win assignment. There was no question that this group needed help. She did like Stella and the project directors and would like to help them out. But working with Buddy could be a major, major challenge. She recalled a workshop at a recent organization development (OD) network conference on working with difficult clients. Unfortunately, she missed that session and now wished she had attended.

If you were Jeanne would you take on this consulting assignment? If not, what would you tell Buddy? If yes, under what conditions would you accept the consultation? What would be your intervention strategy? Would you go ahead with the retreat or would you recommend another approach?

And finally, what tips would you have for consultants working with difficult clients?

We asked four expert consultants—Dennis Mayhew, Kathy Carmean, and Dick and Emily Axelrod—or their advice on this case. Their responses follow.

Dick and Emily Axelrod

Consulting problems can always be traced back to the original "contract" between the consultant and the client. Jeanne does not have a good contract with Buddy and needs one if she is to continue working with him. If Jeanne had a good contract she would not find herself in her current predicament.

If Jeanne decides not to continue working with Buddy, she should meet with him, tell him why she is not a good fit for this work, and provide Buddy with a list of colleagues he could contact should he decide to continue the work.

If she decides to continue, she needs to regroup and hold a series of contracting meetings with Buddy in which she discusses the following:

- Goals and outcomes for the consultation. What will be different as a result of their work together?
- The kind of involvement Buddy wants. Does Buddy just want to sell his idea, or does he want to involve employees in addressing the "raggedy operations"?
- The people who should be included in the process.
- The kind of working relationship Jeanne needs with Buddy in order to be successful and the kind of working relationship Buddy needs with Jeanne.
- Their strategy for achieving the goals and outcomes.
- The method they will use to assess progress.
- Consulting fees and payment arrangements.

Based on these discussions, if Jeanne believes that Buddy sincerely wants to involve employees in improving the organization, is open to feedback, and would listen to her advice, she might want to continue. If, however, Jeanne's gut begins to rumble, she should end the consultation immediately.

Difficult clients present unique challenges. Here are a few tips to follow when working with difficult clients.

- Take time to develop a good contract.
- Pay attention to your gut.
- Watch out for flattery: you are never as good as someone says you are.
- Blend empathy and confrontation. Be able to see the world through your client's eyes and also see the behaviors that prevent the client from being successful.

- Difficult clients require energy on your part. If this client feels like a drain, then this may not be the client for you.

Successful consultations require building strong partnerships with your clients. Most of all, success requires you and your client to become partners in the work. If you cannot become partners, then it's best to move on. Remember: you are only as good as your client.

Kathy Carmean

Isn't it interesting? So often in our work as OD practitioners the client who calls with the presenting problem is the one with the blind spot and in need of as much help as they are often a contributor to the group's effectiveness and performance. Such seems to be the case here.

First of all, let's get on the balcony and do a quick assessment of what the situation appears to be. The company is privately held and in financial difficulty, "living from paycheck to paycheck" according to the business/office manager. Buddy, the boss, appears to be using a command-and-control management style as opposed to one that taps into the strengths of his staff; he may not even have identified their strengths and how best to use them. This is not surprising given his behavior at the non-profit planning session which points to the possibility that Buddy needs to be in the limelight and in control. It also sounds as though he runs the business and develops business strategy in a vacuum as the staff hadn't seen the new technique that was to be the impetus for expansion in the next year.

A peripheral issue that may soon be the demise of the business is that Buddy's staff is "young" and in the "Nexter" Generation. This group was born after 1980, prizes technology, and applies to themselves a constant pressure to excel. If Buddy doesn't quickly engage these talented employees by getting them involved at a strategic level, he will lose them. With the impending dearth of good talent to replace them in the marketplace, his business will be challenged to survive, much less to find the right people to execute his business strategy with his current leadership style.

Given the data in the case study, there really is insufficient information on which to make a decision as to whether I'd take the case. I'd like to have a cup of coffee with Buddy off site where he doesn't have to be on stage. He's a typical hard-charging entrepreneur and a private meeting might increase the likelihood of showing his true self. My initial "intervention" before any contracting would be to gather more data: to learn more about him, his company, and what the underlying issues might be. I'd also want to gain insight into Buddy's motivators and satisfiers. I'd also like to assess his openness to enhancing his leadership capabilities as these might provide some indicators of whether or not he would be willing to change behaviors to save his business.

Would I take the case? Yes, if I got a real sense of his willingness to change and his desire to do what it took to save his business. Tough case? Yes. But that is what we do in this profession and the personal satisfaction derived from helping people move forward and effectively lead others is well worth the challenge of working with "a jerk" that we all know underneath may not be a "jerk" at all.

Dennis Mayhew

Jeanne first needs to center on herself. Buddy will need very strong feedback throughout this engagement around several critical points. Jeanne had a tough time partnering with him in their first conversation, allowing the meeting to be a one-sided affair. Working with strong personalities takes strong personal resolve, inner confidence and a knowledge base on how to handle difficult people in the context of achieving their business goals. The question (for her) is whether she is up to this task.

Assuming she wants to continue, her initial intervention is with Buddy himself. In a case such as this it is essential to help the client understand the consultant's role and the boundaries to the work that will be delivered. Jeanne's approach to Buddy needs to be nonthreatening and personally affirming, and yet needs to be done with strength and integrity. She should broadly outline the concerns she has heard to date, clearly outline her overall plan and advise that a retreat would not be beneficial to his success at this point. Rather, first there is discovery work that is needed to uncover the underlying issues in the organization that are hurting his business. She must be prepared for significant pushback and anger. People don't talk to Buddy this way and she needs to impress upon him that this is exactly why she needs to gather more data. It is imperative to tie her plan to the success of the business and the eventual goals of a future retreat, in an attempt to diffuse personal volatility. Her contract with him should be through data gathering, a feedback report, and potential next steps.

Jeanne should focus on six interviews; three private and three groups. Start the private interview process with Buddy, then Stella and Walt. Next use group interviews with the office team and as well as the key subcontractors. The interviews would certainly focus on interpersonal dynamics, but also on how work is structured, assignments given, decision making, and so forth. A mixture of data prevents it from becoming gripe sessions on Buddy and looks at a systemic picture of what is happening in the business itself.

Jeanne is now ready for the feedback session with Buddy. This is the time to confront Buddy with the inconsistency between the "rosy" picture he presents and the hard reality of what others have stated, while keeping names confidential. Buddy should hear how his behavior is preventing him, and the company, from being more successful. If she is able to work through the walls of defense, she may find he actually appreciates her boldness.

On a personal note she should suggest personal business coaching for Buddy and outline ongoing courses/seminars on leadership development. He also needs to play a leading role creating the culture he wishes to achieve and a learning partnership with his employees. This initial work would help assure the success of a possible future retreat by neutralizing the overwhelming political dynamics and allowing focus on current work flow structure and design, as well as the exploration of new ideas for future business development.

Homer Johnson Responds

Wow! Our experts provided some great advice for a difficult case. Rather than reiterate their comments, let me note a couple of points that particularly struck me.

One of the interesting lessons learned from our expert panel is that all were willing to work with Buddy given that they thought they could be helpful. They seem to be saying that whether a client is "difficult" or "easy" is really irrelevant. The question is whether we, as consultants, can assist the people and organization to become more effective. Each client brings a unique set of problems to the table. The question is can we help, not whether the clients are difficult or easy.

Where do you start? Well, Dick and Emily wisely pointed out that many of the problems incurred in a consulting assignment can usually be traced back to inadequate contracting with the client. They would see Jeanne engaged in a rather protracted consulting discussion with Buddy before any (formal) intervention begins. The list of contracting questions they provided in their response would not only serve Jeanne well in dealing with Buddy, but are, in fact, important questions for beginning any consulting assignment.

All members of our expert panel emphasized the need for some extensive (and probably, intensive) one-on-one discussions with Buddy to clarify the direction this assignment will take as well as their relationships. Designing a planning retreat seems to be out of the question until some other, more basic, issues are worked through. Certainly, the contracting discussions will be an important intervention in themselves. However, Buddy will need considerable additional support in both facing and in working through any feedback he receives regarding his style.

The "balcony view" suggested by Kathy provides an interesting context for the discussion. The balcony view looks at the overall business, as well as how it is managed. For example, Buddy's rather dictatorial style doesn't and won't sit well with the "Nexter" generation. Certainly Buddy needs to understand this. However, a crucial question is whether Buddy can change his style enough to hold on to the young talent that seems to be a key part of his organization. Thus we need to develop a wider lens and consider not only Buddy but all members of the organization as we assist them in becoming more effective.

Speaking of context, the suggestion by Dennis that the intervention focus on improving the business is very instructive. In some sense, this isn't all about Buddy. Rather, this is about improving the business, which Buddy and others describe as not working well. While Buddy's behavior is probably having a negative effect on the business (although we don't know that for sure), there are probably a bunch of other issues that are negatively impacting the operation of the firm. That should be the focus of Jeanne's strategy. That is why she is there—to help improve the business. Her intervention will be a success if the business improves. And as Dennis points out, if Buddy is going to change his style the impetus for the change will be his desire to improve the business.

Thank you Dick and Emily, Kathy, and Dennis for your insight and advice.

ACKNOWLEDGMENT

An earlier version of this article was published in *The OD Practitioner,* *37*(1), 42-46.

CASE STUDY 20

RESOLVING CONFLICT AT INSO

Homer H. Johnson

"Help! They are at it again! Drop everything and get out here as soon as possible! I really need you, now!"

Dicky Knowles, the Organization Development Manager at Integrated Software (InSo), really didn't need any explanation for the message on his voice mail. Without a doubt the caller was Jo Duggan, the Executive Vice President (EVP) at InSo. And the "they" who were "at it again" had to be InSo's VP for sales, Vera Marlo, and the vice president for software design and installation, Alan Brown.

InSo was a quickly growing software company whose major product targeted the manufacturing segment, and was designed to integrate all manufacturing functions and areas. One of the key features of the product was its ability to link customers, company, and suppliers in one system, thus providing a seamless just-in-time inventory and product flow throughout the value chain.

Vera and Alan had been battling for over 2 years and in spite of the peacemaking efforts of EVP Jo the problem certainly hadn't cleared up, and if anything, had escalated. In Jo's mind, the problem was a classic personality conflict between two very different people, who just could not get along together.

Critical Issues in Organization Development:
Case Studies for Analysis and Discussion, pp. 197–205
Copyright © 2013 by Information Age Publishing
All rights of reproduction in any form reserved.

There was some truth to Jo's analysis. Vera was an extravert, very out-going, very personable, very much at ease with other people, and always smiling and joking. Clients loved her, as did her direct reports. Dicky had been in many meetings with her and she quickly made her presence known, not in an offensive way, but by asking questions, making sugges-tions, and cracking a few jokes.

On the other hand, Alan tended to be very quiet and very introspec-tive. He rarely said much at meetings unless asked a question directly. He was seen as being very bright and very competent, and someone who was great at solving complex design and installation problems. His direct reports almost idolized his skill and leadership in the unit, and customers often asked that he be put in charge of their project.

While Dicky acknowledged that their personalities did conflict, he also suspected that more systemic issues added to the problem. For example, the InSo sales people worked on salary plus bonuses. They could do quite well, money-wise, if they made a big sale. On the other hand, if they didn't close a couple of sales each year, there would be no bonus and it would be a very lean year for their bank account. To add to their incentive package, the sales people could also win trips and other awards if they met or exceeded their sales targets.

While the sales people loved the compensation system, the software people thought of it as a source of many of their problems. As they saw it the sales people would promise the client everything and anything just to make a sale. They would guarantee the client software features that the software could not deliver, or couldn't deliver without a lot of extra work and cost. Once the contract was closed the problem became that of the installation people. The sales people got their bonuses and their trips to the Hawaii or Vegas. And the software people were stuck with a bunch of headaches. Compensation for the designers and installers, in contrast to the sales people, was straight salary, no bonuses, and they usually worked long hours when on-site for an installation project.

As one might expect, the complaints of the software people did not endear them to the sales people. Vera and her group were pretty vocal in accusing the design and installation people of being inflexible, not tuned into client needs, being "too anal," and "being a bunch of whin-ers." For the most part, there was very little contact between the two units. In fact, they tended to avoid contact with each other. According to Jo, that was a good way to keep the peace. "The less they see of each other, the better it is," she stated. "That's the only way to handle per-sonality problems."

When Dicky called Jo back he learned that the most recent blow-up was over a major installation at a multifacility manufacturer. Apparently, when the software people began the installation they found (or at least they claimed) that the contract required the installation of special features that were not part of the basic package, and which would involve some time-consuming and costly design work. The client objected to the time delays, and particularly objected to the suggestion that they would be charged extra for the special features.

When Alan complained to Vera about the contract problems, Vera's e-mail response was that while there were some "extras" in the contract, there was nothing "special" about any of them, and anyone with the intelligence level of a pea could install the system on time and on cost. And she advised Alan to stop being "so anal" and get on with the project. Alan apparently responded with something equally blunt.

At this point, the problem is in Jo's lap. The project is now on hold, and Jo is left with an angry client who is threatening to sue, two angry vice-presidents who aren't speaking to each other, and a bunch of confused sales people and installers who are avoiding one another.

As Dicky was calling to book his plane reservations, he was struggling to think of the best way to handle this situation. Jo had often spoken to Alan and Vera separately, and together, about the need for cooperation. That seemed to help for a week or two but then they were at it again. Jo thinks that Alan and Vera should undergo therapy. "It's a personality problem," she has stated, "and the only solution to personality problems is therapy."

InSo's legal counsel recently became involved because of the contract problem and his suggestion was for Jo to fire one or both, probably both. "That would be a great wake up call," he argued, and added, "It sends a clear message that either you work together or else you are history." However, Dicky knows that Jo would like to keep both Vera and Alan with the company. Both are very competent and productive and would be difficult to replace.

What advice do you have for Dicky? How should he proceed, given that he is expected to become a key player in resolving this situation?

And going beyond the specifics of this case, what general advice do you have for OD practitioners who find themselves having to deal with conflict situations? Are there any rules for handling conflict?

We asked four expert consultants to give us their answers to these questions. Drs. Sherry Camden-Anders and Larry Anders are faculty members at the Marshall Goldsmith School of Management, Alliant International University, Fresno, California campus. Donna Hapac is a Learning and Development Consultant at Health Care Service Corporation in Chicago, Illinois, and Lorna Rickard is Chief Workforce Architect at CONNECT: The Knowledge Network, in Denver, Colorado.

Sherry Camden-Anders and Larry Anders

There is a need for a "wake up call" for the individuals involved in this case! The first appears to be for Jo Duggan the EVP because of the way she has managed the differences between Vera and Alan, and the resultant impact on the departments. She has (1) isolated the two departments to avoid conflict, (2) operated as a peacemaker which has not provided positive results, and (3) has concluded that Vera and Alan's difficulty is a personality problem and that "the only solution to personality problems is therapy."

As the OD consultant, Dicky needs to:

- Begin to think through and identify his own feelings about how he received the request to assist. What is his reaction to the message he received from Jo?
- Determine how he plans to work with Jo Duggan, the EVP. What is his role as an OD manager or coach?

It is important that he establish how he would work with Jo and the variety of options for helping the client deal with her situation because she is the primary client. Once this discussion has taken place and a contract established with agreed upon objectives and how they will work together, several options are possible:

(a) Establish the effect of the situation by creating awareness that the situation is at the system level, impacting the customers, the employees, and two departments.
(b) Create awareness that conflict is being avoided by refusing to work through their differences.
(c) Analyze and revise the reward and compensation system to better support and motivate the sales and software departments.
(d) Explore the possibility of bringing in outside resources (coaches, educators and trainers to develop skills in emotional intelligence and conflict management) so that the energy can be redirected positively.

About Emotional Intelligence: The lack of emotional intelligence exhibited in this case has been integrated into decisions and behaviors. Vera acts out her emotions, calling Alan "anal" and alludes to him having "the intelligence level lower than a pea;" Alan fails to see the forest through the trees by being so-called "objective" and unemotional; and Jo in her pursuit for peace between Vera, Alan, and the two departments has attempted over time to oppress or avoid emotional reactions. Successfully managing emotions means that our actions are guided by both thinking and feeling; that allows us to integrate cognition and affect as we generate more effective solutions.

About Conflict Management: When differences occur, the resulting tension stimulates interest and creativity and people begin to search for new approaches. The basic differences can generally be identified by searching through the facts, goals, roles, values and methods. Skills can be developed to use a variety of methods to manage these differences. While it may be advantageous to avoid and repress the differences on occasion, the more positive outcomes can be reached through utilizing the differences for creating problem solving, or sharpening them into a clearly defined conflict.

Donna Hapac

So often in organizations, what looks like a personality conflict is often a result of how goals, incentives, or processes are structured. At InSo, all of these appear to be contributing to the current situation.

Dicky needs to address the immediate crisis. Then, he should recommend a new organization focus and structure that will foster a "one team" mindset.

Crisis Intervention: Immediately, Dicky needs to get Jo, Vera, and Alan to shift focus from the conflict to the client! Meeting contract obligations will cost less than a lawsuit.

Dicky needs to start with three one-on-one meetings (in this order) with:

1. Alan to get his perspective on what the contract has committed InSo to deliver, what the software people are saying, and an estimate of the costs and time delays required to meet client expectations;
2. Vera to understand the Sales perspective; and
3. Jo to share his findings, make recommendations, and coach her on leading Alan and Vera to a solution.

Jo needs to meet with the client herself to show InSo's commitment. And, Jo must point the organization toward cooperatively taking care of the immediate crisis, even if InSo may lose money. If it is true that sales made promises that eliminate profit, then sales might have to take a budget hit. Jo should promise incentive bonuses for the people who put in extraordinary effort to save the project. Jo needs to let everyone know that she wants them to take a team approach to this case and all future business.

Future Crisis Prevention: Today, sales can make promises, throw the contract over the wall, and let software figure out how to keep those promises. The salary structure does not support teamwork or ownership of project completion and profit or loss consequences.

Jo needs to champion a new approach to sales at InSo—consultative problem solving. After sales conducts an initial call to establish a client need, they return with a sales team that includes a technical expert. The expert can address customization requests, calculate cost/benefit analysis, and advise on cost-effective ways to meet client needs before the contract is signed. This individual should be in constant contact with the client, the salespeople, and the software designers to clarify deliverables and deadlines throughout the project.

InSo needs to establish standard products and product capabilities. This should be done by a collaborative product team of software and sales and marketing people. The business goal should be to sell the standard product without customization whenever possible. Customizations that the client requires should be scoped and priced by the product team.

The compensation structure needs to be revamped to support the new sales approach.

Lorna Rickard

Social psychologists and anthropologists have long identified social spaces that exist in all systems—families, workplaces, communities and nations. These social spaces affect our behaviors, often without our awareness, and broadly align with *top, middle,* and *bottom.* Tops have overall responsibility for the system, Bottoms do the direct work of the system, and middles exist between the two, often as supervisors and managers.

In each of these spaces, predictable relational vulnerabilities exist. While personal differences can, and do, lead to conflict, these particular vulnerabilities show up regularly in all systems, regardless of the individuals involved. So, Dickey is on the right track when he suspects that systemic issues are adding to the problem. For purposes of this response, we'll focus on the middle space—where Vera and Allen reside.

There are two characteristics of this space that can lead to conflict. First, middles typically are responsible for some piece of the organization (sales and software design and installation, respectively) and are not collectively responsible for wider organization outcomes such as gross profit, customer satisfaction, and organizational reputation. Second, the tearing-and-diffusing nature of the space often leads to the development of an "I" mentality. Elements of an "I" mentality are that middles often feel that they share little in common, therefore there is little need to work together. They also tend to feel competitive with and critical of one another.

The primary strategy for helping Vera and Allen overcome the limitations of the middle space is exactly the opposite of what Jo has encouraged. Rather than isolating them, Vera and Allen should be working more closely together with a powerful, shared mission as their guide. The primary question they could be working on is: "what's not happening that needs to be happening, and how can we make that happen?"

So much of what occurs in organizations feels personal, but it's not … it's systemic. So far, Jo and the legal counsel have tried to intervene on a personal level. The problem with this approach is that when our diagnoses are personal, so too are our solutions … fix, fire, rotate, send to therapy, and so forth.

When OD practitioners find themselves addressing conflicting situations, they should expand their thinking to include the impact that the system is having on the relationships. As people understand the degree that conflict has on a systemic foundation, they are more open to communicating candidly and with less judgment about each other's motives or abilities, and new solutions can emerge.

Homer Johnson Responds

Our expert panel did a great job of disentangling a very sticky situation. Often conflict situations quickly evolve into blaming, name-calling, isolation and a variety of other unconstructive actions. And attempts to resolve the conflict often focus on surface symptoms and fail to address the underlying issues that caused the conflict. The panel was quick to recognize the complexity of the situation. Not only must the underlying and systemic issues be addressed, but so does the current behavior of Vera and Alan, and so does Jo's ineffective attempts to resolve the issues. Dicky also has to think out his strategy as to how involved he needs to be, and with whom. For example, should he work only through Jo, or directly with Vera and Alan, or with both of the units involved?

Without repeating the excellent advice of the panel, let me note a couple of points that I found very interesting.

Among other insights, I liked Sherry and Larry's discussion of emotional intelligence in the context of this case. I hadn't thought of it but EI would seem to be an effective approach to use in helping Vera and Alan and Jo better understand the impact of what they do and don't do. Actually, EI training may be beneficial for all of the folks at InSo.

Donna provided a nice step-by-step process for dealing with the problem that has general application. And her discussion of "consultative problem solving" illustrates one approach to resolving the systemic problems that often exist between sales and the tech people. It not only turns a competitive situation into one of cooperation, but has the potential of significantly impacting the bottom line through reducing costs and increasing delivery time.

A final observation is that Lorna has given us a nice theoretical framework to look at the roles and relationships in organizations, as well as where the predictable relationship vulnerabilities exist. As she points out middles often are responsible for their piece of the organization and not for overall organizational outcomes, which can often lead to a competitive mentality. The framework also explains why Jo's strategy in handling the conflict reinforced the behavior that she wanted to eliminate; in fact, it probably escalated the conflict.

Thank you Sherry and Larry, and Donna, and Lorna! Great advice!

ACKNOWLEDGMENT

An earlier version of this article was published in *The OD Practitioner*, *38*(3), 49-52.

CASE STUDY 21

RESOLVING CONFLICT AT THE WALBERG BANK GROUP

Homer H. Johnson

"Well, this is going to be a really different assignment," murmured Don Hon as he left the senior vice president's office at the Walberg Bank Group.

Don had been an outside OD consultant to the bank for about 6 years, first starting with a project on succession planning, but more recently had spent a lot of time on change management projects. The bank had acquired several small banks, most of them "takeovers" ordered by the FDIC. So, he had plenty of work integrating the acquisitions into the Walberg system. Jean Lovato was the Senior Vice President at the bank in charge of making sure that the acquisitions ran smoothly. A very bright and talented leader, she was highly respected in the banking community, and Don found her a pleasure to work with. So, when Jean called him in for a meeting he assumed that Walberg had been ordered by the Feds to take over another bank group. But that proved not to be the case.

After they exchanged personal greetings, Jean said, "I have a new assignment for you. I want you to help resolve an interpersonal conflict between two of the managers in our operating units." She went on to explain that both of the managers were very talented and were on the fast

Critical Issues in Organization Development:
Case Studies for Analysis and Discussion, pp. 207–216
Copyright © 2013 by Information Age Publishing
207

track to move up in the bank. However, for reasons she did not quite understand, they were not able to work together. Moreover, their issues were spilling over to the relationships between members of each of their units.

She said she had talked to both of the managers individually and together about ending the conflict, however, she perceived little change. "I made it very clear to them that the conflict was not helping their careers at the bank, and that they needed to resolve it very quickly," she added. She went on to note that she had told them that the bank was considering them for higher levels of leadership in the bank; however, before that could happen they would need to get beyond this problem.

She said she had recommended that the two of them go off-site for a day, with a professional, to resolve their differences, so they could get on with their careers. Both apparently had agreed to such a meeting.

"And I am the professional who will go off-site with them?" Don asked.

"Yes, I thought you could do it," Jean continued, "You have a good reputation in the bank. Also you are an outsider. I don't think it would be good to have one of the bank's people involved. I checked with human resources and they thought you were a good choice to handle this problem."

"I will leave it up to you as to how to proceed," she added. "And I am counting on you to get this resolved quickly. Actually, I think it will be a good learning experience for the two of them." And with that the meeting ended, and Jean was out the door to another meeting.

As Don left the building and walked to his car he found his mind racing. He did know the two managers that were involved in the conflict, but only casually. Both had impressed him as being very competent, highly energetic, and "hard chargers." They were part of a group of young managers that the bank had identified as "future leaders," which meant that they were expected to move up the ranks quickly. Beyond that, he did not know much about them or what the problem was between them.

While Jean had said that she would leave it up to him as to how to proceed, at this point, he was not really sure how to proceed. He remembered taking a conflict workshop at NTL, and attending a session on conflict at the National ODN Conference, but they both were probably 15 years ago. He was also somewhat puzzled as to why Jean had suggested a one day, off-site session with the two managers and him. He regretted not asking her why she thought that was the best approach; however, she seemed in a hurry to move on to another meeting. While that seemed like a reasonable approach, he wondered what she had in mind.

What would be your advice to Don? How would you proceed? Is the one day off-site session a good idea? Or would you suggest another approach—what approach? If a one day session, what would be the agenda for the day? Should Don meet with the managers prior to the off-site session? Should he meet with anyone else?

In general, what would be your suggestions for organization development (OD) consultants who are engaged to help resolve interpersonal conflicts?

We asked three expert OD consultants to assist us with the case and to give us their analyses as to how Don might solve his dilemma. Tammy Seibert has extensive OD experience and is now an Organizational Effectiveness Consultant at Allstate Insurance. Annie Viets has worked extensively in mediation and conflict management, and is an Associate Professor of Management at Prince Mohammad Bin Fahd University in Al Khobar, Saudi Arabia. Ruth Urban is an independent consultant and principal of The Urban Group, with extensive experience in conflict management and facilitation.

Tammy Seibert

This is a complex situation that requires more background information and clarity around client identification and contracting. The other layer of complexity is that the client has been impressed with Don's work in OD, but may not be clear that there are sub-specialties in OD. I would recommend that Don meets with Jean to understand her needs as a client, and to make sure Jean understands his areas of expertise.

From a reset of the expectations of OD service offerings: I would provide an overview of the OD offerings and areas of expertise (as the case presents, it appears that Don does not have a background in interpersonal conflict resolution). I will make the assumption that Jean views Don as a credible business partner since she came to him for this work. So if I were Don I would offer her a process on how to contract and work with a consultant who has expertise in conflict resolution. As an outside consultant, Don would be offering her a way to think about her needs while providing a resource that has expertise in conflict resolution. This should maintain his credibility as a consultant and continue to establish himself as a business partner who knows his limitations, but is creative in continuing to support his client.

If Jean agrees to take Don's approach in having him help her think about the "right" choice for an OD consultant, I would recommend that he helps her become clear on her needs and the contracting process.

From a client needs perspective, questions I would have Jean respond to are: How did the conflict start? How long has the conflict been occurring? What is each manager's role in the conflict? What specific behaviors are being observed that are taking away from their effectiveness as leaders? What behaviors are being demonstrated in each of their teams that indicate the conflict is being carried out into other parts of the organization? What and how has performance been impacted? How is the "system" supporting the fact that the conflict has not been resolved? If the system is part of the problem, what work needs to be accomplished at a system and possibly team level?

From a contracting process, questions I would have Jean respond to are: Who are the "clients" in this situation? Is it only the two managers? Or is it the managers and their bosses? How open are you to a coaching process versus a one day off-site? How open are you to a blended approach of one day off-site and coaching? If you go the coaching route, would you use the same coach for each client or the same coaching? How would you contract determining the success of the coaching? Would you track behavior change and leverage 360 degree feedback tools, or would you leverage your observations? If you go the one day off-site route, what type of conflict resolution process/model would be used? Will there be any premeetings/work prior to off-site and any follow-up work/meetings? Post the one day off-site, what is the behavior change you will need to see to demonstrate success?

For consultants who engage in conflict resolution between leaders, I recommend contracting with each person and their bosses whereby the process and success is clearly defined, and how it will be measured and reported on. In this case "success" could be defined as behavior change and measured through a 360 degree feedback process. As a consultant I would also seek to understand how deep the conflict has filtered into the organization and be prepared to recommend additional OD intervention work at a team and/or systems level.

Annie Viets

This case study presents a situation that is all too common in organizations: two individuals simply cannot get beyond their personal differences to work productively together. Left unaddressed, these types of conflicts, as evidenced in the case, often spiral to impact others in the individuals' environment and, potentially, entire work teams or departments.

Jean's decision to proactively deal with the dispute is therefore sound. Her choice of Don as the agent of conciliation also has its merits. He is known and trusted in the bank and both of the disputing parties have accepted his assistance. He is an outsider who (presumably) has no history with either party so he can be more objective than someone from within the organization. Going off-site to a neutral location also has its benefits, although it is highly unlikely an initial mediation session would consume an entire day and it may also be unrealistic to expect a dispute that has persisted despite possible career consequences can be resolved to the satisfaction of all parties in one meeting.

Don's impartiality in this intervention is critical. The fact he has been appointed by senior management and is being compensated by the bank could introduce bias. He must, therefore, take measures to ensure he does not push for a hasty resolution or one that is not the disputants' own. His first step must be to explain and establish the necessary conditions for a successful mediation with Jean. She needs to understand that to ensure the commitment of the parties to the process, it must be confidential and the parties must be confident Don will not report to her on what occurs in the session(s). Jean must also understand the best resolution may not be achievable in one session and may require additional meetings.

Don should then meet with each party separately to explain the concept and process of mediation and obtain the perspectives of each party in the conflict. The purpose of this step is to enable Don to begin to identify the issues so he can tentatively frame the parties' positions into interests that can be mediated.

As an OD consultant, Don will already have many of the skills of an effective mediator. His knowledge of facilitation techniques and the ability to actively listen will be foundational to his ability to assist these parties to resolve their differences and move on. Before commencing this intervention, however, he should study the structure and sequence of a good mediation in Jennifer Beer and Eileen Stief's *The Mediator's Handbook* (2011).

Don's role as a mediator is to facilitate a constructive and focused conversation between the two that enables them to understand each other's perspectives and create their own basis for a continuing positive professional relationship. Because they must continue to work together, the goal of the mediation must go beyond simple dispute resolution to focus on how the parties will work together in the future. For this to occur, Don must remember the solution is entirely theirs and, as much as he might like to steer them toward a solution he believes is right, he must remain an impartial guide who allows them to create their own path for moving forward.

Jean's prediction that the process "will be a good learning experience for the two of them," can be realized if Don perceives the conflict as one ancient Chinese sage described it: "opportunity riding on a dangerous wind" and provides a safe and objective environment in which fruitful problem solving can occur. Transformational mediation can, indeed, provide the opportunity for mutual learning and respect and an enhanced working relationship neither party might ever have envisioned.

Ruth Urban

I would advise Don to circle back with Jean to clarify what portion, if any, of what she told him could be disclosed to the two managers. Namely, can he share that their interpersonal conflict will be career-limiting if not resolved? This will be helpful to know because part of Don's role in the conflict resolution process is serving as an agent of reality. He also needs to clarify that his work with the managers will be confidential and let her know he will not be releasing any information to her without their permission.

Don needs to meet with both managers together and share with them what he was asked to do, his planned approach, and the confidentiality of the process. For example, he plans to meet with them individually to best understand the conflict from their perspectives and then will meet with them together off-site for a full day. He needs to share some of the processes he will be using during the off-site meeting, answer any questions and concerns they might have about this approach, and mutually decide on a date for the full day. He needs to tell them that he will be looking for mutual issues and themes in their individual confidential interviews. This initial meeting helps to establish the transparency of the process and Don's neutrality sets the stage to empower the managers to resolve the conflict, and get their buy-in for the process.

Don then needs to craft a series of questions to ask in the individual interviews. Two hours should be allotted for each interview. The more entrenched the individual, the longer the interview might go because this is an opportunity for venting and some transformation. The interviews are usually structured with some ice-breaking questions to help develop rapport and then questions that help flesh-out the story-behind-the-story that is the interest basis for the conflict. This is often uncovered when the focus is on discussing feelings. Don might use some visioning questions to see what the managers' view is of an ideal relationship and what they see as standing in the way of achieving a better relationship. This is where Don's role as the agent of reality might be helpful and where he can ask the managers some hard questions and give each an opportunity to save face. Don can also explore at the conclusion of the interview what the individual is willing to do to resolve the conflict.

Don should conclude the interview by giving each manager some homework to complete before the off-site meeting, namely a "needs and offers" negotiation process in the form of a worksheet for them to bring to the off-site for reference. This consists of the following questions: What each manager thinks the other manager wants from them, what they want from the other manager, and what they are willing to give the other manager.

Don's agenda for the full day off-site should consist of the following:

1. The managers establishing some ground rules for their discussion
2. Don sharing the themes/issues that came from the interviews
3. The managers prioritizing the themes/issues as a starting point for their discussion
4. An open discussion of the top two or three themes/issues
5. Don putting on a flip chart any resolutions they reach regarding the themes/issues
6. Don facilitating the *needs* and *offers* discussion between the managers, using the format of the worksheet he gave them. He needs to scribe their responses as this will become part of a written agreement they reach
7. A focus on personality type, as often conflicts are fanned by lack of understanding of one's own personality type and others. (I use a

quick and very accurate self-contained instrument called The PEO-PLE Process)

8. Summarizing any agreements reached and establish next steps

9. Determining if the managers want to meet again with Don to check on their progress

10. Clarification of what information, if any, can be released to Jean, and what the managers agree they want to tell Jean about the process when she asks

11. An evaluation of the process, either in writing or by discussion so Don has some feedback on what the managers found helpful or not and what can be improved

Homer Johnson Responds

Let me first thank Larry Anders for telling me about this case. A former colleague and mentor of mine, Larry has a well-deserved reputation as one of the best OD practitioners in the business.

Don would do well by listening to the advice of the expert panel before he starts his venture. For example, Tammy starts out by asking whether Don should accept this assignment. Does he have the skills to effectively handle a somewhat tricky intervention that seems to be different than that he typically does for the bank? I was reminded of the few times I strayed beyond my skill level, usually with poor results, simply because of pressure from the client. If Don realistically does not think he has the skill set to be effective here he should be honest with Jean, and find her someone who has competencies in interpersonal conflict.

If Don accepts the assignment, our expert panel is unanimous in suggesting that he ask Jean for clarification regarding her expectations as well as what she knows about the conflict. Each of the panel has questions of Jean. I was impressed with Annie's and Ruth's suggestion that Jean be briefed as to the rules of a successful intervention, such as confidentiality, consent, and so on. And all of our experts suggest a meeting (or two?) with the managers prior to going off-site. They have to understand (and agree to) the process. And Don additionally needs to get their take on their differences.

I will not repeat the panel's details of the intervention, except to note that our panel offers some great advice that OD practitioners would be well advised to review. Annie provides a broad overview, as well a valuable reference source which will help where there may be questions. Ruth is more detailed and offers some specific suggestions for an initial meeting with the two managers, as well as an agenda for the day-long retreat. I found it interesting that she suggests using the "Needs and Offers" exercise, which tends to be easy to use and very effective.

Finally, each of our panel members advocates a follow-up. Was the intervention effective? Are the managers working together much better? What else has to be done so that they continue to do so?

Beautiful job panel! Great advice!

Thank you Tammy, Annie, and Ruth!

ACKNOWLEDGMENT

An earlier version of this article was published in *The OD Practitioner, 44*(2), 48-51.

REFERENCE

Beer, J., & Stief, E. (2011). *The mediator's handbook.* Gabriola Island, BC, Canada: New Society.

CASE STUDY 22

THE CASE OF COMPETITION AT CENTRI-PHARM

Peter F. Sorensen and Therese F. Yaeger

One of the critical issues for organization development (OD) today involves OD becoming more strategic-strategic in terms of providing assistance in defining the organization's future, and also in terms of developing necessary competencies to support the change process as the organization prepares for the future. This is the perfect time for OD to make explicit its value to an organization.

Herein lies a challenge: at the same time that OD can make its value more visible to the organization, the human resources (HR) department is also transitioning into new roles. HR finds itself moving into a more strategic role and partnership with management. HR interprets its new role as being increasingly involved in change management, but historically that is the OD zone. This new role of strategic HR complements the role of OD, but also clouds the boundaries between OD and HR.

If HR becomes more strategic and gains a "seat at the table" with change management work, then what is OD's role? Our case deals with this dual transition and the complexities that this OD-HR scenario creates.

We asked a panel of three OD-HR experts to comment on this Centri-Pharm case. Each of the panelists has significant experience in their

Critical Issues in Organization Development:
Case Studies for Analysis and Discussion, pp. 217–225
Copyright © 2013 by Information Age Publishing
All rights of reproduction in any form reserved.

organizations dealing with daily HR, OD, and change issues. Further, each panelist comes from a different industry. Robert Sloyan is Vice President of Human Resources in the manufacturing arena. Sue Sweem is a Senior Human Resources Manager for a healthcare, coatings, and chemical company, and Dr. Tim Goodly is the Senior Vice President of Human Resources for CNN Worldwide.

Case: OD and HR ... Together?

The OD consultant in our case is Gary Jones, an experienced change agent, who has been brought into Centri-Pharm, a large global pharmaceutical organization, with the assignment of creating an internal OD university to prepare HR personnel with OD competencies and skills in change management. Gary knows that Centri-Pharm is a successful leader in the pharmaceutical industry, and that the company likes its internal operations to mirror their external success. Gary willingly accepted this consulting job, as he had previous opportunities with other organizations in creating internal change programs for a broad range of employees, and in a broad range of industries.

The OD and HR departments report to two separate directors who in turn report to the same area vice president. The HR department has a longer organizational history and was previously referred to as *personnel* (it is also considerably larger than the OD department). The HR department is staffed primarily with highly experienced employees who have mixed amounts of formal education. In contrast, the OD department is staffed by a smaller number of employees, all professionals with doctorate degrees. Each department has a corporate staff along with globally decentralized operations. Until now, the two operations have for the most part operated independently. HR has been primarily oriented toward record maintenance, recruitment, staffing, compensation and benefits, occasional downsizing, and legal compliance issues, along with some training and development. But over the last several years many of these operations have been outsourced and the HR function has come under increasing pressure to redefine its role in a manner that demonstrates value to the organization. Now OD sees HR moving close to their change management work.

Historically, the OD department had been involved in strategic tasks such as mergers and acquisitions, culture change, conflict management issues, large group interventions, work process redesign and other related activities. Now the AVP has recommended that OD and HR collaborate in their roles and become strategic partners. Gary, the new internal consultant, recognizes that his OD-university assignment has significant political issues. He realizes that, along with creating an internal OD university, comes the corporate power and political issues of two competing departments during times of change and transition.

We have asked our panel of experts to address some issues related to this case, namely:

1. If you were Gary Jones, how would you approach the shifting roles of the OD and HR departments as they move toward a more strategic partnership with management?
2. Is it possible or even desirable for HR and OD to become partners in strategic planning and change management? What are some of the major issues that need to be addressed?
3. How would you approach developing OD competencies in the HR staff?

Thanks in advance to our panel experts—let's learn from them!

Robert M. Sloyan

This is a common issue in organizations today: OD and HR fighting over the same slice of the strategic pie. If the HR group goes forward with its OD training, it will exacerbate the political tensions between the two groups and likely hurt both departments' credibility. Gary needs to convince his HR sponsor to invite OD into the process.

Together, they should start with the organization's strategy. Imagine the future.

I recommend Gary ask big questions such as:

- What competencies are needed?
- What's the culture?
- What types of communication are needed?
- What policies are in place?

Determine the key gaps between where the company is now and where it needs to be. Then, determine the skills the organization will need from OD/HR collectively. Mutual goals should be established focusing on the organization's strategy with clear understanding of how both departments add value. Once established, the training priorities for both groups will become clear.

OD and HR must become strategic partners or they will do a disservice to the organization. Both departments are so interdependent that neither can be successful without the other. How could even the most successful large group interventions be sustained unless HRM practices support them? Good OD requires good HR and vice versa. OD and HR must be aligned or neither will add value. If OD and HR cannot add value, neither deserves a "seat at the table."

Sue Sweem

If OD and HR are going to become significant contributors or even leaders for organizational strategy, they must work in concert as one combined function. The consultant in this case must recognize that the shift of OD and HR is clearly a change that not only affects the total organization but also greatly improves the value of their combined contributions to the success of the company.

One of Gary's first goals should be to collectively redefine the roles of HR and OD. This needs to be a participative process with both departments so the roles become complementary. HR is no longer an adminis-

trator and needs to prove itself as a business partner. OD needs to have a
stronger voice up front in strategy development. The two departments
need to agree on their combined goals and initiatives, which include
identifying and incorporating the strengths of both areas. For HR it is the
ability to understand the current issues at the site and know what the
leaders are struggling with internally. HR also knows the employees and
what is occurring on a day-to-day basis. OD brings its expertise in terms
of change management and the ability to transfer knowledge. With HR
and OD combined, they can proactively develop strategies to move the
business forward. This is contrary to the reactive stance that HR's role has
taken in the past. Specifically, OD and HR can partner to develop a talent
management strategy that significantly influences organizational effectiveness. Talent management is more than simply hiring the right person
for the right job. It is not an HR initiative, but rather, it is a holistic organizational approach that integrates HR and systems to align talent with
the business strategy. In order to accomplish this feat, OD processes need
to be implemented to ensure the appropriate culture and environment
are established to support it. OD and HR must become joint facilitators
for the process, as together they become the catalyst to develop a sustainable organization strategy that will exert a significant impact on the success of the business.

Obviously, there will be issues and concerns that arise from both OD
and HR that the consultant will need to be sure to address. As neither
department has worked closely together in the past, there may be some
territorial battles. Complementary skills such as consultation and large
group interventions will need to be integrated. HR is no longer simply
the employee's advocate. HR is now the business partner who contributes
to the bottom line and OD must also accept the fact that it, too, has to
prove its value and not simply rely on its perceptions to react. Together,
HR can identify the issues and concerns and OD can assist with the interventions.

There has always been a history of OD not wanting to be associated
with HR and vice versa, but only by combining the two can their expertise
and efforts have the greatest impact on organization improvements.

The competencies of HR are in transition. The traditional functions
have been outsourced (i.e., benefits, HRIS, compensation) and are no longer supported within the internal HR business model. This leaves the HR
professional with employee relations and strategic responsibilities. Therefore, the HR professional needs to develop and use more OD skills such
as facilitation, consultation, and strategic visioning. This is where HR can
establish its value with the operations management. Often this new role is
overlooked and not acknowledged or acted upon. The consultant will
need to help HR, as well as OD, view this new paradigm through a com-

bined lens so they can see how their joint roles can affect the organization's strategy. This becomes part of the talent management evaluation and strategy. A solid foundation from which to build upon already exists with team building and advisory expertise, but additional skills will need to be developed and transferred. This can be developed through experiential projects as well as OD training initiatives. The mindset of the HR professional is now one that encompasses both an advisory role as well as a change agent responsibility. This mindset change also applies to the OD professional.

The ability to obtain the seat at the C-Suite strategic table is greatly enhanced by combining HR and OD. The skill set will require the ability to transfer knowledge, integrate HR and systems, and implement change toward organizational effectiveness. HR and OD can only accomplish this together.

Timothy W. Goodly

The recommended collaboration of the OD and HR departments presents Gary Jones with a great opportunity to merge the capabilities of these two groups to provide a greater strategic and value-added partnership to the business. The OD department can enhance the HR department's various transactional offerings such as staffing, recruiting, and training by systematically linking these processes to larger change and strategic initiatives. The HR department, embedded in the daily operations of the business unit, can enhance the work of the OD department by providing local expertise on implementing various change initiatives, strategic interventions, and real time feedback on the effectiveness and practicality of these OD-driven activities.

At bottom, this HR and OD partnership offers the business an array of competencies that can significantly augment its effectiveness. By collecting feedback from his HR and OD management teams on current and desired capabilities, and validating these capabilities with key business partners in the various business units, Gary Jones will be in better position to develop a plan that will help the HR and OD partnership realize its full potential.

Issues to overcome include Gary working with the OD and HR leaders on the roles and work responsibilities of the various professionals in both groups. Collectively, they must establish clear boundaries that both segment and integrate HR and OD work assignments. These various roles and boundaries must be communicated to and understood by their business partners. Gary must also ensure that leaders of both groups establish protocols of partnership that facilitate intergroup teamwork, promote mutual respect of and professionalism within both groups, and prioritize the needs and expectations of business partners. Lastly, on-going training and education issues need to be resolved. In theory, the HR department will be involved in more strategic activities as these related competencies are developed through its partnership with the OD department.

Peter Sorensen and Therese Yaeger Respond

OD consultants often encounter broader organizational issues than that which they initially contract for—in this case, while his assignment is to create an OD university for HR, Gary encounters the HR department's desire to demonstrate value to the organization in terms of strategy and change management.

This Centri-Pharm case symbolizes increasingly more organizations today, as HR needs to expand their skill sets. But a suggestion by the AVP for HR and OD to collaborate can also be perceived as clouding one another's value to the organization. Our panelists each recognized the element of collaboration as a means to improve any HR and OD tension. Each panelist made unique suggestions as well, namely:

Rob Sloyan reminds us that we have to ask the right OD questions before we can create action. Concerns regarding culture, communication, policies, and even present and future scenarios can help to see the strength of listening to organizational members. Further, Rob mentions a large group intervention and the interdependencies of the two departments. Good OD work, Rob!

Sue Sweem recognizes the need to agree on combined goals and initiatives, finding strengths from both departments. Redefining goals, proactively developing strategies, and a holistic approach strengthen the possibility of HR and OD becoming better business partners. Sue also mentioned the development of a talent management strategy to align talent with strategy. Novel idea, Sue!

Tim Goodly recognizes the positive business outcomes—that merging both departments' capabilities can significantly augment the organization's effectiveness. Tim is careful to recognize that, amidst collaboration, the departments must also establish clear boundaries to both segment and integrate HR and OD work assignments—thanks for thinking about the bottom line, Tim!

Overall, we feel that collaboration, as well as integration, are necessary to move ahead with the OD University and build competencies. We suggest that Gary not forget what a true OD consultant can bring to this scenario. For example, can he be seen as a collaborative peacemaker and not a disruptive troublemaker? Is he capable of staying on task to deliver an internal corporate university and stay out of cross-departmental politics? If Gary understands his potential contribution to the organization with the knowledge he can deliver to HR, he is more likely to succeed at Centri-Pharm. Finally, Gary should consult with both HR and OD to determine the OD course content required, thereby making explicit OD's value to the organization.

ACKNOWLEDGMENT

An earlier version of this article was published in *The OD Practitioner*, *39*(4), 55-59.

CASE STUDY 23

THE CASE OF BAD NEWS AT GREAT NORTH INSURANCE

Homer H. Johnson

"I think we've got big problems," exclaimed Janice Rashid to her consulting partner as she looked over the data from the employee focus groups. "It's nothing but negative." Janice and her partner Jim were scheduled to present the focus group data to the executive team at Great North Insurance next Monday morning, and she knew that the team was expecting that the employees would have nothing but praise for the change efforts going on at Great North. After all, at least in the minds of the executive team, their efforts were saving Great North. However, the employees saw none of that—they were angry, frustrated and fearful.

Great North Insurance Company was founded over 2 decades ago by a group of small business owners who felt ignored by the large insurance companies. The founders' vision was to become the premier provider of casualty and property insurance for the specific needs of the small business owner. And to a great extent they succeeded.

"The family spirit" is the motto of Great North, which translates into superior customer service. Each customer has his/her own personal service representative. Questions are answered, policies are issued or changed, and claims are settled "hassle-free." The 350 person staff is prompt, informed, and courteous.

Critical Issues in Organization Development:
Case Studies for Analysis and Discussion, pp. 227–237

The founders of the company thought that one of the keys to a successful business was a great deal of support, collaboration, and family spirit internally. That is what would give Great North the competitive edge. Over the years, Great North became known as a great place to work, with good pay, benefits, and a "family" culture.

In the last couple of years, Great North has operated in the red. Several major competitors have targeted the small business market, and the increased competition has forced the company to lower rates. However, the company continued to focus on personalized customer service, and as a consequence, Great North has had the highest ratio of employees to policy holders among their competitive groups. The decreasing revenues combined with the high costs of service resulted in ever-increasing losses for the company.

After about two years of deliberation, the Great North executive team decided that a dramatic restructuring was the only way Great North was going to survive. The company would focus exclusively on business insurance and drop (unprofitable) side products such as insuring the business owners' pleasure boats and homes. The core processes would be reengineered and computerized using an enterprise-wide software installation. Many processes within Great North would be redesigned, and approximately 20% of the workforce would be let go. The latter would occur over the next 2 or 3 years, primarily through attrition and early retirement packages.

During the restructuring a variety of mechanisms were used to keep employees informed and involved. The changes were widely publicized in company meetings and newsletters. A change "hotline" was established in which employees could get their questions answered. And there were a variety of "design teams" of employees formed to assist in the redesign of processes. A primary goal in the change effort was the preservation of the "Great North family culture."

Janice and her partner had been hired to assist in the change effort and, sensing that not all was going right, they urged the executive team to "take the temperature" of the employees regarding the change. To accomplish this, they suggested conducting focus groups with a cross section of employees. The use of focus groups would allow the consultants ample time to explore issues and feelings in some depth and also allow time for the employees to present and explain their concerns. The executive team somewhat reluctantly agreed and 12 focus groups were conducted, each facilitated by two consultants and each having a recorder present.

The focus group results were very consistent and overwhelmingly negative. Employees were very angry about the restructuring. They thought that management had destroyed the Great North culture that they so cherished. In their minds, corporate greed was driving the change process. They did not trust the information being given to them by management. There were widespread concerns that many of the current employees would not fit into the new job positions and thus would be let go. Many employees thought that they would be replaced by younger workers who would be paid a lower salary. The president of Great North and one other key officer were particularly singled out for some very unkind personal attacks.

Certainly the data was not in line with the executive team's perception as to how the change effort was going. The team seemed energized by the change efforts and they were proud of the progress that had been made over the past year. They saw this change as "saving" Great North. While they acknowledged that there were some "bumps in the road," they talked about how it would, in the long run, create a future for Great North and would preserve jobs. And it was the family culture of Great North that would be instrumental in making this happen—dedicated employees pulling together to create this better future. However, the employees had a very different view of the change effort, and were angry and fearful at what they saw.

The consultants were in a quandary as how to present this information. They had a session scheduled with the president and the Great North executive team next Monday morning at 9 A.M. at which they were going to present the results of the focus group. This was going to be tough!

Typically, the consultants would have started the presentation by listing some areas that the employees thought were going well, and then they would move to areas that were not working well and which needed to be addressed by the team. However, in this case there was little positive information to report.

Moreover, the goal of the feedback meeting was to have the management group take action to address the employee concerns. However, the consultants feared that the vast amount of negative information and personal attacks would cause the executive team to become defensive about their behavior. The team seemed to think they were managing the change nicely. The consultants feared that the meeting could end up with the executive team becoming offended and hurt by the feedback and not handling the employee concerns constructively.

Janice and her partner began speculating how they might handle the overwhelmingly negative data. Maybe they should cancel the meeting and do some one-on-ones with the president and other key people? Or perhaps only present some of the negative feedback-have the executive team work on a limited part of the feedback and then present the rest of the negative feedback at a later time. Should they delete the data regarding the personal attacks on the president and the other key officer? That data would be sure to offend the people targeted.

If you were the consultant in this situation, what would you do? Would you cancel the feedback meeting? If not, how would you structure the agenda of the feedback meeting? Would you present all of the data? How would you assist the executive team in examining and understanding the concerns of the employees? How would you help the executive team to take some constructive action in addressing the employee concerns?

We asked a panel of organization development (OD) experts what the consultants should do in this situation. Their responses are as follows.

John McCall

I believe I am effective as a consultant because of the positive relationships I have with my clients and because I believe in my clients' success. This case presents a dilemma for me. I read that the focus groups were commissioned because the consultants were "sensing that all was not right" and that the executive team "reluctantly agreed" to them. I hope that we, as a consulting team, helped the executive team explore their reluctance and that we had approval of the focus group design. Working under this authority, I find it difficult to imagine surprisingly negative data.

I also find it difficult to imagine being stuck with presenting surprising data after twelve focus groups. I hope my colleague and I discussed the situation before now and modified the focus group design if we could. One possibility is we set up the data collection to be overwhelmingly negative to prove that "all was not right." If we believe we "set up" the data, we need to carefully own our actions and take responsibility. Regardless, my colleague and I need to support each other as we foster continuing positive relationships with the client.

And here we are, just before the data presentation. I would check our contract and work with our client contact, if not a member of the executive team, to enlist support. Because we perceive the data will be a surprise, I believe we should give the president and the other key officer a heads-up. I would structure the agenda to focus on the outcomes of the change effort saving Great North AND preserving the family culture. During the meeting, we can pay attention to signals of defensiveness and help the team work with the data rather than defend against it. As we focus on the results of the change effort and envision success, we can help Great North achieve positive outcomes.

David Coghlan

My first reflection on the case is to note that I am not happy with what has taken place. Janice and her colleague had set up the focus groups as an intervention. Focus groups are essentially consulting without responsibility. To provide the forum for the employees to simply vent their feelings and, in effect, dump their frustrations without assuming responsibility for the future of the company wasn't good OD process. The consultants did not anticipate or consider that there might be views of the events other than those presented by senior management. Other interventions, such as a confrontation meeting or some form of large group intervention, which would have aimed at not only taking the temperature but generating ownership of the current situation, would have been more useful.

Given the situation as it is now, Janice and her colleague do face a tough meeting with the executive team. In my view, they need to meet with the president and present the data to him/her. S/he is the key stakeholder and, as CEOs typically don't like surprises, it is critical that the two consultants provide the feedback from the employees to him/her first. They have to face the president's reaction, in all likelihood denial of the data and anticipated dodging and blaming. They have to take responsibility for how their intervention backfired and accept the president's anger at them. This will make big demands on them to listen actively and not appear to be defensive. They need to move to explore how such a gap in perception exists between what the executive thinks about the progress of the change and the employees' perception. Then they need to argue the following case: If the president wants to fire them, then that is likely to exacerbate the employees' feelings and in effect may make the situation worse. They have to convince the president that they can take the situation forward and then if the contract is confirmed together with the president, they plan the meeting with the executive.

The meeting with the executive team will go over the same ground as the meeting with the president. Janice and her colleague have to face the executive team's denial of the data, dodging, blaming and anger at them. They have to re-argue the case for their retention as OD consultants. One of the key things they need to watch out for is how the executive team takes in the data from the employees. The negative data may produce dissention in the executive team and blame towards the one(s) who hold(s) one position or another. The president may blame individuals in the executive team or the executive team may be blaming the president obliquely. If the contract is confirmed, then they need to plan a number of meetings with the employees. These meetings need to focus on recognizing the imperative for change, setting a shared direction and articulating the role of the employees in shaping a portfolio of insurance products for customers and influencing customer needs for integrated insurance packages.

Paula Wilder

Janice and Jim should first manage their own anxiety about reporting "negative" data to the executive team. While the focus groups revealed negative data and angry, frustrated and fearful employees, Jim and Janice can frame this as an opportunity for the company to build on its professional, courteous employees, develop renewed profitability, and recommit to its "family spirit." The data belongs to Great North. But data is just data. It's the meaning people make of it and the actions people take as a result of it that count.

Assumptions

1. Frontline employees are feeling vulnerable.
2. Leading complex change means meeting people where they are while continuing to paint the long-term, big picture. Often the executive planning world puts top leaders ahead of where employees are-creating distrust and disconnection.
3. Design teams have not integrated the company's executives and personal service representatives.

Framing the Data

1. Seek and build on the positive.
2. "Negative" data is opportunity.
3. Format the data to make it actionable. Shed light by applying the data to an organizational change model (hopefully Great North's own model). This will leverage increased clarity and understanding and enhance effective strategy development.
4. Employees' emotional states are solution indicators. What's frustrating them? What do they fear? What is making them angry?
5. Communication breakdowns during tough economic times are common across organizational levels.

Process for Reporting Back the Data

1. Give the president a "heads up" prior to the feedback meeting. Enlist him/her as supporter in a productive feedback/action planning process.
2. Paraphrase any inflammatory language to convey the message, not the drama. Acknowledge you have done this.
3. Extract all personal feedback and share in individual meetings with the president and other executives following the session. Coach executives on how to productively deal with their feedback.

4. Format data so that the executive team can see possible actions. Engage executives in actively working the data: What surprises them/doesn't surprise them? What is easy to address? What is most important? What information gaps exist? What can they do next week?

5. Encourage the executive team to develop personal, collective, participative processes to create partnerships with employees. Possible strategies for Janice and Jim to suggest include:

    (a) Share data with design teams. Enlist their ideas and efforts to improve morale, communication, processes, and feedback systems and examine implementation of the enterprise software.
    (b) Share data with focus group participants. Enlist their ideas and efforts.
    (c) Share high quality relevant information on the current reality of the company directly with employees—including financials, larger industry context and specific 3-year strategy to deliver profitability.
    (d) Partner with design teams so that they become powerful integrators of the change processes system-wide.
    (e) Develop personalized vehicles for executives and workers to communicate directly.

If Janice and Jim contracted well at the onset of their consulting activities, they should be able to facilitate Great North's navigation over these bumps in the road well.

Homer Johnson Responds

Organization Development consultants are often the bearers of bad news, particularly in conflict and change situations, and how to present this information is often a challenge to the consultant. The Great North case is a particular challenge in that the bad news is really bad; it is not expected by the executive team, and some of it is very personal.

Before going into the presentation of the data, two of our panel of experts raised questions about the focus group approach. John McCall questions whether, after 12 focus groups, the consultants would really be surprised at the consistently negative information. They should have been aware of how the data was going long before finishing the final group, and could have made adjustments, or at least discussed how to handle this. He also suggests that the consultants need to examine their own actions to see if they "set up" the data.

David Coghlan has raised a more basic issue regarding the intervention strategy chosen by the consultants. He states that using focus groups to provide a forum for employees to "dump their frustrations without assuming responsibility for the future of the company wasn't good OD process." Relatedly, there seems to be an assumption, both on the part of the executive team and possibly the consultants, that the responsibility for making the key decisions, and for solving all problems, resides with the executive team—the executive team is charged with saving Great North! This type of paternalism and lack of stewardship would likely put Peter Block into a rage.

David suggests that a more appropriate intervention would have been a large group intervention (whole systems change) or a confrontation meeting. Certainly some intervention to engage the employees early, to let them express their fears, and to engage them in both finding solutions to the issues as well as actions that will create a future for Great North would have been more productive. And it probably would have avoided the mess that the executive team, employees, and consultants find themselves in now. We don't know the dynamics of the situation. Perhaps the focus groups were the best "collaboration" the consultants could get out of the executive team and those who are implementing the software. However, there is better OD available.

Certainly one positive outcome of the focus groups was that the issues are now out in the open and there is an opportunity to deal with them constructively as well as to move in the direction of a more collaborative change effort. Our expert panel had some valuable suggestions as to how to progress towards that goal.

Paula Wilder's suggestions for writing the feedback report are worth noting. Paraphrasing the inflammatory language to convey the message, not the content, and extracting all personal feedback are good suggestions. Both Paula and John suggest the presentation of the latter should be handled one-on-one with the president and the other executives. All of our panel members would meet with the president first to prepare him for the data and the meeting, and enlist his/her support in the presentation. And their strategy is to present, as scheduled, the feedback to the executive team, and not sugar coat the bad news.

Finally, the panel saw this as an opportunity to move the executive team toward a more collaborative partnership with the employees as well as to rekindle the Great North "family spirit." The panel suggests that the consultants need to pay attention to signs of defensiveness and blaming in the executive team, and move the team to working constructively with the data. A modification in strategy is also needed. The executive team, indeed Great North, should embrace a change strategy that involves and engages the employees, as well as one in which the employees share the responsibility for restoring the financial viability of Great North and its family culture.

ACKNOWLEDGMENTS

The author wishes to thank Phyllis Schrage for her assistance in writing this case. An earlier version of this article was published in *The OD Practitioner*, 35(2), 39-43.

CASE STUDY 24

RIOTING IN THE THIRD WARD

Homer H. Johnson and Richard T. Johnson

News broadcasts stated that the trigger event for the rioting in Central City was a police shooting involving a 15-year-old boy in the Third Ward. The police had responded to a call of armed robbery, and upon arriving on the scene, saw three males running away from the apparent victim. A chase ensued, and a police officer encountered what he believed to be one of the suspects hiding in a dark alley. The officer called for the suspect to surrender, but instead the suspect pointed what appeared to be a handgun at the officer. The officer fired two shots, seriously wounding the suspect.

The shooting occurred around 8:30 P.M. on a hot Friday night in August and the rumor quickly spread that the police shot and killed an unarmed teen. By 9 P.M. crowds were gathering on the streets of the Third Ward, and by 10 P.M. cars were being turned over and several stores were being looted and set on fire. The rioting lasted well into Saturday morning. By mid-Saturday the area was calm. Much of the credit for ending the riot was given to a group of Third Ward ministers led by a Reverend Wells, who spent Friday night and Saturday on the streets asking people to remain calm and to stay in their homes.

Central City was once a fairly prosperous midsized city, and the home of several steel plants. These plants had spawned a large, diverse population and a bustling economy. However, about 25 years ago, the plants

Critical Issues in Organization Development:
Case Studies for Analysis and Discussion, pp. 239–248
Copyright © 2013 by Information Age Publishing

began to close and the economy soured. Central City is divided into six wards, and the Third Ward was hit hardest by the downturn in the economy. The last census listed the Third Ward as 80% Black, with an unemployment rate of about 32%, in contrast with the numbers for all of Central City, which were listed as 67% White with an unemployment rate of 13%.

The Third Ward was also perceived as a "high crime area" and targeted for "extra policing." While the stated reason for the extra policing was to ensure the safety of Third Ward residents, it was quite obvious that many residents of the Third Ward did not see the extra policing as adding to their safety. Instead, there were periodic complaints against the police for racial profiling, illegal search, and use of excessive force. The police denied such charges and countered that "aggressive" police work was necessary in order to keep gang and drug activity at a low level. All of this led to considerable tension between the residents of the Third Ward and the Central City police.

It was not more than a week after the rioting that Linda Bruce received a request for a meeting from the Central City Police Chief, James Stevens, and early in the following week Linda met with several police and city government officials and Reverend Wells. Much of that discussion concerned the need to improve communication between the police and the residents of the area, particularly those in the Third Ward. The outcome of that meeting was the police department offering a contract to Linda and her organization development (OD) consulting group.

Over the next 10 months, the OD group became very active in working with the community. While the police chief was only initially interested in diversity training for the police officers, Linda convinced him of the need for a broader-based approach. An ad hoc committee, chaired by Reverend Wells and made up of representatives from various groups and agencies in the Third Ward, was formed. This committee met weekly both to improve communication as well as to resolve police-community issues that might arise. A minority hiring plan was implemented for the police and city government. All police officers and many other city employees received diversity training, and a community relations officer was assigned to the Third Ward area, who proved to be well-liked and respected by the younger residents.

The efforts of the OD group received much praise from almost all parts of the community, and therefore Linda was a bit surprised when Reverend Wells asked if she would attend a "private meeting" at his home. In attendance at the meeting were several of the leaders of the Third Ward African American community. Reverend Wells began the meeting by praising the work that Linda and her associates were doing with the police and the community and stated that he thought that police-community relations were the best they had been in many years. He also expressed his confidence that Central City would not see a summer like the one they had the previous year.

However, he quickly added that the people assembled in the room did not think the Third Ward was any better off now than it was a year ago. In fact, he thought that it actually might be doing worse since many of the shopkeepers who suffered damages in the riot "took the insurance money and skipped town." He added that unemployment was still very high, the community was still very segregated, and there were many more vacant stores and buildings.

He went on to add that while they appreciated the many good things Linda had done for the community, they (apparently referring to the people in the room) saw her as "working for the police," and "taking a police view of things." The bottom line was that they wondered if she would consider working with them to help restore the vitality of the Third Ward. In the ensuing conversation a variety of goals were expressed, including the need to revitalize the business community, to find jobs, and to improve the schools. Apparently funds were available from the state for such projects and the local state senator had already received some commitment of funding to start the initial planning. They hoped that Linda would assist them in this planning phase. The meeting ended with Linda telling the group that she would need a little time to think about their offer.

Linda left the meeting not knowing whether to feel hurt or flattered. She was a bit shocked that some of the community people saw her as "working for the police," and particularly bothered by a statement by the school principal, who said they wanted her "to switch sides." On the other hand, she was flattered that the group trusted her and thought enough of her skills to ask her to undertake this assignment.

As she reflected on the meeting, she noted that she was still under contract (for at least 4 months) by the police department and had been discussing additional projects with Chief Stevens. While she thought the police department had made considerable progress in the last few months in understanding and addressing the needs and concerns of the Third Ward residents, much more work needed to be done in order to make a significant change in the department culture. Having developed strong relationships within the department, she thought she would be in a good position to facilitate the changes.

On the other hand, the project proposed by the Reverend Wells' group, while admittedly at a very formative stage, had the potential of making a significant change in the lives of the residents of the Third Ward, and Linda found that possibility very exciting. She also was aware that there was still considerable apprehension among Third Ward residents regarding the police, as witnessed by the principal's statement about her "switching sides," and she wondered if she could (or should) continue working with the police department if she decided to take this new offer.

Linda saw herself in a very real dilemma. She wanted to help both the police and the Third Ward residents. However, she wondered if this was an "either/or" situation. If so, which client should she work with? If you were Linda, how would you handle the situation? Are there any rules that OD consultants might use for handling situations like this involving potential client conflicts?

We asked four expert OD consultants—Sherry Camden-Anders, Larry Anders, Therese Yaeger, and Jeremy Lurey to tell us what they would advise Linda to do. Homer and Richard add their comments following that of the expert panel.

·

Sherry Camden-Anders and Larry Anders

Linda has apparently done a credible job in her initial work with the police department. She now finds herself in a very real dilemma due to the dissonance and negative comments of the Third Ward residents; she wants to help both the police and the residents of the Third Ward. A way to deal with her situation is to view it as a both/and situation rather than trying to solve it as a problem—the police and community are interdependent (one cannot exist without the other) and each contributes to the success of the whole. Linda can work with both the police and the community-planning group. The ambiguity and uncertainty presents a great opportunity to bring the community and the police together in an open and trusting forum to build the community-planning process. Together, this opportunity could increase the range of possibilities and impact what transpires and happens to increase the economic, social, and political development of the Third Ward. Using the both/and approach, Linda might:

1. Explain to the police chief, James Stevens, that while there is more work to do within the police department, there is also an opportunity to further work with the community residents who are expressing pain and discontent about the Third Ward.

2. Explain that she would like to set up a meeting between Reverend Wells, the community relations officer, and the police chief to explore how they might support one another in a community-planning process. She would also explain her plan to Reverend Wells and the community relations officer, asking for their support and assistance.

3. Assuming an agreement to work together, they would invite key people in order to gather data and create a plan.

4. The invitation would establish a focus group designed around a two-ring dialogue. The inner group would consist of the residents discussing what they would like to see happen in the ward with the outer group listening and taking notes. The inner circle would then switch and the police would discuss how they might help in the political and social aspects of assisting with a community development plan while residents listen to the discussion. Then, both groups would come together to discuss what they heard and what they believe could happen if they combined their resources (this design could also include some of the city government officials Linda interviewed following the riot, which would then involve a third inner circle).

It is important to create a clear contract regarding how the two groups will work together and the role of the consultant. Linda and the police chief will have to decide what will happen to her 4-month contract since she would be entering into two contracts, one with the police and one with the community development planning group. She could fulfill the contract by setting in place future plans for the police department and a transition plan for turning over that contract to a lead consultant in her group.

Therese Yaeger

This case reads like a West Side Story, or Romeo and Juliet, in which someone has to be rejected, hurt, or killed before the story ends. So for Linda Bruce, the dilemma of which group to support is critical and gut-wrenching. But does there have to be winners and losers, haves and have-nots? Could there be a mutually beneficial resolution for the Central City Police, the Third Ward African American community, and Linda as well? Perhaps we should propose a "win-win-win" solution.

Linda's dilemma of which group to support is not so easy to resolve, given the power of Reverend Well's statement that she is "working for the police." However, there may be some possibilities. Knowledge of Linda's expertise might help to strengthen a win-win-win solution. For example, what is:

- Linda's success with different clients—past OD consulting projects and personal learnings from projects that included political or community groups?
- Linda's OD consulting group—who, how many, the diversity of the group? What is the willingness (capability) of this OD group to work with these two groups collectively?
- Linda's ability to work for both clients collectively? How really different are the needs of the two groups? How willing will they be to let Linda's group work collaboratively with both groups?

Linda might:

- See similar, not different views of the situation, as both parties are concerned about the Third Ward. She could renegotiate the police contract to include the Third Ward needs. This collaboration may be quite attractive and it may also be cost-effective for both groups.
- Reflect on the fact that Linda's consulting contract initially came from the Central City Police Chief, which may have triggered Reverend Wells' animosity toward the police (and Linda's efforts).

- Explain to Reverend Wells that the Central City Police do not know that he (or the Third Ward African American community) feels this way.
- Demonstrate the win-win-win benefits to both groups if they were to agree on Linda's consulting group, helping to create an alliance between the police and Third Ward.

Linda should:

- Begin interfacing more with Reverend Wells, as he appears to be a powerful, respectable leader of the Third Ward who is capable of influencing others.
- Remind each group that they are more alike than different in their wants and needs for the community.
- After renegotiating the consulting contract, begin to resolve inter-group conflicts using an intergroup conflict resolution strategy.
- Focus on OD ethics!

    (a) Respect the client-consultant relationship, regardless of which group is ultimately the client.
    (b) Be open about the desire to work for both groups, and the commitment to avoid conflicting interests.
    (c) Maintain professionalism, and remember that inclusion and collaboration are what strengthens OD efforts!
    (d) Above all, know thyself (skills, limitations, values, assumptions, etc.).

In my view, Linda, the police, and Reverend Wells want the Third Ward revitalized, with mutually beneficial goals achieved for all. It doesn't have to be either/or for Linda. Instead of a West Side Story, think of historically competing groups such as U.S. Postal and FedEx, who now operate a business alliance together.

Jeremy Lurey

What a wonderful opportunity, Linda! This case presents an incredible chance for you to give back to society and help influence positive change within the community, one which is undergoing a grand transformation due to organizational changes in the surrounding environment. I would welcome such a rewarding engagement within my own practice.

In their willingness to engage a consultant in this process, it seems like the police department recognizes the need for change. Having the support of your primary client is a great start; however, there are two client organizations to consider. It is critical that you work closely with Reverend Wells and the residents of the Third Ward to ensure that their voice is represented—and heard—throughout this process. Your initial meetings with the Reverend will likely prove useful in building the foundation for an ongoing relationship, so I recommend you create an open dialogue with community residents, too. Given the heated emotions of the situation, I strongly encourage you to take this important first step through in-person communications and open forums. Town hall meetings with local church groups and school-sponsored parent-teacher associations might be a good way to start. In this context, you are likely to make some direct connections with local constituencies, earn some much needed respect, and build the trust necessary to succeed in this endeavor. From there, you will be able to use more formal communication channels, like monthly updates about the initiative, e-bulletins describing recent achievements, and even short articles in local newspapers to elicit greater awareness of the problems.

At the same time, it is important to remember that the police department is in desperate need of change, too. Whether their tactics were justified or overly aggressive, this situation did not occur because of one "bad cop." The situation is far more complex and warrants further investigation as your effort continues. Personal interviews and focus group meetings with police officers who work in Central City as well as first-line supervisors who understand their tactics should be conducted. These inquiries will likely yield information about what specific changes are needed within the Department. The police officials you met with earlier probably offered some preliminary suggestions regarding the issues, but their "answers" to the current problems would not address all that is wrong within the system. They are too close to the situation and may be biased by the recent shooting.

Perhaps your longer-term goal should be to create broader whole-system change—to have a group of police officers and residents united in building a brighter future —but this dream may take time to materialize. The recent shooting is likely just one incident in an ongoing cycle of vicious activity. For this reason, it is important to start slowly and take smaller steps to put both groups on the path for success. Forcing them to come together before they are ready may have a devastating effect by creating a more hostile environment for everyone involved—those who live in the community as well as those sworn to protect it.

Homer Johnson and Richard Johnson Respond

Client conflicts are not uncommon for OD consultants; however, the current case portrays one such conflict that has significant implications for the residents of the Third Ward. Our panel is unanimous in pointing out that this should not be viewed as an either/or situation, but rather as a unique opportunity for our consultant to bring together groups that have been in conflict and to help them create a better quality of life for the residents of the Third Ward. This is the type of situation that brings out the best of OD practice—an opportunity to make a significant difference in the lives of people.

But, as our panel points out, this is a very delicate process since there remain some deep differences between the parties Linda will be bringing together. While the panel doesn't explicitly posit a theory of change, it is interesting to note that they have nicely outlined some key elements of best practice in their responses. For example, they talk about moving slowly, about getting a good understanding of the problem, about building relationships with the key decision makers such as Reverend Wells, about convincing all parties involved that they can gain much more by working together, and about being open and honest with all parties. Great advice and strategy!

Finally, it is interesting to note that each of our experts recommends a slightly different intervention. Sherry and Larry recommend an "inner circle" approach (fishbowl), Therese recommends an intergroup conflict approach, and Jeremy suggests a town hall approach. Other OD consultants might offer other recommendations. These approaches are not in themselves conflicting; rather, each is designed to bring people together in open dialogue to facilitate understanding. They speak to the richness of OD technique.

Which approach should Linda take? It will all depend on what Linda thinks is the one that will best move the groups forward, and she probably will not know the answer to that until she better understands the people and issues involved.

Thank you Sherry, Larry, Therese, and Jeremy for your great insights and advice.

ACKNOWLEDGMENT

An earlier version of this article was published in *The OD Practitioner,* *36*(2), 40-43.

SECTION V

GLOBAL ORGANIZATION DEVELOPMENT AND CULTURE

CASE STUDY 25

A CASE OF TOO
MUCH DIVERSITY?

Homer H. Johnson

"This is crazy," said Michael Obedaye as he pretended to pound himself
in the head, "I think we might have created a monster that is out of control. Maybe we have too much diversity?" He was talking to Donna Fer-
nandez, the Regional Director of organization development (OD) for
Soap Products, and added "I really need your help on this one!"

Michael is the General Manager of a Soap Products manufacturing
plant in the central city area. An African American himself, he was given
the charge to diversify the workforce when he was appointed to the job 3
years ago. He recounted to Donna the conversation he had with the corporate execs when he took over the job. "Diversify, diversify, diversify,"
was the message. The execs were upset that the plant consisted primarily
of White males, whereas the central city site had large numbers of Hispan-
ics and African Americans. "Diversity is your #1 priority," they told him.

With the help of Donna he embarked on an intensive recruitment
effort to diversify the workforce. And now 3 years later, the plant was
roughly about one-third Hispanic (almost all immigrants from Mexico),
about one-third African American, and about one-third White, mainly
recent immigrants from Poland. These numbers pretty much matched the

Critical Issues in Organization Development:
Case Studies for Analysis and Discussion, pp. 251–260
Copyright © 2013 by Information Age Publishing
All rights of reproduction in any form reserved.

demographics in the area around the plant. The gender ratio was about 3 to 2 male to female. Not quite 50/50, but certainly much, much better than 3 years ago. The supervisory and administrative staffs were becoming more diverse, although the progress here was slow.

The efforts of Michael and Donna did not go unnoticed at corporate headquarters—last year both received a special award at the annual management meeting for "creating a diverse workforce."

Not only was the Soap Products workforce diverse, but they were also very motivated and committed. Certainly one contributing factor was that the salary and benefits were quite good and much higher than other plants in the geographical area, and there was no shortage of people who wanted jobs in the plant. Moreover, the skill level was likewise very good. Donna had instituted a mentoring program for new employees such that every new hire was trained by an older employee who spoke the language of the new employee. The older employee had to train the new employee to a specified competence level within three months to five months (depending on the job). If this was accomplished, the mentor received a bonus, and the new hire went from "probationary" to "regular" status. This program was so successful that Donna introduced it to other plants across the country.

However, the diversity effort had not been without problems. Language differences were just the beginning. Most of the employees spoke a little English; however, for many employees it was only a "little." This presented communication difficulties between line employees and supervisors, between employees, as well as in understanding company policies and procedures (the manuals were all in English).

One of Michael's gripes was that he seemed to be continually involved in deciding minor issues that he thought should be resolved by others. For example, the latest involved semi-nude pictures of women that several men had on the inside of their locker doors. The women employees complained; the men didn't understand why; and it all got pushed up for a decision by the "boss."

Michael thought that the employees were too "boss-conscious"—too dependent on the boss to handle problems. They always seemed to want the boss's opinion or decision on all sorts of issues. Many of these issues, he thought, should be handled by the employees themselves, maybe with the assistance of human resources (HR).

Of more serious concern was that productivity had been flat over the last few years, and was actually slightly lower than when Michael took over the plant. Michael's manager at corporate was pretty blunt in telling Michael that his new priority was to get the production numbers up. "You got the diversity you needed, now the target is productivity," was the clear message.

Employee skill level didn't seem to be the problem, thanks to Donna's mentoring program. And employee motivation was high. The problem seemed to be more in the areas of communication and coordination. Everything just took too long. If there was a problem on the soap line, it seemed to take forever to fix. Retooling the line for a run of a different soap product likewise took forever, it seemed—usually 4 or 5 hours for what other plants could do in 90 minutes or less.

"They are not working as a team," was Donna's diagnosis. "They are pretty good as individual performers," she said, "but they identify more with their racial and nationality groups, rather than with working together for the company. That makes sense given the language differences. They just feel more comfortable with people with whom they can best communicate. For example, if there is a problem on the line they look for their mentor, who may not be around, rather than informing the supervisor. We have to get them more focused on working together. If they can start working together better, I am convinced that productivity will increase."

"I agree," said Michael, "I think you are right on, and I am counting on you to put this together."

If you were Donna how would you handle this situation? How would you proceed? What interventions would you put in place? Looking more broadly at the diversity question, what advice would you give OD consultants or managers for working with diverse workforces?

We asked three expert consultants, Diana Montalto, Kathy Woodrich, and Matt Minahan to tell us what advice they would give Donna in handling this difficult situation. Diana is a Management Development Specialist at Exelon Corporation in Chicago; Kathy is the president of Woodrich Consulting in Venice, Californa; and Matt is the president of MM and Associates in Silver Spring, Maryland.

Diana Montalto

Is Soap Products pursuing diversity for diversity's sake or to enhance organization effectiveness? Perhaps Donna should reflect on how the diversity initiative was "mishandled" before attempting to "handle it!" Did it promote inclusion or cultivate a culture of exclusion? What are the core business needs driving the diversity initiative?

Donna should conduct a needs assessment focused on individual, team, and organizational levels. The workforce is currently engaged, motivated, and committed; yet thirsting for a sense of teamwork and camaraderie. Perhaps a "pulse survey," produced in several languages, could unveil the root causes behind the symptoms. Diversity training for employees would create value—especially one designed to reinforce the concept of diversity of thought. This may help employees feel more accountable, and less "boss-conscious." Management could also sponsor a potluck lunch to honor and recognize various cultural traditions and cuisines. Soap Products could invite guest speakers from the community to the event to convey multicultural thoughts and views that resonate with the employee population. The company could sponsor activities to facilitate integration such as on-site English as a second language courses, cookouts for all of the shifts, or interactive team building activities. In the spirit of safety and operational performance, they could start producing policy and procedure manuals in other languages. This should also result in a product changeover time reduction. Regardless of the intervention used, a feedback mechanism and control plan should be instituted to remain focused on continuous improvement.

I would advise OD practitioners faced with multicultural challenges to focus on realizing the inherent potential of a diverse workforce. Soap Products has been operating in a tactical, compliance mode to meet a predetermined directive. Now it is time to focus on promoting a unified culture by replacing ethnic cultural differences with shared goals and values. I challenge them to take a hard look at the organizational climate and move toward a place of inclusion. The cultural landscape has changed drastically; this has created the ideal opportunity to implement organization-wide initiatives to help manage change more effectively. How can an organization orchestrate the cultures, ideals, and myriad perspectives in a way that stimulates, rather than stifles, creativity and efficiency? How does the dissimilar nature of the current workforce support the organization's sustainable competitive advantage? Could the diverse employees possibly generate new business through product diversification resulting in greater market share? Perhaps the language barrier can become a conduit by utilizing the workforce to translate product names, taglines, and instruction manuals into multiple languages.

Another dimension for OD practitioners to explore is a focus on targeted development and retention of their workforce. With the average cost of replacing an employee at 1 to 2.5 times base salary, attracting and retaining talent, lowering absenteeism, and reducing overtime has a significant impact on the bottom line. Soap Products will begin to realize productivity gains if they implement programs designed to leverage the benefits of a multicultural workforce. In conclusion, it is imperative that Donna remembers her most effective "tool" in leading organization development and change is herself!

Kathy Woodrich, Venice, California

It is unclear what the organizational objectives were for the diversity initiative, but it appears they were EEOC-related. Thus the plant is experiencing problems related to polarization along ethnic and gender lines, and an apparent lack of strategic focus is having unintended systemic impacts. Redefining diversity and clarifying the initiative's objectives are needed, and team building and translating the policies and procedures manual are obvious solutions.

Donna and Michael have identified some issues, but their assessment is incomplete and not validated. Employees are motivated but not empowered or engaged with respect to the issues. Assessment and employee engagement seem the logical place to start.

If I were Donna I would begin by performing a preliminary assessment by interviewing a representative sampling of the workforce. Next I would engage employees in clarifying the issues and formulating action plans through a series of focus groups—multiethnic, with translators. (A large group change intervention could also be effective here). Focus groups would cover the following objectives:

- Why we are here: Clearly communicate the purpose of the focus groups and management's desire to empower employees in creating and implementing solutions;
- What success will look like: Clarify the ideal state regarding production goals, roles and responsibilities, and team functioning;
- Where we are now: Communicate Donna's preliminary assessment of the issue, and invite employees to challenge and validate those findings;
- What we are going to do about it: Identify opportunities and recommend actions:

o   A team-building component that engages employees in refram-
ing the concept of diversity from the narrow sexually—and eth-
nically-defined EEOC definition to one that respects and values
diverse perspectives: experience, authority, knowledge, skill,
strengths, relationships, communication styles (e.g., Hofstede's
cultural dimensions).

o   Determine how the teams' diversity can be leveraged toward
issues such as team functioning, and strategic and operational
goals.

o   Identify other opportunities such as those related to systems,
processes, structure, leadership, and team awards versus individual rewards.

From the data acquired through the focus groups, I would organize a task
force to create the action plans and oversee their communication and
implementation. I might also consider implementing the following interventions, based upon available resources and their potential strategic
impact:

*   A leadership succession program and diversity program that incorporate and reinforce the new definition of diversity,
*   Training on policies and procedures, and
*   Expansion of mentoring to include cross-cultural mentoring with
specific objectives, aligned with organizational objectives, outlined
and rewarded.

Working with diverse workforces can be challenging, yet if approached
intelligently and strategically, can yield organizations great cultural richness and competitive edge. OD consultants and managers need to be
clear about objectives and cognizant of how the organization is defining
diversity. If defined too narrowly, diversity can tend to polarize employees
(as in our sample case, by ethnicity and gender). Instead, OD consultants
and managers can help organizations to define diversity through a collective process of identifying and leveraging its diverse resources toward a
rich organizational culture and the achievement of common goals.

Matt Minahan

In my opinion, the seeds of the problem at Soap Products lay in the
guidance from corporate, "Diversity is your #1 priority." Unfortunately,
Michael and Donna took that advice literally, and what should have been

the real number one priority—production—got lost, and the plant is now paying the price.

I don't think that Michael is right when he says, "Maybe we have too much diversity," though. I think it's hard to have too much diversity. But, when diversity is promoted as aggressively—and successfully!—as it has been at Soap Products, it can become the end rather than the means. It appears that this plant has lost sight of its true goals, and now has to find them again.

The presenting problems are quite clear—productivity is down, lateral communication among employees is inadequate, cultural "clans" have formed which make the workplace unsavory for some, and there is an over reliance on the boss to solve problems.

If I were Donna, my *short* term solutions would be to:

- Agree with Michael and corporate what the real goals for the plant are for the next 2 years.
- Post the production numbers for the plant and the different production lines, including the "down" times for retooling. Knowing how we're doing is the first, and best, way to get employees to do a better job.
- Convene a standing committee of first line managers and line workers, representative of the plant in terms of nationality and gender, and work with them to review the productivity patterns over time, and ask them to make suggestions for improvement.
- Start an optional English speaking class for all employees, across nationality and language lines. This class would focus on the terminology needed to operate the production lines, and would also model solid employee-to-employee problem-solving skills and practices.

If I were Donna, my *medium* term solutions would be to:

- Engage volunteers and an outside consultant to conduct a corporate culture audit of the plant. This would likely include a focus group or three, a survey, and a representative steering group drawn from across the plant to help interpret the data and guide the action planning.
- Engage a coach for Michael and myself, to help us discover how we lost sight of the larger goal, and to help keep us from doing it again.

For HR and line managers, I would strongly advise getting outside help. When you're in the problem, you can easily lose sight of the solution, and end up trading means for ends, as happened here at Soap. A solid outside perspective is critical, and a good OD or diversity consultant would help you to keep an eye on the larger goals, while still pursuing the diversity goals. An outsider's perspective is critical when you're tinkering with the internal workings of your organization, so that you don't become "snow-blind" from all of the details.

For OD consultants, we don't know why corporate has made diversity such a big priority at Soap, but this points out again that we draw the real meaning of anything not from the content of the thing, but from the con-text in which it occurs. Soap's diversity initiative is being presented to us, and, I assume, to them, without any context, and so it's no wonder that the initiative can be wildly successful, and still fail. Without a reason why, all we can do is execute smartly, and smart execution is never enough when the larger context is ignored.

Homer Johnson Responds

Great job, panel! Very insightful and helpful!

Nice insight in pointing out that the diversity intervention appeared to be more about compliance than it was about diversity. As Kathy notes, the corporate office was probably under pressure from the EEOC to change the ethnic and racial numbers quickly or face some sort of penalty. In the company's very narrow view, diversity was all about headcount and not much beyond that. And while Donna's mentoring intervention had the positive effect of getting new workers up to speed very quickly, it also may have contributed to splitting the workforce into ethnic and racial divi-sions. As Diana points out, the overall process created more "exclusion" than "inclusion."

In hindsight (which is always 20/20), the initial intervention was very shortsighted, and was more of a short-term fix than a strategy to move the organization to a higher level of effectiveness. The company missed a great opportunity to create both a diverse and a high performance work-place.

I thought it interesting that all of our expert panel members advised starting the change process with a new look at the issues facing Soap. Each has a slightly different approach: Diana suggests a needs assessment or pulse survey and Kathy suggests interviews followed by focus groups. Matt's initial step includes a standing committee to analyze and take action in the production area, and then a follow-up culture audit.

The point, at least in my mind, is that Donna and Michael have a lot of assumptions about the problem, some of which may be correct, and others may be totally wrong. Before they jump into trying to change things, they better find out first what the real issues are. This could be a little tricky considering the language problems, but it is absolutely critical. I like Matt's suggestion of bringing in outside consultants to assist in the diagnosis. I am fearful that Donna and her people may have already decided what needs to be done, and some "fresh eyes" may come up with a different, and more valid, perspective. Matt's suggestion of a coach for Michael and Donna will hopefully turn this into a learning experience for both.

Finally, our panel of experts suggested several possible ways of creating an inclusive and high performing culture at Soap Products. I won't elaborate on the suggestions here, but want to echo the panel's view that a single and one-time intervention will not change much of anything (except for another short-term fix). Real change requires multiple strategies focused on a single objective. And the objective here is the creation of a high performance organization.

Thank you, Diana, Kathy and Matt. Great analysis and great suggestions!

ACKNOWLEDGMENT

An earlier version of this article was published in *The OD Practitioner.* *39*(2), 45-48.

CASE STUDY 26

IMPLEMENTING "NO CHILD LEFT BEHIND"

Is There a
Role for Organization Development?

Jan Rashid and Homer H. Johnson

"No Child Left Behind will be the downfall of the Medville School System," was told repeatedly to Anne Baxter when she interviewed for the position of the superintendent of elementary schools in Medville last year. In fact, No Child Left Behind seemed to be the only topic of discussion in the interviews. "Whoever gets this job has got to fix this mess quickly," was the school board president's parting comment to Anne as she left the final interview.

Well, Anne got the job! She became the superintendent of Medville's eight elementary (K-8) schools, and "the number one priority is to fix the mess, before the entire system collapses," as the board president told her when she was hired.

No Child Left Behind (NCLB) is a federal mandate, which simply stated, requires that schools make adequate yearly progress (AYP) each year until 2014, when every child has to perform at grade level in reading

Critical Issues in Organization Development:
Case Studies for Analysis and Discussion, pp. 261–269
Copyright © 2013 by Information Age Publishing
All rights of reproduction in any form reserved.

and math. For example, 100% of third graders must be reading at the third grade level and also have the skills to perform third grade level math. And to assess whether the schools are meeting that mandate, schools give students a standardized exam in third through eighth grades. The mandate also includes sanctions on schools and districts for failure to meet the expectations stated in the NCLB mandate.

While the idea is attractive, the reality is that there is considerable variance in reading scores and math scores in, say, the third grade. Some students develop their reading and math skills quickly, and some are slower to develop. Moreover, these skills seem to be more difficult to develop in schools that serve lower-income and/or immigrant communities. There are other issues that add to the controversy, such as who decides the grade level standards and what standardized test to use. Usually the state board of education makes these decisions.

Anne inherited two big problems. The first is that six of the eight elementary schools in the district did not meet NCLB standards. Moreover, in the last 3 years these schools had not made much progress toward meeting the standards. Actually, two schools had lower scores. Thus, the schools seemed to be stuck in place. This lack of progress did not please the State board, which was considering sanctions against the district.

The second problem was related to the lack of progress, and that was the schools themselves seemed to be in disarray. The principals were in a panic because if they didn't turn things around soon they would be the first to go. The teaching faculty was frustrated and angry and felt they were being unfairly blamed for the problem. Moreover, there had been considerable turnover in both the administrative and teaching ranks. Teachers complained that nobody knew what to do and consequently did not do anything.

Much of this discontent spilled over to the parents who were putting considerable pressure on the school board. Parents were concerned about their children being in a system that was not up to national standards, and moreover, the board wasn't doing anything about it.

The board seemed to put the blame on Anne's predecessor, who was known as a rather authoritarian, tough, no-nonsense administrator. His strategy for NCLB was to give the principals and teachers their "marching orders" and expect that they would "perform or else." He didn't seem to offer much help and expected the principals and teachers to "figure it out for themselves." For those who didn't meet standards he was forever threatening to "move them aside." And in fact he did remove three of the principals of the under-performing schools over the last three years. While the teachers are unionized and could not be "moved aside" easily, he did replace several probationary teachers in the underperforming schools.

So, as the school year was about to begin, Anne was struggling with putting together a plan to (again) implement NCLB and realized that this was a very tricky situation in which she was going to need some professional help. She had worked with Manny Chico in her previous school district and asked him to assist her. Manny was an OD consultant who had helped the previous district design a collaborative approach to managing the system change necessary to implement NCLB.

As she and Manny had their first meeting some things were becoming evident. One was that there was no "magic bullet." Change wasn't going to happen overnight, the plan would have to unfold over the next 2 or 3 years. Second, the principals and teachers were the key to implementing any plan, but they had been "burned" before and getting them on board was not going to be easy. There were a lot of negative feelings associated with the past efforts. Moreover, the principals and faculty couldn't be left out on their own to "figure it out." They needed support and resources.

Assume you were the OD consultant (Manny) working with the superintendent on this project. What might be the OD consultant's role in this change effort? What are some of the major steps or actions that you see as important in implementing the project? How would you deal with the negative effects (resistance) left over from the previous attempts to implement NCLB? How would you help take the emphasis away from the Federal and state mandates and sanctions, and put it back on student growth and achievement?

Finally, the bigger question: We keep hearing about the "crisis in education," particularly in the United States. How might the OD profession contribute to the changes that are occurring, or that are necessary, in the educational systems in both the United States and internationally?

We asked a panel of experts what advice they would offer Manny and Anne. To start, we thought it important to include a principal as part of our expert panel so we asked David Russo, the Middle School Principal of Fairview South School in Skokie, Illinois, to give us his understanding of the problem. David brings the perspective of being in the trenches as one who has been implementing NCLB. Ken Williams is our second expert, who is an associate professor at the School for International Training Graduate Institute in Vermont, as well as an independent consultant, and who has extensive experience in education. Our final expert is Cathy Royal from The Royal Consulting Group in Riverdale, Maryland, who also has a strong background and passion in educational issues.

David Russo

As coprincipal of a K-8 school in suburban Chicago, I see how relatively high achieving schools interact with NCLB legislation. In 2011, AYP benchmarks will push past 85% and districts such as mine are facing the reality of not meeting standards for the first time. I offer the following as a suggested course of action that can be applied to the Medville case as drawn from measures taken in my district designed to remediate our NCLB status.

It appears Medville took the approach of many districts at the onset of NCLB, which included identifying the tenets that make one compliant with the law and moving forward with those administrative tasks. Fundamentally, NCLB aims to improve instructional practices, which leads to increased achievement. Anne's predecessor failed to provide a focus and vision for innovative instruction. This created paralysis among the building administrators. They lacked capacity to implement programs designed to improve their school's performance through better instruction. Time was lost analyzing outcomes through student test scores without reflection on instructional practices.

Currently, Medville's principals and teachers mistrust the superintendent's office because it represents authoritarian rule and the abdication of responsibility by failing to provide thoughtful leadership during NCLB years. To rectify, Manny can fill these voids by generating ideas formed from previous experiences, which might serve as a buffer between Anne and her district until such time when she can restore confidence in her office through the implementation of purposeful change. Anne and Manny need to work in concert to develop a mechanism for problem solving system-wide issues and restoring order to the chaos created by NCLB failures.

Regaining trust begins by engaging those who have been most disenfranchised by processes under the previous administration, most notably building principals and teachers. Manny could oversee the creation of a standing committee with the specific purpose of establishing structures for dialogue and shared governance to problem solve issues of district-wide significance. Membership would be comprised of individuals from each building drawn from teachers, administrators, parents, and community members. This would be the first step in changing the top-down culture of the district. Yielding the chair to a building level administrator could be a symbolic gesture that the new superintendent will work in a more collaborative spirit. For the situation to improve in Medville, the efforts of each building and central office need to be coordinated through some measure of shared governance and decision making.

Once formed, the initial charge would be to examine the successes and failures in methods to determine how to fundamentally change instructional practices to improve student learning. This group would have an excellent starting point by reviewing the practices of the two schools that continue to meet AYP benchmarks. The committee has to create a centralized vision for instructional reform that both define the efforts of each building, while establishing standards to which building principals will be held.

Ken Williams

This case appears to be an example of a highly charged political environment. The school board president's warning to Anne, "Whoever gets this job has to fix the mess quickly," presents the critical element as to what is wrong in this case. The school board president abdicated his responsibility leaving Anne to solve the problems. Having candid conversations with all of the stakeholders prior to accepting jobs can help determine the types of resources needed, provide leverage for the interviewee in ascertaining the necessary resources prior to job acceptance, and help to hold employers accountable for solving problems.

The strong political nature of the case signals a collaborative role for the consultant. Anne would be actively involved in data gathering and analysis, setting goals, and developing action plans as well as sharing the responsibility for success and failure with Manny. The relationship will serve as a model for interactions across the district.

Building a set of alliances and finding out who is really committed to solving the problems in a way that focuses on student growth and achievement and keeping students and quality education at center is critical. Doing the political mapping and consulting with the real allies should be followed by a renegotiation of the terms of the contract to include board involvement, support, and accountability. They need to develop a shared vision that focuses on quality education for healthy students. Alliances must also be formed with parents, businesses, and other community partners. A key element is to get the parents fully involved in the school and understand the needs of students from their perspectives. Keeping focus on the "whole" child and healthy home environments need emphasis. Developing a strong parent-teacher organization and utilizing resources from alliances and strategic partnerships, so that parents can get their children ready for a good education, is important.

Another major step is to provide support for teachers and principals, involving them in ongoing professional development. However, before Anne can get to the support she needs she must have candid conversations with them to gain trust. Measures to shift the culture of apathy are needed with culture destruction and creation. Celebrating positive achievements and identifying changes needed for the new beginning are important.

Using a data-driven approach would be useful in this case to help create trust. Involving teachers currently in the system in data gathering is important. Painting a clear and accurate picture of the state of affairs is important (involving the main stakeholders in this as much as possible) without fixing any blame on the teachers and principals. Anne must be careful to ensure that she focuses on where they can go as an organization and provide hope for turning the situation around.

In an attempt to change the culture I would recommend that Anne focuses on what is working well in the system and identify, with the assistance of teachers and principals, what is not working well also based on the NCLB standards. Collaborative structures need to be set up and determinants must be on how teachers will be rewarded for collaborative and team efforts. A merit pay system can be created but this needs to involve teachers and principals for it to work and provide hope that they can achieve what is desired. Anne must send a clear signal of her commitment for the "long haul" if she is to get the support that is needed here.

The crisis in education in the U.S. is connected to the fact that education funding is controlled by external sources, and allocation of resources at the state level is tied to a funding formula that is mysterious and not transparent with property taxes playing a major role in the educational funding at the local level. Additionally, there is an unhealthy tension between local and federal control of education. There is a great deal of resistance to change in education settings even in the face of the need for rapid changes with a growing multicultural and immigrant population. The OD profession can provide tools for educational institutions to learn about themselves and to become adaptable in the face of change. The OD profession can also provide tools for the education profession to study itself as a system and help develop practitioners as systems analysts using a data-driven, decision-making approach to leadership. There are large group methodologies from the OD profession which can help education systems to better understand themselves and there are several tools from OD on how to develop a multicultural organization that is needed in education at the national and international levels. The OD profession also can assist in the arena of overcoming resistance to change, which plagues education in general.

Cathy Royal

Manny Chico, the OD consultant, is critically positioned to use both traditional OD theories, and strength based OD theories such as appreciative inquiry and strength based learning modules to implement sustainable,

innovative change. I support using these processes for helping the Medville community come together to address their possibilities for NCLB and
collaboratively "fix the mess."

Manny could assist Anne in implementing a three phase change initiative. Taking an inclusive and affirmative stance in the consultation will do
much to generate a "space of good will" for Anne as she assesses and lis-
tens for what are the possibilities for the school district.

**Phase One: Individual Community Engagement and Information
Gathering**. The key of this phase is listening and gathering the community. Taking into consideration the need for stakeholder commitment and
a compelling shared vision of each school's preferred future avoids the
pitfall of a "one size fits all" process of improvement. This is also an
important step in helping the system to heal. His role here will be to convene various stakeholder groups and create a strategic series of common
ground meetings. This phase will be the opportunity to ask the questions
about, "What will be important for Anne to know about your work and
needs as a member of this school (each school should have their own
meeting with the consultant) as you create a blueprint for student success?" In each phase it will be important to be as transparent with the
community as possible.

**Phase Two: The All Schools Community Summit: Reporting back
to the stakeholders as a total school community**. The all school system
summit invites the stakeholders and citizens of each school community
to participate in a school district summit. Manny's task in this phase will
be to coach Anne on the guidelines and assumptions for the summit. A
key community question for the summit is, "What should be present in
our schools for each child to feel safe and confident that s/he can
succeed?"

Phase Three: Anchors and Blueprints: Success from the Summit.
The consultant will play a critical role here as he now holds an important part of the system's institutional memory about commitments,
dreams of a preferred and shared successful future, and the activities
that have created trust and transparency with stakeholders. This is the
phase where all opportunities to redefine the NCLB challenge and
restate the roles of all stakeholders will be created by Anne and the community stakeholders.

It is time to rethink how we engage the stakeholders in communities in
the critical activity of educating a nation and preparing students to be citizens and leaders. Using innovative and critical OD skills can redefine
public education toward preparing citizens to be prepared for scholarship
and self efficacy, and lifelong learning.

Jan Rashid and Homer Johnson Respond

Very nice job, panel! Great insights and suggestions!

While not attempting to summarize the insights of the panel, it struck us that all three of our experts strongly advocated a collaborative approach to change. Principals, teachers, and parents not only have to be involved in the implementation, but also have to be the key players in the data gathering and planning, and implementing the efforts in their own schools. Not only is this the way to overcome resistance, and to build trust, but also is the key to successfully implementing NCLB.

To accomplish this collaboration the panel suggested a couple of approaches. David suggested a standing committee made up of teachers, administrators, parents, and community members, and chaired by a building administrator, as a key initiative. Ken talked about setting up collaborative structures, including linking rewards for collaboration and team efforts, as well as the use of OD tools such as large group methodologies. And Cathy was more specific in suggesting a three phase process, the center of which is an all-school system summit involving the key stakeholders. Which of these will be most effective in, or best fit, the Medville situation is something that Anne and Manny (and others) will have to decide based on their diagnosis of Medville's issues and capabilities.

It is also obvious from the responses of the panel that, yes, OD has much to offer in the massive change efforts that our schools are undergoing. We have several effective change processes to offer, as well as tools to overcome resistance, facilitate wise decision making, and enhance commitments.

Thank you David, Ken, and Cathy for your wisdom and provocative ideas!

ACKNOWLEDGEMENT

An earlier version of this article was published in *The OD Practitioner*, *43*(2), 53-56.

CASE STUDY 27

THE CASE OF CAMWELL HIGH SCHOOL

Homer H. Johnson

The consultants were first contacted in early July by Marian Alonzo, the principal of Camwell High School. She told them that she had recently completed her first year as the head of Camwell and needed help to "change the culture at Camwell High."

Alonzo explained that she had spent her first year at Camwell ensuring that the school was running smoothly and getting to know the faculty, staff, and students. Now that the school year was over, she was ready to start thinking about what changes Camwell needed, or as she put it, "to start thinking about my legacy."

Under the previous principal's administration, decision-making was centralized at the principal or associate principal level. Although chairpersons were in place for all curriculum areas such as science, math, and English, these persons had little authority or responsibility. Several older teachers supported the previous principal's management style and thought his "tight ship" approach was necessary in order to run a large high school. However, the newer teachers were less supportive. They believed this style blocked new developments in teaching. For example, Camwell was the last high school in the area to introduce computers as

Critical Issues in Organization Development:
Case Studies for Analysis and Discussion, pp. 271–281
Copyright © 2013 by Information Age Publishing
271

instructional tools. The previous principal thought they were too expensive and unreliable, and he was not convinced of their educational value.

Alonzo's vision for Camwell, as she told the consultants, was to develop a collaborative learning community, one where teachers would have high standards for themselves and for their students. They would have the freedom to design and teach a curriculum that would meet these high standards and—as importantly—they would be held accountable for their performance. She thought that this could happen only if decision making was decentralized down to the department level, putting the faculty in charge of setting standards and designing a curriculum that would deliver those standards. However, she did not want to impose her structure on the faculty and thought the new structure and culture would be "self-organizing," emerging out of collaborative discussion.

The consultants had worked with another school in the district and had some familiarity with Camwell. After two meetings with Alonzo, the consultants agreed to work with her in this change effort. Their primary role would be as advisor and coach to Alonzo on change management. In addition, they would design and facilitate the retreat scheduled for the beginning of the school year, and would serve as process consultants at subsequent meetings. Because they thought it was important for Camwell faculty to take ownership of the change, the consultants suggested they provide a supportive role, rather than assume leadership in this process.

As a first step, the consultants advised Alonzo to have lunch with most, if not all, of the department chairpeople individually over the summer to share her vision with them and to elicit their ideas and support. Because they would be the key people to implement the change, obtaining their reactions and suggestions prior to suggesting any change would be important. She did so, and reported that the meetings went quite well.

In mid-August the school traditionally held a 2- or 3-day retreat with the entire faculty and administration. Under the previous principal, a typical agenda for this retreat was, as one teacher described it, "getting our marching orders:" outlining the schedule for the coming year, making teacher assignments, and reviewing school rules and regulations. Alonzo and the consultants decided that the retreat, which would be facilitated by the consultants, would be a good time to introduce and model the new culture.

The first day of the retreat was designed to get to know each other, to welcome the new teachers, and to discuss school start-up issues. On the second day, the faculty met in their departments, and the facilitators led them in a team-building exercise. They provided rules for effective meeting management and asked the department groups to develop their own ground rules. After this, the departments discussed start-up and curriculum issues. On the third day, Alonzo shared her vision for Camwell. The department groups provided feedback on the vision, added to it, and later offered suggestions on how to proceed. Feedback from participants indicated that the retreat had been very successful.

One decision made during the retreat was to form a 14-member committee, which would serve as the major vehicle for change. This committee would consist of the department chairpersons plus several faculty members who represented a cross-section of the school. Alonzo would chair the committee. The committee planned to meet every three weeks depending on the school schedule. The consultants would assist in the design of the meetings and function as process consultants during them. Alonzo (as chairperson) would run the meetings.

There was considerable excitement and enthusiasm during the first several meetings. The committee spent a lot of time in the first meeting defining its members' roles and responsibilities and discussing the expected outputs. In the meetings that followed, the "vision" was discussed and clarified, including specifically what would be expected of each stakeholder group—administration, chairpeople, and teachers. A draft of this document was presented for comment at a teacher in-service meeting in late November. Although it did not generate a lot of discussion, the faculty was very supportive.

After the first of the year, much of the work was to take place at the department level (in which the consultants did not participate). The agenda for the department meeting was not specified, although the committee suggested they work on issues of curriculum and standards. The committee met monthly and functioned as an advisory board to Alonzo, giving her input on several pressing issues.

The only major task that the committee undertook in the spring was to redesign the annual performance review process for teachers. In the past, the principal and associate principal had done all reviews with no input from the teacher or the teacher's chairperson. The criteria for evaluating the teachers and the outcomes of the review were often times a mystery, unless, of course, you were fired. Of all the issues raised at the August retreat, this seemed to be the one issue that the faculty unanimously wanted to see changed.

After much discussion and several visits to a high school in an adjacent district, the committee decided to adopt the process used at that high school. In the new process, each teacher submitted a portfolio of his/her lesson plans and other materials, as well as examples of student work. This was given to the department chairperson, who was responsible for meeting with the teacher. The two of them would then design a development plan for that teacher. The process is fairly standard in many schools, and puts the emphasis on teacher development rather than evaluation. Most of the Camwell faculty agreed to the new approach.

With only a month remaining in the school year, the consultants received a call from Alonzo who requested an emergency meeting with them at 8 A.M. the next morning. At the meeting she told them that she was very discouraged and frustrated about the progress that had been made to date and was considering dissolving the committee. She was disappointed that they had been working on this change effort since last summer and didn't have much to show for it. In her opinion, the committee had spent a lot of time discussing change; but when it came to actually making changes, not much had happened. For example, while the departments had spent a lot of time discussing curriculum changes, only two had anything to show for it: Math had revised the curriculum to include two new honors courses, and Science was writing a grant proposal for a computer-based biology lab class.

The final straw was the annual performance review. While she was pleased that the school had adopted a new and developmental process, the chairpeople had refused to implement the process in their departments. Their excuse was that this was the end of the school year—they were already overloaded with tests, grading, graduation, band concerts, and other work, and couldn't take on any additional responsibilities. Further, some of the older teachers objected to the new process, and the chairpeople wanted to avoid a confrontation with them.

Alonzo added that she believed that Camwell's culture had changed, but not very much. She conceded that the faculty probably felt more involved and more committed to the school, but she felt that their involvement was primarily in giving advice. Her belief was that, in order to change a culture, people have to take action—not just give advice. With that said, she had to run a district meeting and excused herself, adding that she would like to discuss this further with them later in the week. The consultants sat in stunned silence as she left, wondering what next step to take. They hadn't seen this coming.

Let's assume that you are the consultant in this case. What do you think is going on with Alonzo, and the faculty? Looking back over the last eleven months, what, if anything, could or should you have done differently to avoid the current problem? When you meet with Alonzo later in the week, how would you structure that meeting? What advice and help would you give her for moving forward? Or would you suggest she throw in the towel on this effort?

Arnold Minors

These consultants negotiated a primary role as advisor and coach about change management to Ms. Alonzo. More precisely, the change involved here is implementation of culture change. It is not apparent that they advised Ms. Alonzo that culture change is a relatively long-term process, particularly where the expected outcome is a collaborative learning community. It was predictable that the way in which this community would unfold would be uncertain.

Principals in Ontario—and I suspect elsewhere—would be pleased at the progress that was made in such a short time, especially given the unpredictable resistance that would come from "several of the older teachers."

In light of the experience so far at Camwell, I would:

- Ask Ms. Alonzo what specific actions she was expecting, given her choice to allow a "self-organizing structure and culture";
- Discuss, in some depth, the nature of organization change—speed, issues of resistance, identification of things which would have to remain unchanged, and so forth;
- Acknowledge the changes which have occurred and encourage Ms. Alonzo to continue with her dream;
- Suggest that at least one of the two consultants be replaced with one who has expertise in change management and that this person's function would be to work directly as Ms. Alonzo's coach;
- Propose that the new coach negotiate a more specific contract for advising and coaching (frequency of meetings, nature of information that Ms. Alonzo might need, etc.); and
- Negotiate the process consultation contract so that the terms are clearer about potential outcomes.

I know that principals in Ontario, where I live, would be delighted to get that kind of help. So would Ms. Alonzo and Camwell High.

Beth Applegate

I believe poor management and the transition process was the root cause of the client's frustration, which took the consultants by surprise in the Camwell High School case. Together, we can change many things in organizations. However, if the individuals who make up the client system don't actually make a shift—go through the process of letting go—they will keep showing up the same way.

If I had been consulting with Alonzo, I would have better determined who the client was and more thoroughly clarified the client system's need and readiness for change. I would have helped Alonzo set realistic expectations about the scope of the change process and her goals. Finally, I would recommend that we begin our work together by utilizing action research.

To prepare Alonzo for her one-on-one meetings, I would have suggested that they begin a data gathering process with the staff to determine the external and internal forces that maintain the status quo. Next, I would have helped her develop a set of talking points and questions to: introduce the idea of a change process; and gather data from the faculty about their vision for a desired future state.

At the faculty retreat, I would have assisted the whole system with analyzing the factors identified in the data collection through a force field analysis. And, in addition to helping them understand the tenets of organizational change readiness and resistance, I would have helped faculty understand change at a personal level.

With the 14-member change process advisory committee, I would have assisted them to identify the committee's mission and clarify roles, goals, process and relationships within the committee, and among the rest of the faculty. Additionally I would have helped them to determine what norms or rules made sense and which worked against their desired state. Finally, it would be critical that the committee and department heads agree to clear, prioritized and measurable outcomes and that ongoing communication and coordination between the change committee and departmental heads was ensured so that they could manage unexpected side effects resulting from the change effort, and make adjustments accordingly.

At the faculty in-service meeting, I would have encouraged Alonzo to share the implementation plan and timeline with the faculty and enlist their measurable involvement. I would have recommended that results be evaluated and communicated to all faculty on an ongoing basis and that incremental successes were celebrated.

If I had received the emergency call, I would have needed to resist the temptation to overfunction by offering expert advice on how to solve the problem she raised. I would continue to hold an objective mirror before her as she experimented with answers. Finally, I would have asked her what she believed were the appropriate steps and how I could assist her in taking them. I would not have thrown in the towel; I would have continued to trust the process.

David Moxley

Let me use this opportunity to inventory all of the tactical errors I made as the Camwell consultant. I didn't get Principal Alonzo to pause when she took ownership of the "vision" as her legacy and instead I merely accepted it without clarifying the need to engage faculty from the very beginning. Faculty needed time to frame the change process for themselves and their school. They needed time to honestly reveal their preferences about the direction and tempo of the project. Adequate time was needed to reduce the gulf of differences in preferences for change between younger and older faculty members who held substantially different styles, expectations, and aspirations about school management. There is a real need at Camwell for faculty members to understand and respect differences among themselves while they discover unity, a process that requires adequate time.

Principal Alonzo needed to trim back her expectations. Perhaps I could have framed the coming academic year as a preparatory one in which faculty members would contemplate the change process, simply work on getting ready during the first year, and produce a plan of action. To satisfy her desire for action and concrete results, we could have identified several pilots or experiments—identifying areas of the curriculum for improvement, implementing new faculty evaluation protocol in one department that could champion this change, and restructuring some courses. It does sound like the accomplishments of the first year helped faculty members to ready themselves for future challenges. Some important outcomes were achieved regarding curriculum change, the design of new courses, and the preparation of proposals for external funding. These achievements deserved celebration since the recognition of small victories can sustain the morale and elevate the energy of participants.

Principal Alonzo needs energetic allies. So I would encourage her to recruit individual faculty members from both the new and senior generations who could take on some of the pilots. They could exemplify change at the individual faculty level, collaborative learning with colleagues and students, and how to use portfolios as springboards for professional development. Involvement of both young and old faculty members as role models may come to symbolize Camwell's commitment to transgenerational change.

When I meet with Principal Alonzo, I would simply apologize for misdirecting her. I would suggest that we needed to respect the first year for what it was: a time to get ready and a time to get people on board. "Principal Alonzo," I would say, "it's time to walk the razor's edge." "What?" she may say with some irritation in her voice. As the Buddhists suggest, we need to walk between the long and short term, between action and reflection, between outcome and process, and between hard work and celebration. Principal Alonzo's legacy could emerge out of a balance of polar opposites—a school whose resilience and vitality are its principal's resources.

Homer Johnson Responds

Our panel of expert consultants did a great job of identifying the major issues in this case and suggesting alternative strategies. Let me highlight a few points that I see coming out of their analysis. The panel apparently did not have too much of a problem with the overall agenda set by the consultants. That is, the summer meetings between the principal and the department chairpersons, the new look for the beginning of the school year retreat, the 14 person transition committee, and so forth, seemed to provide a reasonable structure and process for changing Camwell's culture. However, the panel did have some issues with what went on in those meetings.

1. "Self-design" doesn't mean "laissez faire." There seems to be an underlying theme among the panel that the consultants may have been too laissez faire in assisting Alonzo and the faculty, particularly in the area of setting realistic expectations (see below). We don't know why this occurred, whether by design or lack of knowledge. One might speculate that Alonzo's insistence on a self-designing process may have caused the consultants to back away from giving too much input. Whatever the reason, there was a clear need here for more active consulting. Helping the clients articulate a mission, and a focus, and reasonable goals, and helping them understand the change process would have been helpful. Having the client group look at themselves and how they are working together, and urging them to celebrate accomplishments, is a critical part of any consulting process, which for some reason the consultants failed to do (or didn't do enough of) in this case.

2. Whose vision, Alonzo's or the faculty's? A couple of the panel members were uncomfortable with starting the process around Alonzo's vision for Camwell High. Her meeting with the department chairpersons over the summer to share her vision and to elicit their support, as well as using her vision to kick off the change process in the August faculty retreat focused the change effort around Alonzo's vision of Camwell. Both Beth Applegate and David Moxley suggested starting the process by having the faculty develop a vision for Camwell. Although they suggest slightly different processes, either would have developed more ownership by the faculty and would have helped the faculty "let go" (see below) of the past.

"Whose vision" is an interesting issue that OD practitioners frequently face. One could also argue, from the perspective of those in Whole Systems Change, that all stakeholders, for example, parents, students, faculty, and community members, should have been a part of developing a vision for Camwell, not just the faculty. And certainly for those who work in the private sector, having top management develop the vision is standard practice, and it is often the OD consultant's job to implement the vision throughout the company.

3. Make sure the expectations are very clear. As the panel pointed out, Alonzo had very different expectations as to what she expected could or would be accomplished during the school year than did the faculty. Actually, there were probably several sets of diverse expectations among the faculty itself, as well as with the consultants and with Alonzo. A major agenda item for both Alonzo and the faculty should have been the development of a consensus on what they would like to accomplish, and what they could reasonably accomplish, in the long term, and particularly in the current school year.

4. Set reasonable (and "doable") expectations. Following up on the previous point, the panel noted that Alonzo's expectations were unreasonable given what we know about culture change. In fact, this probably was the major cause of her suggestion to call off the change process. She apparently thought that they could change the culture in nine months, and one suspects she thought she could ram it through. It was the consultants' responsibility to help her be more realistic both in terms of what was possible, as well as suggest a more effective way of accomplishing the change. This should have dealt, at the very start, with the relationship between the consultants' and Alonzo. Culture change usually takes several years. The message here is don't expect too much in the first year.

I like Beth Applegate's idea of using William Bridge's transition management as a framework for this change effort, as well as her suggested agenda for the first year. The first year might have been more focused on "letting go of the past," rather than pushing ahead into the (somewhat unspecified) future. David Moxley made the same point from a different perspective by suggesting the first year should be focused on "unfreezing," a la Kurt Lewin. "Letting go" or "unfreezing" would have been a major accomplishment, may have brought the different factions together, and would free the faculty to move on to the future.

5. Use pilot projects which have a high probability of success. An old piece of wisdom for starting a Total quality management process in a company was that you start with a manager and a department who is both competent and excited about the process, and do a pilot project in that department. Early success will build confidence and you can move from there. David Moxley suggested just that strategy for the transition committee. In the first year, focus on a couple of "doable" projects. Get some early "victories," and Camwell will be ready for a more extended effort in the second year. Good advice for any change project.

6. Celebrate accomplishments. Arnold Minors pointed out that principals in Ontario would have been pleased at the progress that Camwell made in such a short time. Much was accomplished, although Alonzo apparently didn't appreciate the amount of progress. All of the panel members noted the need for celebrations, even for small accomplishments. These reward people for their efforts and also send a signal as to what is important.

7. Renegotiating the contract with Alonzo and the faculty. So, what happens now? What should the consultants tell Alonzo at the next meeting? The panel agreed on a couple of points. One was that there had been some important accomplishments in the school year. A second was that the change effort should continue. The question is how the consultants should handle the meeting. Beth argues for a more reflective approach and "continue to hold an objective mirror before the principal as she experimented with the answers." David proposes a somewhat different approach, asking Alonzo to look at the first year in a different framework. Arnold suggests, among other input, discussing the nature of organizational change. I realize that I have oversimplified their positions, but my point is that there are a couple of ways of handling this meeting. Whatever way it is handled the panel suggests, some more directly than others, that it is time for a renegotiation of the contract, with a better understanding of expectations, of the role of the consultants, as well as a redesigning of the change process.

Finally, I think it important to note that even considering the above comments, the consultants had some good points in their design and facilitation. They did get the change process off of the ground, and as Arnold pointed out, many principals would have been pleased at how much was accomplished during the year. Our purpose here is not to nitpick the efforts of other consultants, but rather to look at problems that arise in consulting and examine what we might do better. It is with the hope of improving OD practice that these suggestions are offered.

ACKNOWLEDGMENT

An earlier version of this article was published in *The OD Practitioner*, *34*(4), 60-64.

CASE STUDY 28

ORGANIZATION DEVELOPMENT'S ROLE WHEN GOING GLOBAL

Therese F. Yaeger and Peter F. Sorensen

Pharma is a successful pharmaceutical company operating, until now, solely in the United States. As a result of their successful hard-line sales history, the environment at Pharma has been described as entrepreneurial. Pharma's corporate culture has always been aggressive, competitive, and power-oriented, which has contributed to its success.

However, being U.S.-centric must now change, and Marcus, the new CEO at Pharma, has charged the organization to become global by next year. Marcus has identified three global regions—India, Asia, and Africa—to begin Pharma's global efforts.

You are the U.S. organization development (OD) consultant reporting directly to Marcus. Marcus wants to involve you in the overseas future growth development for Pharma. He has told you, "Failure is not an option. We might be a great U.S. pharmaceutical corporation, but as CEO, I insist that we become global, and make it happen now. The announcement of our new global efforts will be in the press next week."

As the OD consultant, you have expertise in global OD, with limited exposure to regions in Africa, India, and Asia. You understand Pharma's past culture, but you are also aware that in these different national cul-

Critical Issues in Organization Development:
Case Studies for Analysis and Discussion, pp. 283–292
Copyright © 2013 by Information Age Publishing
All rights of reproduction in any form reserved.

tures, start-ups do not succeed as quickly and aggressively as the U.S. Pharma culture. In fact, with your global knowledge, you know of instances where start-up efforts failed because U.S. management teams were unaware of the context in which they were operating.

You understand the no-fail approach that Marcus has taken. But you also wonder what will be needed to support all the future efforts. Perhaps with the right people and the right knowledge, this global effort might just work. But you realize that this effort is bigger and broader than OD.

Right now, more questions than answers exist. Some of these questions include:

- How might OD be of strategic relevance in helping Pharma?
- Does Pharma understand the economic, political, and legal issues that must be addressed?
- Does everyone understand the societal and national cultural values?
- How will the role of OD be perceived?
- What specific OD strategies would you incorporate with on-ground Pharma management?
- Finally, how would you measure success on this global undertaking?

We have asked three consultants with global expertise to help unpack all the answers and questions for this huge corporate global project: Nazneen Razi, with human resources and OD knowledge operating globally, particularly India; Dalitso Sulamoyo, with first-hand change experience in Africa (particularly Malawi); and Katherine Shroeder, with expert OD knowledge and experience working in Japan.

Nazneen Razi

The challenge of doing business globally cannot be underestimated, particularly in a country like India, one of the most culturally, socially, and politically complex countries in the world. The initiative to take Pharma across U.S. borders provides tremendous opportunity for an OD consultant who can leverage both local OD talent and healthcare experts to assess the current situation and develop an outcome-based strategy for success.

According to a recent IMS (2010) report, the pharmaceutical industry in India is a $10 billion business and among the top four emerging markets, forecasting double digit growth over the next 5 years. If Pharma wishes to enter the Indian market, the role of OD will be critical in assessing and addressing the following:

- Market strategy
- Launch readiness
- Acquisition of key talent
- Cultural and societal forces
- Legal and regulatory environment
- Competitive landscape

The pharmaceutical industry in India is extremely fragmented. Large retail drug chain stores like Walgreens or CVS do not exist; rather, pharmaceutical retail outlets are operated by local small business owners who are well known by the communities around them, including medical practitioners and hospital staff. If Marcus wants a plan that is guaranteed to succeed, several key decisions will have to be made, guided by good research and advice. Various scenarios can be contemplated with varying outcomes. For example, should Pharma sell its own U.S.-manufactured products in India, or leverage the low cost, highly intelligent pharmaceutical local labor market to do the R&D work, and then market products to India and potentially to other markets? Should Pharma penetrate one geographic market one product at a time, or proliferate rapidly?

To optimize the decision-making process, the following five-step process should be proposed to Marcus for implementation this year to ensure a successful launch next year, using OD interventions that are conducive to large-scale initiatives:

1. Quarter One—Select High Powered Teams: A strategic sourcing strategy should be deployed to engage a group of skilled local OD and business consultants who are also market and industry experts. A global leader, either an expatriate from within the firm or a qualified local hire, should be appointed to lead the strategic effort. Using the right assessment tools to select and develop a strong leader, who has the cultural sensitivity to lead teams in a very diverse setting, is critical to this initiative.

2. Quarter Two—Conduct Rigorous Research: The OD and business teams should focus their energy to collect data on the technical aspects of the industry as well as around the societal, economic, and regulatory aspects of doing business in India. Marketing and legal experts should review the competitive and legal landscape of the business, while cultural OD experts should examine the behavioral norms that define consumer habits and employee needs.

3. Quarter Three—Apply Research to Inform Key Decisions: Once this data is collected, the teams should bring key stakeholders together, including healthcare practitioners, pharmacists, doctors, chemists, and others to develop a powerful global strategy. Scenario planning should be used to create a variety of possible future scenarios in deciding which direction Pharma should be headed using the data to support its trajectory.

4. Quarter Four—Define Strategy and Criteria for Brilliant Execution: In Weisbordian (1987) fashion, the team should gather the entire system in the room, using an "all-purpose view finder" to understand the market, economic, and government forces at work in this business. During this session, strategy, structure, design, and other organizational constructs can begin to form and get vetted.

5. 2012—Launch and Measure for Global Success: The launch should be a collaborative effort by marketing, human resourses, and the business teams. Appropriate financial and nonfinancial metrics and measurements should be developed to keep plans on track.

The OD function should continue to monitor progress on an ongoing basis to ensure that both top line and bottom line objectives are being achieved and teams are engaged and productive for continued success.

Dalitso S. Sulamoyo

Marcus should be commended for his vision to expand Pharma's operations globally. He should also be commended for engaging the services and expertise of an OD consultant to aid in the facilitation of this expansion to Africa, India, and Asia in general. There are indeed many questions that need to be considered and answered with regard to the role that OD should play with this expansion, particularly on the continent of Africa south of the Sahara. My OD approach to this proposed growth and expansion onto the continent of Africa would involve a two-pronged approach designed to address the critical questions.

The first order of business would be the identification of local African OD practitioners that would partner with me in the specific African countries where Pharma intends to set up its operations. The partnership with these local African OD practitioners would first serve the purpose of gaining and building trust with the local workforce and operations. Relationships are very important in any African setting, especially if they involve any cross-cultural work. It is important to recognize local African talent in an age where Africa is going through a rebirth that some have described as the African Renaissance. Global operations have tended to focus more on bringing expatriates with less recognition of existing talent on the continent of Africa. A partnership that is built on cross-cultural OD would be beneficial to its implementation in this new venture by Pharma. Second, since many of the OD applications and techniques are Western-developed, it is critical that these local OD practitioners serve as the cultural translators and indigenizing agents for their acceptance and success. Indigenization in this instance would be the convergence of these OD techniques and approach with local African culture. Third, the local OD practitioners would assist in the identification of successful indigenous applications, such as the utilization of African metaphors and proverbs to facilitate change and convey OD practices to the local setting. Fourth, the local African OD practitioners would assist in designing appropriate surveys to assess and understand the political, economic, social, environmental, technological, and legal issues that need to be considered as part of Pharma's strategy in establishing its operations. It is critical to utilize the local OD practitioners so as to ensure that the questions that might be in a survey are appropriate.

The second order of business would be to educate Pharma about African culture, particularly the collectivist culture of Ubuntu, whose principles are common in Sub-Saharan Africa. Pharma's corporate culture which has been described as aggressive, competitive, and power oriented has contributed to its success. However, those cultural factors are in many respects the antithesis to the prevalent African culture found in sub-Saharan Africa. Ubuntu represents a powerful philosophy and cultural approach whereby Africans view their existence through others in their society. The approach for Pharma would be to utilize Ubuntu and its principles as the cultural integrator for strategic OD. The western world, as exemplified by Pharma, emphasizes efficiency while the five principles of Ubuntu emphasize effectiveness in relationships. I would propose the convergence of these two approaches to productivity to design an indigenized approach for Pharma. These five principles should provide Pharma with a different approach to competitiveness as follows:

1. Importance of Relationships with Others—Relationships are very important in an African culture. Africans view relationships as being reciprocal. The whole notion of people viewing themselves through others, or the existence of empathy, is an important dimension in African relationships. Pharma should consider this as it establishes its operations in Africa, because people are intrinsically motivated to contribute more when they are valued members of the work place. Solidarity and social harmony are also important components of African culture when viewing relationships. In an Ubuntu culture, Pharma would have sustainable and competitive advantages due to the strong loyalty Africans have to group goals. Pharma could utilize this cultural component to foster group synergy when developing new ideas and products.

2. Shared Decision Making—Participatory decision making will be important in gaining commitment to Pharma's goals and the effectiveness of its operations in the long run. Africans like to reach decisions by consensus where dissenters are recognized so as to foster harmony. This would be a different approach for Pharma, where perhaps decisions are primarily top-down. Creating and fostering harmony builds a strong sense of commitment in an African setting.

3. Time—An observation that is generally shared by those who visit Africa for the first time is the difference in the perception of time between westerners and Africans. In Ubuntu, time is recognized as not being a finite commodity, but a healer if enough time is allowed for important decisions to be made. Western perception is that Africans are not punctual and treat time carelessly, while Africans' perception of time as a healer could offer Pharma a competitive advantage. If more time is taken on thinking things through, then all aspects are considered and decisions are rational as opposed to rushed. It would offer Pharma a competitive advantage in the sense that the best decisions for the corporation can be made. Africans also value and respect older workers because they bring experience and wisdom to the workplace. This would be a competitive advantage for Pharma if some of the organization's leadership consists of older workers. There is great respect for the elderly which would result in a more cohesive work setting for Pharma.

4. Belief Systems—Africans subscribe to belief systems that are based on both organized religion from the East and the West and traditional African spiritual beliefs. These belief systems are, in most respects, part of the African psyche. To respect them would be to allow the best in people to come out for the betterment of the workplace.

5. Loyalty—Africans in an Ubuntu culture place their personal interests secondary to the collective, tribe, or the workplace. There is an African saying that states "the river that forgets its source will soon dry up." If the Ubuntu or components of African culture that have been discussed here were considered as part of Pharma's OD approach in Africa, then Pharma can expect to have loyalty and commitment from its workforce which are very valuable dimensions in the long term.

In generalized terms, Africans view their place of work as their second home. Ubuntu would help to facilitate the human touch and family-driven environment in the workplace. This does not mean that Pharma should completely negate its competitiveness. What this means is that Pharma can maintain its competiveness while being culturally appropriate in an African setting. Then the Pharma OD approach will be more successful at the organizational and group levels.

Katherine Schroeder

While "going global" is attractive for many industries in this day and age, particularly pharmaceutical organizations, it is imperative that top executives undertaking such a venture are grounded in the reality of what it truly takes to complete such a task. The first step, of course, is a clear commitment from top leadership not only to globalize, but to devote the resources that it takes to be successful. While Marcus's decision is clear, I would recommend several probing conversations with him and his senior leadership team to ensure that they have a solid understanding of the organizational resources—time, energy, and money—that are required for success. You can present various case studies of other U.S.-based pharmaceutical companies who have made the attempt to go global, highlighting key elements for success and pointing out the many quagmires Pharma may face. It is critical that you erode any false sense of confidence Marcus has about how simple and straightforward this will be. Globalizing requires developing the best laid plans, but remaining open to the unknown factors, which will most certainly be encountered on the path.

After grounding Marcus and the senior leadership team with a less rosy and more realistic perspective of what it takes to globalize, I would focus on negotiating a realistic time frame for the globalization process. There is no magic wand to wave that "makes you global" by next year just because the CEO proclaims it should be so. Part of your job as the OD Consultant is to ensure development of a realistic timeline. Of course planning the trajectory of this organizational change depends primarily on the methodology Pharma will follow to globalize. Make sure that Marcus hires a business development resource with solid pharmaceutical experience who can do the business analysis to recommend the best way to expand globally. A strategic alliance or acquisition may prove to be more effective than a straight expansion of the Pharma organization into these markets.

To ensure that the legal, political, and market perspectives have been assessed, you should ensure that the business development resource does a thorough assessment of the markets in Asia, India, and Africa to ensure that these truly are the best options for expansion of Pharma's footprint. While it is unlikely that Marcus came up with these areas by throwing darts at a world map, you need more data to ensure that targeted expansions fit with your overall strategic plan and that the markets can support your entry. Also, choosing one entry point for 2012 is worthy of serious consideration and would narrow your scope, increasing your possibilities for success.

If Marcus and the senior leadership team do decide to expand into Asia, your work shifts into not just ensuring effective execution of the business strategy, but providing the context for effective cross-cultural relationship building that will be imperative to Pharma's success. Help the senior leadership team begin with the position that you do not know enough to make assumptions about what it takes to create a successful partnership. Humility in this regard will serve you better than false confidence.

As you target your territory in Asia, expand your "cultural due diligence" to the specific country you have targeted. You may want to find a resource that can provide you and the senior leadership team with key cultural guideposts to avoid major stumbles out of the blocks. For instance, the Japanese approach to partnership requires an extended period of due diligence not just to do fact finding and data analysis, but to build a strong working relationship. What may appear as secondary "socializing" to the US executive is an essential part of business in Japan. In fact, key conversations that may make or break a partnership occur over drinks and dinner in the evening.

A global expansion such as the one Pharma is considering is complex on many levels. This broad focus makes your OD role even more critical. Your job is to not only draw attention to key OD perspectives, but ensure that key areas of the business are coming together to make sound decisions. In the end, your most important work is to probe and ask the questions that will keep Marcus and his senior leadership team focused on the reality of what it takes to succeed as Pharma begins the journey to globalization.

Therese Yaeger and Peter Sorensen Respond

Applause for these three exceptional OD contributors who have three very different approaches to assist Marcus at Pharma! Nazneen, Dalitso, and Kathy illustrate how different OD can look when delivering OD support in three different cultural regions—India, Africa, and Asia. But even beyond the three different regional perspectives, these three respondents have provided different approaches specific to assisting Marcus at PHARMA .

Each respondent begins their discussion by emphasizing the complexities of working in a global environment. Nazneen integrates business and OD strategy, and builds on and uses some of the best in OD work (i.e., high-powered teams, data collection, and measurement).

Dalitso does an exceptional job of integrating his understanding of the African culture with western OD. He reminds us of the need to identify local African OD practitioners to partner with, and to understand the collectivistic culture and Ubuntu principles when working in Africa.

The cautions of going global cannot be emphasized more, as Kathy Schroeder reminds us of the importance of a realistic strategic plan. The macro business issues of "cultural due diligence" and continuing to evaluate whether all of the business components are coming together make good business sense. Often, as consultants we have exceptional OD knowledge to assist the client, but we are naïve at the larger global business plan that OD must contribute to.

Thank you again to our expert respondents; and again, remember to be culturally aware when going global.

ACKNOWLEDGMENT

An earlier version of this article was published in *The Old Practitioner*, *43*(1), 45-49.

REFERENCES

IMS Health. (2010, March 16). IMS announces 17 countries now rank as high-growth "Pharmerging" markets; Forecast to contribute nearly half of industry growth by 2013 [Press release]. Retrieved from http://www.imshealth.com/portal/site/imshealth/menuitem.a46c6d4df3db4b3d88f611019418c22a/?vgnextoid=01624605b5367210VgnVCM100000ed152ca2RCRD

Weisbord, M. R. (1987). *Productive workplaces*. San Francisco, CA: Jossey-Bass.

CASE STUDY 29

IMPLEMENTING A GLOBAL CORPORATE STRATEGY

The Role of Organization Development

Therese F. Yaeger and Peter F. Sorensen

This case deals with two of the most important issues that face the field of organization development (OD): (1) OD as a partner in the development and implementation of strategy, and (2) the implementation of strategy on a global basis. In other words, OD as a partner with management in dealing effectively with critical issues of survival and growth. These are not new issues. Over the last 10 years a number of prominent contributors to the field have argued that OD must become a strategic partner in order to survive. We believe that by increasing numbers OD executives and practitioners have, in fact, become partners in strategy.

This case is real, but rather than a single organization case, it is a composite of experiences of several organizations that are dealing with strategic global initiatives. As a composite, it represents generic issues faced by global organizations.

We have asked three expert panelists to comment on the case. Two panelists represent a team from Abbott, the largest Chicago-based global

Critical Issues in Organization Development:
Case Studies for Analysis and Discussion, pp. 293–303
Copyright © 2013 by Information Age Publishing
All rights of reproduction in any form reserved.

organization and one of the largest health care companies in the world. Abbott has an exceptional history of performance, and was one of the organizations featured in the best seller *From Good to Great*. The panelists are Dr. Philip Anderson, Director of Corporate Global OD for Abbott, and Dr. Ghazala Ovaice, Manager of Strategic OD at Abbott. Both are experienced OD practitioners, but with different educational backgrounds—Phillip has a PhD in OD, while Ghazala has a background in human resources/HRD. We asked both to comment on the case expecting that their educational backgrounds would contribute different perspectives to the case commentary.

The third expert panelist is Jennifer Smith, a Benedictine University student in the master's OD program and Corporate Manager of Training & Development for Molex Incorporated, another Chicago-based global organization with an exceptional performance record.

The Case

You are an experienced OD practitioner with responsibility for the implementation of organizational change projects within your corporation. Although you are the Director of OD you have a limited number of OD personnel working with you. Your strategy has been to elevate the role of OD in your corporation and, on the U.S. side, that has been fairly successful. In fact, executive management has asked you to play a role in domestic strategy and future vision, and to develop a global strategy representing the work developed at corporate headquarters.

Your company is 100 years old with a reputation for high quality manufacturing products. Thirty years ago the company began international activities; now the organization has manufacturing and sales operations in 20 different countries including the United States, Scandinavia, Central Europe, Africa, and Asia, including recent activity in China and South America. Each of the regions has its own sales, marketing and production functions and has operated on a decentralized, fairly autonomous basis. The organization has been successful in each of its regional operations with only minor difficulties that were successfully handled.

Generally, the immediate past administration was relatively passive, resting on a history of success, and leading to a tradition of strong, highly decentralized regional operations. This has created a situation where there is some discontinuity in the perceptions of the mission of the organization, and agreement as to its future. The strong decentralization has had the advantage of building robust regional managers with the ability to adapt operations to regional cultures and political and economic environments.

The one consistent core value across all regions is the commitment, tradition, and dedication to high quality products. Also, there is a strong commitment on the part of employees to each of the regional operations, but not necessarily to the corporation or the U.S. home office.

The organization recently experienced a change in top management with a new CEO. The previous administration was fairly passive in their acceptance of OD, although not resistant. As they had not been terribly encouraging, the OD function had to be highly innovative in developing support among line managers. Now the new administration is more receptive to OD initiatives and also is more aggressive in shaping the future of the organization. The CEO has a desire to create greater identity and continuity of operations, consistent with the U.S. corporate culture and vision.

It is your job as the director of OD to develop and implement this executive vision. what is your strategy and recommendation to your OD director who has successfully become a partner in developing domestic strategy and change, and as a consequence, is faced with this global challenge?

Jennifer Smith

I would first look at how the domestic organization viewed my role in assisting with the implementation of strategy and future vision. I attribute the success I have experienced thus far to the knowledge I have gained in understanding the business itself. By engaging with individuals throughout various levels of the organization, I have been able to understand the pressure points critical to the business and align the work I do with the key critical business indicators identified by management. When I approach a situation, I view it not only from the human aspect, but also from a business aspect, to determine how potential solutions align with the business model. My intention is to show value to the organization in a language the executive level speaks-increasing revenues and profits or decreasing costs. This strategy can be labeled: engagement, understanding, and language.

The strategy to implement a consistent identity and provide continuity throughout worldwide operations would be similar: engagement, understanding, and language. This might be challenged by various cultures, and perhaps is a role not as recognized across the world. One recommendation I would make to the director of OD is to not only understand the business as a whole, but to concentrate on understanding the business practices that have been in place in each region that have made them successful. Prior to implementing a corporate strategy, it is crucial to understand how it will fit within each region's current business model.

The director of organization development could suggest that evaluation research be initiated with data compiled, and feedback reported to the executive level management team. This would give the OD director the opportunity to engage and learn practices in the other regions with senior management. It will be important for the feedback to be given using business language. This would be sensitive research, as any time thoughts of structure change are suspected, individuals tend to become protective of their territory. Patience will be critical in order to gain credibility and respect in other regions. It will be the director of organization development's role to help facilitate the breakthrough of these barriers and communicate the message to improve the whole organization in order to attain accurate feedback.

A second recommendation is to engage the employees in the formulation of the strategy. the director of OD can orchestrate a worldwide survey and focus group project to gather input on globalization. This will give the employees a sense of belonging and identify pressure points throughout the worldwide organization. the message the director of OD needs to communicate to this team is that if the employees feel a part of the strategy, the implementation will be more successful. Data gathering, synthesis and feedback presented to executives in a company-specific manner demonstrates the value OD can play in the organization.

A third recommendation for the director of organization development is to help the executives see the effect of aligning the organization strategy in order to achieve long-term high performance. This can be accomplished by identifying critical gaps that occur when strategy is not clearly planned or executed and the impact that has on both short- and long-term business goals.

Philip Anderson

This is a classic dichotomy in our field—OD needs to become more strategic, yet rarely is the OD function sufficiently resourced to allow them to make significant strategic investments.

However, there are a myriad of strategic OD interventions going on in all successful organizations—that is what makes them successful. In some cases, it is not the exclusive domain of OD practitioners. Most OD activities are designed and executed by organizational leaders. Successful organizations are inevitably led by people who have good OD skills. Often those skills are indistinguishable from their overt leadership style. After all, our field embraces the same values that constitute good leadership behavior, that is, participative management, equal opportunity, autonomy, fair rewards, and cooperation. In the end, OD is simply "just in time" leadership.

Our job is to support leadership, not take ownership of it or claim exclusive rights to the field. To do so is the antithesis of what we claim to value. So, rather than asking how OD can become more strategic, the real question is how OD practitioners can become strategic partners.

With that said, let's turn our attention to our OD Director. There are a number of things she can do to be seen as a strategic partner, most of which must be done through influence rather than direct authority—a competency that is often underrated by internal practitioners.

First, she should look for strategic alliances. OD is not the exclusive domain of OD practitioners, nor is it only a leadership style. Marketing, human resources (HR), training and communications professionals are deeply vested in OD practices. She can use these alliances to build a robust internal practice.

For instance, most companies are financially driven. It is usually a financial crisis that spawns significant organization change. Market analysis is the vehicle by which the organization assesses future financial stability. It is the primary function that keeps the company attuned to changes in their external environment—the very essence of strategic management. The OD Director can help by assuring the internal climate is congruent with the external environmental changes. Research shows that there is a correlation between customer and employee satisfaction. Knowledge like this can be the foundation for a culture assessment that would provide leaders with compelling data that can be translated into a corporate strategic plan for OD.

However, a corporate plan is not enough. If the OD director is to be successful, she must somehow connect with the business leaders. One avenue could be the HR function. The organization depicted in the case has a divisional structure. In a divisionally structured corporation, the corporate function (in this case where OD sits) is responsible for prescribing in what business (products, services, etc.) the company should be involved. The business units or divisions are responsible for producing those products or services. In this type of structure, the OD director will rarely have the opportunity to work with business leaders—she will be relegated to working with staff functions because she is too far away from the business. However, HR professionals are often matrixed. In addition to corporate guidance, they have direction from the business and they understand its culture and leaders. By developing a partnership, she can gain access to the business and identify issues with which leaders are struggling. If OD professionals want to become strategic partners, we must gain access to leaders and help them solve their problems, not problems we perceive them to have.

Ghazala Ovaice

My response to this case will focus primarily on the assessment and joint diagnosis stages. Specifically, the political and cross-cultural implications of building a global strategy for operations will be discussed from the perspective of the director laying the foundation for managing this change.

While the director of OD has domestic success in partnering with business leaders, the director will need to make political connections globally. Her first line of action should be around understanding the expectations of the CEO and his staff regarding creating a vision of global operations. Second, the director needs to have a champion in the senior vice president of HR as well as the senior vice president of operations, both who were privy to, and benefited from, domestic partnerships with this director on local OD initiatives. These key individuals will serve as "plants" in building a coalition for OD support (i.e., they have reaped the benefits of previous partnerships with OD). The hard reality of internal consulting (and consequently internal politics—especially in a large organization) is that once OD has had a successful client intervention, they have built trust with that client. Third, the director must understand the needs and expectations of the various stakeholders globally.

The director must also realize that she or he is working on two levels: (1) building a global vision for operations, and (2) building a global partnership for OD. The latter will be a consequence of successfully achieving the first.

Through clarifying expectations, building a need for change, working with the client to create a desired end state, and understanding the needs of the various stakeholders globally, the director is laying the foundation for the change process (i.e., a new global strategy for operations).

Through the act of garnering sponsorship and setting expectations, the director will also need to assess the readiness for change. Is a global strategy for operations (GOS) prudent for the organization? Is the organization ready for a global strategy? What are the benefits and threats of having a GOS? What are the various stakeholders likely to gain or lose with a global strategy? What are the cross-cultural implications of a GOS? How will a global strategy translate literally and figuratively across cultures in the various international regional offices?

During an assessment with the CEO, his staff, and key global stakeholders, such questions must be flushed out to jointly determine if a global organization strategy is the right strategy for this organization. More importantly, going through this process will allow the key stakeholders to assess their own readiness for change (both individually as well as for the organizations they represent) as well as garner support and commitment for this process. These discussions tend to be cathartic in nature because often times this is the first opportunity key stakeholders have to sit at the same table discussing options, opportunities, threats, history, and expectations together.

One caveat to note at this point is that the key stakeholders and champions should drive these discussions of problem diagnosis, creating expectations, and envisioning a desired end state. The OD director's personal bias should not be present. Moreover, the director should simply serve as a process consultant. While this viewpoint seems obvious to most OD professionals, in the heat of the moment even the best of OD professionals must hold themselves back from interjecting their opinions or preferences. The OD director's domestic success with her key internal clients rested on the fact that the domestic operations strategy was rightly perceived by the organization as being driven by the CEO and not an HR or OD professional. The OD and HR directors domestically took on the mantra that, "my job is to make my leader look good—consequently the employee populations shouldn't even know who I am." Therefore the owner of the GOS should be the global vice president of operations with sponsorship from the CEO and his executive staff.

Once the expectations have been set, the current situation assessed, and the problem jointly diagnosed, the OD director can work with the CEO, his executive team, and global stakeholders to align expectations regarding a GOS with the overall strategy of the organization. In other words, now that the decision has been made for a global strategy, and the readiness for this change assessed, how will this strategy align with the organization's global business strategy? What are the implications domestically and internationally for design and implementation around structure, people, processes, and culture (both organization culture and the various regional cultures affected by this new strategy)? Ensuring alignment among stakeholders, across structures, and between cultures will allow for commitment, ownership, and execution of the proposed strategy.

Included in this strategic alignment is the need for a robust communication plan. Ideally, the global communications director will be involved from the initial sponsorship discussion to ensure consistency of message, alignment with other global initiatives, and timely communication among and between employees.

Once these key elements of sponsorship, readiness for change, strategic alignment and strategic partnerships are in place, the key stakeholders can build a strategy. The reality is that these are not linear processes and that many of these steps and discussions will happen simultaneously and may be revised and revisited. Yet, starting with these key elements will lay the foundation for successful strategy building especially given the global nature of this intervention.

Therese Yaeger and Peter Sorensen Respond

Each of our panel experts focuses on both different and common aspects of the case. Each draws on their own unique experiences and history in the field. Jennifer, our first expert, with extensive international training experience, stresses the importance of understanding the business, key critical business indicators, and the language of the executives.

She also stresses the importance of understanding the complexities introduced by national cultural differences, the fit of the business model with each region, building credibility, and patience. In addition, her comments include the role of providing data, building inclusion, and working as a partner with management, and understanding the role of strategy for short- and long-term performance.

Our second expert, Philip, immediately identifies the dichotomy of having significant responsibility and limited resources. He makes the point that OD extends beyond OD as a specific function and is a set of skills and actions that characterize effective leadership. His sensitivity to working with limited resources is probably a result of many years of experience as a director of OD. His comments include influence through demonstrated competence, compensating for limited resources through building alliances, including marketing and particularly Human Resources. As a corporate director of OD he reflects an understanding of the potential in working with the HR function that frequently has a longer history and is embedded in the business units and/or divisions. Building alliances is one of the key functions in working with limited resources.

Our third expert, Ghazala, focuses on the need to clarify expectations, and again the need to build alliances and support. Her comments also add the critical factor of building trust. She emphasizes the role of national culture and introduces the classic and essential OD concept— readiness for change. Ghazala provides a number of insightful comments regarding the role of OD which is nicely summarized in her statement 'my job is to make my leader look good.'

Each of our experts expressed the desire to move beyond the limits given to them for their response. Their comments might easily include considerably more analysis and suggestions. However, if we were to attempt to summarize the extensive insights, recommendations and experience that our experts were nevertheless able to provide within the given limits, they would include the following points:

- Know the business and the language of management.
- Identify key critical business issues.
- Understand the complexities of cultural differences and have patience.
- Employ the use of global data collection, feedback and focus groups, and identify common pressure points and create a common identity through inclusion.
- Understand the development of influence through competence and demonstrated value.
- Acknowledge that OD skills and competence are the domain of management as well as OD.
- Recognize the limitations of being corporate OD and the need to be close to operational leadership at the regional, divisional, and departmental levels.
- Understand the business, the language, critical issues, and working with the leadership in terms of actual needs and problems, as opposed to making assumptions.
- Build alliances.
- Create and build on trust.

ACKNOWLEDGMENT

An earlier version of this article was published in *The OD Practitioner,* *38*(2), 49-53.

CASE STUDY 30

ORGANIZATION DEVELOPMENT IN AFRICA

Therese F. Yaeger and Peter F. Sorensen

In an earlier case we introduced organization development (OD) practitioner readers to Marcus, the new CEO of Pharma, a successful pharmaceutical company which is in the process of becoming a global organization, expanding into China, India, and Africa. Based on recommendations from our panel, Marcus has moved ahead with Pharma's global initiatives. However, Marcus has discovered that each of the three areas is more complex than anticipated—China with its major economic and political transformation and large geographical area with high degrees of diversity across regions, and India with its growing population and ongoing conflict with geographical neighbors. But it is Africa, where Marcus has placed his early initiatives, which he is finding most challenging. Africa is a continent of highly diverse traditions, many of which have their roots in the early colonial history. These traditions are as diverse as the histories related to British, French, and Dutch colonialism, and a history of nation creation across tribal boundaries and dictatorships, which have added to the complexities for Pharma.

Marcus has been doing his homework on OD applications and the exceptionally high OD success rates in developing areas of the world, as

Critical Issues in Organization Development:
Case Studies for Analysis and Discussion, pp. 305–315
Copyright © 2013 by Information Age Publishing
305

well as OD applications in general, including the work of Robert Golem-biewski. He has also reviewed OD practices specific to Africa and the work of Louw du Toit and Joanne Preston, and others in South Africa during the transition from apartheid.

However, in doing his OD homework, Marcus also realizes that even though OD has high rates of success in Africa, it is also vulnerable to fail-ure if the practitioners are not sensitive to important cultural differences. So, Marcus is again asking for more guidance as he becomes more famil-iar with the complexities of doing OD work in Africa. He realizes that he needs a better understanding of cultural issues in order to be effective at strategic planning. He needs knowledge of different regions in Africa, including Ghana, and how different that West region of Africa is from the Sub-Sahara region. What are the social factors and how is competition viewed? These are just some of the concerns that Marcus brings to us.

We have selected three African OD experts to help Marcus with Pharma's entry into the continent of Africa. Our first contributor is Chiku Malunga, a seasoned consultant with African and European nongovern-ment organizations. Our second is Betty Nanor Arthur, faculty at the Business School, GIMPA (Ghana Institute of Management and Public Administration), Accra, Ghana, in Western Africa. Thirdly, and as a fol-low-up to Pharma's earlier case, is Dr. Dalitso Sulamoyo, who has spent several years studying, publishing, and presenting on OD in Africa. He will be publishing his new book, *I Am Because We Are: Ubuntu as a Cultural Strategy for OD and Change in Sub-Sahara Africa*, this fall as part of the series in Contemporary Trends in Organization Development published by Information Age Publishing. Together, our consultants have over 60 years of experience working on management and organizational change in Africa. Here are their responses.

Chiku Malunga

The OD practitioner for Pharma will need to understand the importance of African culture and heritage and how that can be effectively utilized when dealing with organizational capacity issues. The rich and
diverse African heritage can make a considerable contribution towards
addressing many political, economic, and sociocultural challenges that
the continent and the world face today. African cultural heritage, passed
on from generation to generation, has been a source of guidance for African communities in times of peace, uncertainty, birth, life, and death. It
has been a basis of their self-identity, self-respect, and self-confidence. It
has enabled Africans to live in harmony with their physical, social, and
spiritual environments.

It is important for the OD practitioner to understand that traditional
wisdom contained in African proverbs can be applied both to understanding organizations and to improving their performance. The use of African
proverbs in this way presents a new and creative way of communicating
and discussing organizational principles that transcends the common
communication barriers. It therefore offers an important means to making capacity building more effective. Proverbs are an integral part of African culture. They are simple statements with deep meaning. Proverbs can
be understood where literacy is low, and appreciated by the most educated. They are guidelines for individual, family, village, and community
behavior, built upon repeated real life experiences and observations over
a long period of time. Proverbs play different roles in traditional African
society. Some of these roles are:

- **Identifying and dignifying a culture**. Proverbs express the collective wisdom of the people, reflecting their thinking, values, and
  behaviors. Using proverbs to communicate and understand organizational issues is, therefore, a very powerful tool in the quest for a
  genuine African identity.
- **Unlocking "stuckness," clarifying vision and unifying different
  perspectives**. Proverbs add humor and diffuse tension around otherwise very sensitive issues. Every African society has used proverbs
  for centuries to ease uncomfortable situations, confront issues, and
  build institutions and relationships.
- **Proverbs are metaphors and they explain complex issues in simple statements.** For example, two villages in conflict may be less
  likely to fight after reflecting on the proverb "when elephants fight,
  it is the grass that suffers." The meaning behind the simple statement about elephants is a powerful message about the negative
  effects that a disagreement between two chiefs can have on inno-

cent villagers. The proverb "when spider webs unite, they can tie up a lion" communicates the importance of unity and collaboration in tackling problems and inspires people with faith that they can address problems together, no matter how big.

- **By being metaphorical, proverbs create strong mental pictures**. This is a powerful way for motivating people into action.

Proverbs are like seeds. They become "alive" when they are "sown." They are simple statements until applied to real life situations, which then bring them to life and expand their meaning.

OD practitioners would need to familiarize themselves with the utilization of African proverbs in organizational assessment processes, but also in strategic planning, team building, leadership development, board development, and self-development interventions. Some key lessons and advice to be shared with the OD practitioner on the practical utilization of proverbs in an African setting are as follows:

1. In the proverbs-based self-assessment tools, the proverbs act as a communication aid or amplifier.

2. It is necessary to use the most fitting proverb to the intervention or situation at hand. Using "loose" proverbs without a clear link to the intervention or the situation may confuse people and disrupt the process. The practitioner must always ask himself or herself the question, "What is the most effective proverb that I can use in this situation?" In a role and responsibility clarification intervention, for example, proverbs like "if the sun says it is more powerful than the moon, then let it come and shine at night" and "the cat in his house has the teeth of a lion" may be very appropriate. In communicating the importance of learning from practice, a proverb like "a person is taller than any mountain they have climbed" would be appropriate.

3. In training workshops, it is important to use only a few proverbs to maximize their impact. Too many proverbs may lead to loss of interest in the proverbs. This also applies to carrying out assessments using the proverbs-based tools. In a three-day team building workshop, for example, we use about three proverbs to bring issues and insights to the surface for discussion at the beginning. In the proverbs-based assessment tool this may mean that not all categories may need proverbs—only those where proverbs will add significant value.

4. It is important to use reflective questions in order to bring out insights from the proverbs. Since proverbs may mean different

things to different people at different times and in different contexts, the questions must be properly phrased and focused to enable them to solicit only those insights related to the issue at hand.

5. Proverbs can be used as reflective case studies. To do this most effectively, it is important to know and use the story upon which the proverbs are based. Using a story is especially useful when there are complicated issues which are difficult to communicate. For example, it is extremely difficult to teach and communicate organizational identity issues. But using proverbs case studies easily transcends such a barrier. One of the proverbs the OD practitioner could use in identity interventions is the story behind the proverb "an eaglet that does not know that it is an eagle may live like a chicken."

6. Finally, proverbs must be used naturally and flexibly, not mechanically. If used mechanically, the proverbs may actually become a hindrance to the process. The power of proverbs when used properly is their invisibility, as they serve to facilitate the process rather than draw attention to themselves. This means that proverbs must be used only when their use will add value to the process. Development practitioners must not get too excited with the use of proverbs to the extent of "using crutches when they can walk on their own feet." Every different culture has its own ways of communicating – for some it may be stories, for others music, for others pictures, and in some parts of the world today MTV-style videos. Proverbs are still important in many parts of Africa. The important lesson for an OD practitioner is to embed the process within the cultural context in ways that not only bring greater understanding and engagement with the issues, but also motivate and energize the participants towards change. OD practitioners working in Africa need to understand and appreciate the contextual power of proverbs in eliciting the understanding, ownership, and commitment essential to any successful capacity-building process.

Betty Nanor Arthur

My response for Marcus and Pharma will be specific to OD in the Western region of Africa, particularly Ghana. It is not surprising that some OD programs are successfully implemented in Ghana, Africa, the reason being that these programs draw on Ghanaian cultures and local knowledge that promotes the use of OD. Moreover, companies and organizations are applying OD concepts and processes without naming them as

OD. Therefore, any OD intervention that is based on the known can be used to achieve the unknown, resulting in successful implementation. However, most OD changes fail.

In Ghana, the Akans believe that there are dynamic forces, both internal and external, which impinge on the society and bring about changes in the society. Individuals, communities, and institutions are urged to adapt to suit the changing times and conditions as indicated by the expression *mmere dane a, dane wo ho* (when times change adapt yourself). I would therefore recommend the following culturally acceptable approaches for OD application in Ghana.

In designing programs and activities for managing and implementing change, it is important to include consultations, discussions, consensus building, and coalition formation. These collective processes of problem solving are practiced in families, communities, and organizations. It provides the opportunity for the group to collectively identify the problems, voice their understanding of the root causes, provide strategies for addressing the issues, and embrace alternatives. A process the Akans describe as *tikoro mu ni nyansa* literally means "wisdom does not reside only in one head." The belief in the participatory approach is also described as *wonsa da mu a, wonni nnya wo* (if your hands are in the dish, people do not eat everything and leave you with nothing). The process therefore ensures a sense of responsibility and ownership to help bring about change and to avoid or minimize resistance.

Another important cultural issue that the OD consultant should be aware of is designing programs that take into account both group and individual performance to promote good behavior at the workplace. The culture in Ghana promotes teamwork in projects based on the traditional notion that when strands of a broom are put together to form a broom, it sweeps better than when taken individually. The culture also places high value on individual achievement. This is captured by the expression *woforo dua pa a, na yepia wo* (when you climb a good tree you are given a push). Therefore, systems designed to improve performance must take care of both groups as well as individuals.

Healthy competition is part and parcel of the Ghanaian way of life, especially in the Asante culture, where the saying *kum apem a, apem beba* is translated as, "when you kill a thousand, a thousand more will come." The OD consultant can tap into this challenging and competitive behavior to develop programs that will encourage healthy competition both internally and externally.

Yet another vital cultural difference is the process by which Ghanaians resolve conflict. While most developed countries use the formal legal process, Ghanaians value the informal way of diplomacy and peaceful means of resolving conflict. Most often an elderly person within the company or an outsider leads the process. The negotiation principle is based on tact-fulness and patience, as the negotiators believe that however difficult or thorny an issue may be, it must be settled through counseling and negoti-ation and not with an axe. It is therefore crucial that the OD consultant design effective and efficient systems that will reduce formal legal proce-dure in handling conflict, especially when an employee is involved.

Dalitso Samson Sulamoyo

As the OD movement takes root in Africa, and particularly Sub-Saha-ran Africa, there are background and contextual factors that need to be taken into consideration by OD professionals intending to work in that region. The collectivist culture that permeates most of Sub-Saharan Africa was discussed in the Winter 2010 *OD Practitioner* case as a major factor for OD professionals to be cognizant of when working in that environment. However, culture is not the only factor. There are other factors that OD professionals need to be aware of in order for them to successfully bring change in an environment that others have inaccurately portrayed as pes-simistic and inhospitable to OD. These factors need to be discussed and understood in the context of alignment with OD values and opportunities for change and development in Sub-Saharan Africa.

As an OD professional, I would borrow the environmental scanning framework from strategic management that would enable me to analyze the social, legal, economic, political, and technological (SLEPT) environ-ments of a particular country in Sub-Saharan Africa for purposes of align-ment and indigenization of OD applications. Before this analysis is done, it is important to understand the history of African countries, particularly their colonial history, because it may provide some context to the results of their SLEPT analysis. All of the countries in Sub-Saharan Africa except for one were, at one time, colonized by a European country. After these countries gained independence, most of them became autocratic, and some are now pseudo-democracies. One could argue that the legacies of that colonial, postcolonial, and now pseudo-democratic experience has influenced the social, legal, economic, political, and technological factors in that region of the continent. Many of these countries can be described as being in transition because of the changes and challenges they con-tinue to experience today.

The questions I would then ask as I begin to conduct my analysis are as follows: What role does OD have in countries that are in transition? How does OD adapt and indigenize to the environment described after a SLEPT analysis has been conducted? How can OD contribute to not only change within organizations but large-system changes at a national level?

How does a SLEPT analysis that provides macro-environmental reports impact organizations at a microenvironmental level? For purposes of this response I will only focus on two dimensions of the SLEPT analysis, social and political, to illustrate their importance within the context of OD.

An OD professional should have an understanding of how social factors play a role in the subcultural context of organizations in Africa. Some of the social factors that would be part of an analysis for OD would deal with how segmental cleavages defined along tribal, racial, and ethnic lines may influence the climate and structure of certain organizations. In South Africa, for instance, you had for many years the apartheid system that was designed to place White South Africans in positions of power and deny Black South Africans the opportunity to hold those positions of power. It is important to understand the legacy of that system because of how it may influence organizational culture and, to some extent, organizational structure today. In other places like Malawi, there have been assertions that positions of power are being held by people who belong to the President's tribe. This has created consternation among those Malawians who do not belong to that particular tribal or ethnic group. Understanding the intricacies of this rather complex and dominant issue in most parts of the African continent should be a prerequisite before any OD work is done because of the implications it has organizationally.

There are obviously many other social factors to consider when doing OD in Africa. However, as an OD professional I would be looking for opportunities to align OD, or indigenize OD, so that those factors are not hindrances, but enablers for change and development. There are gender issues where OD could play the role of providing the vehicle for empowerment within organizations and the community at large.

These are a few social factor questions I would ask: Can OD play a role in addressing the various segmental cleavages found in Africa organizationally? How can OD facilitate the building of effective teams when working with groups that perhaps have had a history of conflict? What OD strategies would be effective in engaging communities for change to occur when they have high illiteracy rates? How does the HIV/AIDS pandemic affect organizations? How does one conduct effective leadership development?

Politics, political systems, and political environments play an important role in Africa. These factors have some influence on the culture and climate of organizations because they also affect the legal and economic dimensions. Again, this is an area that requires astuteness and sophistication because in some countries, it could mean a life-and-death situation or even a legal situation if OD work is perceived to be in conflict with the power structure. Some of the questions I would be trying to address when looking at the political environment would be as follows: How do you deal with engagement if the organizations exist within a political system that does not accept openness, or even criticism? How does corruption impact effective change within organizations? What role can OD play in facilitating large-system changes? What lessons can Sub-Saharan Africa learn about large-system change from its Northern Africa counterparts who are democratizing? Can OD play a role in that type of change?

There are indeed many opportunities for OD in Sub-Saharan Africa, particularly its alignment with the potential for an African Renaissance as described by Terence Jackson in his 2004 book, *Management and Change in Africa*. The African Renaissance entails the values of OD that are humanistic, democratic, and optimistic. I think with the understanding of the SLEPT factors, successful OD in Africa can occur through its indigenization without compromising its values. There may be instances where the OD work itself is risky but generally speaking OD professionals have to understand African countries from the perspective of Africans given the complexities of culture, politics, social structures, economics, technology, and legalities. This understanding coupled with indigenization would lead to this movement being more acceptable in all sectors of organizations in Africa.

Therese Yaeger and Peter Sorensen Respond

Thank you to our African OD experts, Malunga, Arthur, and Sulamoyo, for their important OD insights. What is most helpful for us (and Marcus) is understanding the cultural differences in the various regions of Africa. In particular, Malunga addresses the concept of proverbs. He helps us understand that proverbs are powerful but should not be overused. Arthur helps us tremendously by focusing her contribution specific to the Western region of Africa—Ghana. She emphasizes that the cultural context is critical, and that some approaches are more culturally acceptable than others. Sulamoyo provides his insights on the Sub-Sahara region, and focuses his approach to be more strategic with the elements of environmental scanning for better alignment and indigenization.

With this new knowledge, perhaps Marcus can better address different OD approaches in different regions on the continent of Africa, to promote more successful efforts for Pharma. Again, thanks to our African OD experts for such insightful input!

ACKNOWLEDGMENT

An earlier version of this article was published in *The OD Practitioner,* *43*(3), 50-54.

REFERENCE

Jackson, T. (2004). *Management and change in Africa: Cross-cultural perspective.* New York, NY: Routledge.

ABOUT THE AUTHORS

Amy Alfermann is a member of the Monsanto Technology Pipeline Solutions Training. At Monsanto, Amy brings training and organization development to a department that provides IT applications to Monsanto's Technology organizations enabling the scientists in these organizations to perform the research and development necessary to drive Monsanto's technology pipeline. Amy has over 5 years experience creating training and OD functions in various industries. She is currently enrolled in the OD doctoral program at Benedictine University. She can be reached at amy.l.alfermann@monsanto.com.

Larry Anders, PhD, is a seasoned executive and organizational consultant. He held varied and responsible positions as Vice President, Human Resources for Allstate Insurance Company, Group Vice President and Partner of Harbridge House, Inc., and Director, Labor Relations for Frito-Lay Company. Since 1965 he has provided executive coaching, consulting, leadership development, and educational programs to a wide variety of public and private sector systems. As an organizational development practitioner, he has particular expertise in consulting with top executives on leadership issues and personal growth, problems of administration and organization, strategic direction, helping create productive environments in multicultured diverse workforces, conflict resolution, and team-building efforts. Dr. Anders' primary focus is helping organizations manage transitions and revitalization in the fast-changing, culturally diverse environments. He has both national and international experience as a consultant and currently in retirement serves as an adjunct professor for the California School of Professional Psychology at Alliant International University. He can be reached at Lbanders@cox.net.

Phillip Anderson, PhD, is the Director of Leadership Development for the YMCA of the USA headquartered in Chicago, Illinois. He is also a faculty member at Benedictine University in Lisle, Illinois and the Chicago School of Professional Psychology located in Chicago. He holds a PhD in Organization Development from Benedictine University and a MEd from the University of Illinois in Human Resource Development Leadership. His work has been published in Training Today Magazine, International Organization Development, and the Organization Development Journal. He can be reached at sfcpta@aol.com.

Beth Applegate, MSOD, has over 2 decades of consulting experience with nonprofit organizations, governmental agencies, and socially responsible corporations. She is the owner of Applegate Consulting Group (ACG). ACG assists organizations in a wide arena of industries both nationally and internationally. Beth has taught at Indiana University in Bloomington and American University in Washington, DC. She can be reached at beth@applegateonline.com.

Betty Nanor Arthur is the Senior Academic Registrar at the Ghana Institute of Management and Public Administration in Ghana, Africa. She has served as coordinator of Women-In-Management program and designed the nonprofit management program run by the Institute. She is completing her doctoral degree on African studies at Benedictine University. She can be reached at bettynanor@yahoo.com.

Nancy Ashworth, MSOD, is an executive coach and leadership development consultant in the Denver, CO area. She has considerable experience coaching C-Suite and global leaders at VP and Director levels, and has shared her expertise in high-tech, manufacturing, healthcare, and hospitality arenas. Currently, Nancy is the Director of Organizational Change Leadership at Catholic Health Initiatives and teaches at the University of Denver.

Dick Axelrod, MBA, cofounded with his wife, Emily, the Axelrod Group, Inc., a consulting firm that pioneered the use of employee involvement to effect largescale organizational change. Before forming the Axelrod Group, Dick was an organization development manager for General Foods, which was among the first companies in America to use self-directed work teams (a strategy whose philosophy made a great impact on Dick). He now brings more than 35 years of consulting and teaching experience to this work, with clients including Boeing, Coca-Cola, Harley Davidson, Hewlett-Packard, Novartis, and the United Kingdom's National Health Service. He can be reached at info@axelrodgroup.com.

Emily Axelrod, MSW, is cofounder and principal of the Axelrod Group, Inc, created with her husband Dick. For more than 30 years, Emily has used strategic visioning, work redesign, team development, and good old common sense to build sustainable, fun, and dignified enterprises. Her clients include: Barrington 220 School District, Boeing, British Airways, Calgary Health Authority, CAPE, First Union Bank, HSB, Intel, the Parliament of World Religions, and ThyssenKrupp AG. She can be reached at info@axelrodgroup.com.

Jerry Bell, MBA, is a former aviation officer and medic, and graduated from the United States Military Academy. He was deployed overseas in support of U.S. initiatives, and culminated a 12-year career as a senior captain after successfully commanding a unit in the Washington, DC area. Bell is a member of the Management Consulting Division of the National Academy of Management. Currently, he is a doctoral candidate in Benedictine University's Organization Development program.

Marilyn E. Blair, PhD, is a principal and Senior Consultant at TeamWork in Denver, CO. Marilyn consults with CEOs in groups and individually utilizing a Leadership model she designed while working in Silicon Valley, California. She is the immediate past editor of the OD Practitioner where she served for 9 years. Marilyn can be reached at marilyn292@aol.com.

Dorie Ellzey Blesoff, MSOD, is an independent consultant/coach/facilitator and serves as adjunct faculty at Northwestern University's Center for Learn ing & Organizational Change, where her courses are "Learning Organizations" and "Designing Sustainable Strategic Change." Her expertise includes designing and implementing sustainable strategic and culture change that engages all levels, and leadership team development, particularly with family businesses, healthcare, and non-profits. Dorie can be reached at www.dorieLZblesoff.com or dorie@dorieLZblesoff.com.

Val Brown, MSOD, is the Communications Manager for the city of Carlsbad, CA. She has received numerous awards from the National Association of Telecommunications Officers and Advisors for her video production work on several projects. Val can be reached at val.brown@carlsbadca.gov.

Kathleen Buchman, PhD, has extensive experience in both Human Resources Management and Organization Development in healthcare. Her positions have ranged from the Corporate Director of HR to the Senior VP, Organization and Leadership Development for the Wheaton Franciscan Healthcare System, where she was responsible for aligning development initiatives with the values and strategic business goals of the organization. She currently serves on the Sponsor Member Board for the Wheaton Franciscan Healthcare. She is a Managing Partner for Buchman Consulting Partners LLP., and an Adjunct Professor at Benedictine University. She can be reached at kathleenbu@sbcglobal.net.

Anthony F. Buono is Professor of Management and Sociology and founding Coordinator of the Alliance for Ethics and Social Responsibility at Bentley University. He is Editor of the Research in Management Consulting series (Information Age Publishing) and a past Chair of the Management Consulting Division of the Academy of Management. He can be reached at abuono@bentley.edu.

Paul Cadario, MSOD, is an Engineer whose integrity and organizational skills have shaped a successful 32-year career dedicated to fighting poverty and improving the living standards of people in the developing world. His current position in Washington as Senior Manager, Trust Fund Quality Assurance & Compliance for the Bank is just the latest of several noteworthy achievements. Following his Oxford studies as a Rhodes Scholar, Cadario went to work for the World Bank in 1975 as a young Transport Economist in West Africa, soon developing a keen nose for corruption and a determination to help the Bank reduce this barrier to the effective use of its funds to reduce poverty. His career has taken him in Western Africa as countries began economic reforms in the 1980s, to an emerging China working to integrate into the world economy, and to the countries of the former Soviet Union as they joined the World Bank in the 1990s. As the Bank's decentralized operations were ramping up in the late 1990s, he led the change management for the worldwide renewal of the Bank's information systems. In late 2001, Paul Cadario was appointed to his present post, where he oversees the Bank's trusteeship of donor countries' contributions to development activities outside the Bank's normal lending business. The grant portfolio has nearly quadrupled in these 6 years, as the Bank "put the trust back in trust funds."

Sherry Camden-Anders, PhD, has been an organization development (OD) consultant and provider of employee education and management development since 1978. As a free lance consultant, she has consulted to a variety of clients in both public and private sectors domestically and internationally. She has held executive management and senior consultant positions during her career within major corporations. In both experiences her involvement ranged from Fortune 500 to small entrepreneurial companies. She has provided service to companies in high technology, financial, utility, oil, insurance, health care, consumer products, manufacturing, retail industries, and not-for-profit social service and governmental agencies. She currently is the Program Director for the Organizational Psychology programs at the Fresno Campus for the California School of Professional Psychology at Alliant International University. Sherry can be reached at scamden-anders@alliant.edu.

Kathy Carmean, MBA, is the SVP, Talent Development Solutions Director, at Lee Hecht Harrison in Washington, DC., where her responsibilities for leadership development and coaching span an 11-state territory. Her career has been spread over several industries, including airlines, banking, management consulting, and home health services.

David Coghlan, PhD, is a member of the faculty of the School of Business Studies, University of Dublin, Trinity College, Dublin, Ireland where he teaches organization development and action research and participates actively in both communities internationally. He has an MSc in management science from Manchester University (U.K.), an SM in management from MIT's Sloan School of Management, a PhD from the National University of Ireland and an MA from the University of Dublin. He is coauthor of *The Dynamics of Organizational Levels* in the Addison-Wesley OD series (1994), *Changing Healthcare Organizations* (Blackhall, 2003), and coeditor of *Managers Learning in Action* (Routledge, 2004), a collection of research accounts of managers who engaged in action research in their own organizations. He is a member of the editorial advisory board of *Action Research*. He can be reached at david.coghlan@tcd.ie.

Anthony Colantoni, JD, MSOD, is a senior organization development consultant and principal in the SGC Consulting Group, and adjunct faculty at Northwestern University, DePaul University, and Elmhurst College. He focuses his practice on supporting large systems change efforts, strategic planning, and leadership development. He believes that sustainability should be integral to the strategy of every organization. He can be reached at tony@sgcconsultinggroup.com.

Rosa M. Colon-Kolacko, PhD, is VP of System Learning for Christiana Care Health System, one of the largest nonprofit, teaching health systems in the United States, with approximately 10,000 employees. With a PhD in OD from Benedictine University, she is also an active researcher and a Professor of Professional Practice at Bowling Green State University. She can be reached at RColon@christianacare.org.

Jim Dunn, PhD, is the Chief Learning Officer for Texas Health Resources, one of the nation's largest faith-based health systems. Prior to joining Texas Health, Jim served as the National Vice President, Human Resources and Talent Retention Strategy for the National Home Office of the American Cancer Society. Jim holds an undergraduate degree from Howard University, a master's in Public Health from Emory University, and a PhD in organization development from Benedictine University. His article, "Strategic Human Resources: An Alliance for the Future" was published in the Fall 2006 issue of the *Organization Development Journal*.

Sharon L. Fletcher, MS, PHR, is the manager of learning and organizational development and an independent consultant in the health care industry. Sharon also serves as an adjunct faculty member for several universities. She has obtained her credentials through Northcentral University PhD program in Organizational Leadership, and is currently finalizing her dissertation work. She can be reached at sfletcher@altru.org.

Eileen Gomez is the Human Resources Director for the city of Boulder, CO. Her background includes a variety of line and staff positions with a large utility company, an international human resources consulting firm and an e-learning start up. Most recently, she was the VP of HR for a General Electric business in Lakewood, CO. Eileen is a certified Senior Professional in Human Resources through the Society of Human Resource Management and has a master's degree in Human Relations and Organizational Behavior and a bachelor's degree in Business with an emphasis in Human Resources.

Timothy Goodly, PhD, is Senior Vice President of Human Resources, CNN Worldwide. He is responsible for HR policies and procedures for more than 4,000 employees across the globe. Goodly joined Turner Broadcasting System, Inc as Director of HR for Turner Sports. Goodly's career also included serving in HR roles at Mobil Corporation and Pepsi-Cola Company and as an officer in the U.S. Army. Goodly earned a BS in Mechanical Engineering from the U.S. Military Academy at West Point and an MBA from Tulane University. He received his PhD in Organizational Development from Benedictine University.

Donna Hapac, MSOD, is a former HR Generalist and an OD Consultant for a major global manufacturer. She is currently a Performance Consultant at Health Care Service Corporation, providing consulting services to the Finance and Administrative Resources Division. Knowledge areas include talent management, leadership and professional assessment and develop ment, team building, and professional coaching. She can be reached at donna_hapac@bcbsil.com.

Corinne Haviley, RN, MS, is currently the Associate Chief Nursing Officer at Central DuPage Hospital for Emergency and Outpatient Services. She has held a variety of leadership roles in the health care field including clinical, faculty, and research positions within hospital, government, industry, and academic settings. She has authored more than 30 professional articles and book chapters in the areas of clinical oncology, radiology, patient care, management, and leadership. She can be reached at Corinne_Haviley@cdh.org.

George W. Hay, PhD, is a scholar-practitioner of management with global experience in academe and business. Most recently George was a Director of Global Consumer and Business Insights at McDonald's Corporation. Over his 15 years at McDonald's, he led domestic and international research initiatives involving the business disciplines of strategic planning, marketing and promotion, new products, operations and service, and human resources. George's current focus in on the practices of collaborative management and business research, the publication of scholarly and practitioner articles on organizational change, and the teaching of the next generation of organizational leaders. He can be reached at geowhay@hotmail.com.

Gina Hinrichs, PhD, is president of Hinrichs Consulting and an adjunct professor for Capella University, Benedictine University, and Lawrence Technological University. She brings over 25 years of for-profit and non-profit organizational experience as both an internal and external consultant. Gina's areas of expertise are: innovation, strategy, process improvement, communication, culture change, team building, organizational design, and executive coaching. She has authored several articles and books including *The Thin Book of SOAR: Building Strengths-Based Strategy*. Gina can be reached at ghinrichs517@gmail.com.

Rose Hollister, MSOD, is the Senior Director of the Leadership Institute at McDonald's Corporation, where she provides guidance and development to the organization's officers and directors. She has over 10 years of Learning and Development experience, and was an adjunct faculty member in Northwestern University's Learning and Organizational Change master's program.

Homer H. Johnson, PhD, (editor of the Case Histories) is a professor in the Graduate School of Business at Loyola University Chicago and directs the specialization in organization development. Homer can be reached at hjohnso@luc.edu.

Richard T. Johnson is the Dean of College to Careers at Harry S Truman College in Chicago. Prior to this, Richard held the positions of Dean of International Programs for Texas A&M University in the United Arab Emirates, Associate Dean for Northwestern University and Chief Operating Officer of a consulting firm. Mr. Johnson has been a featured presenter at many conferences and is an adjunct professor at Texas A&M University's National Emergency Response and Rescue Training Center (NERRTC).

Kathryn Kasdorf/Dodds, MSMOB, has over 15 years of experience in the Human Resources arena. She has held Organization Development and Change Management positions at companies such as Sears Holdings Corporation and W.W. Grainger.

Angie Keister, MSMOB, Owner of Cairn Coaching and Consulting, LLC is a passionate OD consultant and leadership coach with 10 years of experience in Organizational Development. She began her career as an internal OD practitioner designing and facilitating OD projects first at a truck and engine manufacturing firm transitioning later to the heath care industry. She is certified as a Professional Coach, through the International Coach Federation and is currently a PhD candidate with the eighth cohort in Organization Development at Benedictine University. Her research interests are understanding how thriving relates to organization change and team performance.

Rob Kjar, PhD, has spent the last 18 years working in large corporations in the areas of OD, talent management, and T&D. He recently returned from a year-long expatriate assignment in Osaka, Japan. Presently he is in OD at Astellas Pharmaceuticals. Rob can be reached at rkjar@wi.rr.com.

Tracy Lenzen, MSOD, is an Organization Development professional with particular expertise in working in technical organizations. Over the past decade, she has utilized her expertise with companies such as United Airlines, U.S. Cellular, and the University of Chicago Medical Center; she also founded her own consulting firm, Lenzen & Associates Ltd. Currently Tracy is Organizational Change Manager at Beam.

Jeremy Lurey, PhD, is the CEO and Chief Architect of Plus Delta Consulting, LLC. in the Los Angeles area, and has nearly 20 years of management consulting experience. His clients have ranged from start-up companies and nonprofit organizations to multinational corporations. Jeremy is the author of several OD publications, and serves as an adjunct professor at the Graziadio School of Business and Management. He can be reached at jslurey@plusdelta.net.

Bruce Mabee, MS, CPLP, is Managing Partner at Milestone Partners, LLC. Bruce has consulted over 125 organizations in strategic change, leadership, and organization development, half this work serving clients for 5-10 years or longer. He has also trained over 1,000 corporate professionals and leaders in Strategic Consulting Skills, and he has served as adjunct faculty in the graduate schools of Benedictine University, the Chicago School of Professional Psychology, and the University of Chicago. He can be reached at bmabee@aol.com.

Chiku Malunga, PhD, is a consultant and author with OD experience among African and European NGOs. He is currently director of Capacity Develop ment Consultants (CADECO), an organization that promotes African-centered organizational improvement models. His books include: *Understanding Organizational Sustainability through African Proverbs, Organizational Wisdom in African Proverbs,* and *Making Strategic Plans Work: Insights from African Indigenous Wisdom* (2009). He holds a doctorate in Development Studies from University of South Africa. He can be reached at cadeco@sdnp.org.mw.

Dennis Mayhew, MSOD, has over 15 years of OD experience as both an internal and external consultant, working for such companies as United Airlines. Currently, Dennis is a Senior OD & Talent Capability Consultant with Lockheed Martin Space Systems Company in Littleton, CO, where he supports internal clients through various business development, strategic planning, change management, and leadership development efforts.

John McCall, MSOD, is the Program Assistant, Department of Defense Third Party Education Assessment for Management and Training Consultants, Inc. He has over 15 years of consulting experience as an internal consultant and owner of McCall and Colleagues. McCall is a member of NTL Institute for Applied Behavioral Sciences and an adjunct faculty member at American University, where he also received his master's degree in Organization Development.

Michael F. McGovern, MSOD, has been a practicing Human Resources, Leadership Development, and Organization Development professional for more than 25 years and has worked as an internal consultant/professional in both the public, nonprofit and for-profit sectors for companies such as Abbot Labs, BP/Amoco, and the Chicago Transit Authority. He has also been and is currently the Principal of his own consulting firm:

Turn-Key Performance Solutions. He has a master's degree in Organization Development from Loyola University of Chicago and a bachelor's degree in Education from DePaul University. He currently resides in Park Ridge, IL with his wife Susan and their son Michael. McGovern can be reached at michaelfmcgovern@gmail.com.

Matt Minahan, EdD, is president of MM & Associates, specializing in strategic planning, organization design and development, leadership development, and implementing enterprise-wide change programs, including business strategy, mission, business process simplification, new structures, and communications. He has more than 25 years' experience partnering with HR VPs and their staff. He has taught Strategic HR in the MBA programs at Johns Hopkins and the University of Maryland, and regularly offers workshops at OD Network conferences for HR staff who want to expand their skills into OD. He was the Senior Management Consultant, Institutional Change and Strategy for the World Bank. He is a member of NTL Institute, where he delivers training programs to OD and HR staff and where he does consulting projects to help strengthen the HR and OD functions in organizations.

Arnold Minors is Coordinating Associate of Arnold Minors and Associates, which he formed in 1984. The company provides organization effectiveness consulting services, mediation services for couples and groups, and training in negotiation and dispute resolution. Arnold has been a manager of a moving company in Bermuda; National Trainer for Merit Students' Encyclopedia in Montreal; a biochemistry technician at the Royal Victoria Hospital in Montreal; an Organizational Effectiveness Consultant at Imperial Oil; an Associate of the Kaleel Jamison Consulting Group, a top U.S. diversity consulting firm; and Press Secretary to the Premier of Bermuda.

Diana Montalto, MBA, has over 15 years of combined HR and OD professional experience. Stationed in the Chicago area, she has utilized her skills in higher education, public transit, technology, and energy organizations. Diana is founder and Principal of Unconventional Consulting LLC, which specializes in leadership development, teambuilding and group process, career coaching, and professional assessments.

Jay Morris, PhD, JD, is Vice President of Education and the Executive Director of the Institute for Excellence at the Yale New Haven Health System. He is currently collaborating with the Yale School of Management on an action learning/succession process for midlevel managers including

nurses and physicians across the health system. Jay can be reached at
jay.morris@ynhh.org.

David Moxley, PhD, DPA, is a professor of Public Health and Social Work
at the University of Oklahoma's School of Social Work in Norman, OK.
Prior to his appointment there, he held several academic positions at
Wayne State University in Detroit, MI at the Developmental Disabilities
Intitute, Graduate Concentration in Community Practice and Social
Action, and the School of Social Work. He has published numerous works
in the fields of social work, psychology, and social policy. He can be
reached at david.moxley@ou.edu.

Dawn Newman, PhD, is a Lean+ Employee Involvement Consultant for
The Boeing Company in St. Louis, MO. In her role she integrates knowl-
edge of Organization Development, Executive Coaching, and Business
Operations to create a high-engagement work environment. She received
her PhD in Organization Development from Benedictine University.
Dawn can be reached at dawn.m.newman@ boeing.com.

John Nicholas, PhD, is a professor of operations management in the
School of Business Administration at Loyola University in Chicago. John
s research interests are lean production, project management, and organi-
zational change. He is the author of Lean Production for Competitive
Advantage, The Portal to Lean Production (with Avi Sony), and Project
Management for Busi ness, Engineering, and Technology (with Herman
Steyn). He can be reached at jnichol@luc.edu.

Kathleen O'Donnell is an MSMOB student at Benedictine University in
Lisle, Illinois. She works in Human Resources at Tectura Corporation,
specializing in learning and development initiatives both locally and
globally. She has extensive experience in virtual teamwork. She has also
worked in the academic arena at Marquette University in Milwaukee, Wis-
consin and Benedictine University. Kathleen can be reached at kath-
leen.f.odonnell@gmail.com.

Deb Orr, PhD, is Assistant Professor of Organizational Leadership in the
Evelyn T. Stone College of Professional Studies at Roosevelt University.
She holds a Bachelor's degree in Fine Arts, a master's degree in Organizational Leadership and a PhD in Organization Development. Her research
has focused on the use of aesthetic epistemology in organizational settings and how art influences thinking and behavior. An award-winning
writer, ongoing researcher in leadership and organization development,
business consultant and frequentacademic presenter, Debra is a scholar-

practitioner concentrating her efforts on bringing the newest academic research to life within the context of organizations, specifically within the Healthcare arena. She was also the Midwest Academy of Management's Program Chair for 2012. She can be reached at dorr@roosevelt.edu.

Ghazala Ovaice, PhD, is Director of Global Organization Development (OD) at Abbott where she leads the OD center of excellence by providing consulting for strategic performance needs with specific concentration in culture change, change management, M&A, employee engagement, organization design, and organization research. Her research interests include trust in the workplace, cross-cultural issues in work related values, and the relationship of organization culture and performance. Her background is in Organization Development (OD), Organization Research, Leadership Development, and Evaluation. As a result of her educational, corporate, and consulting experiences she has worked in the healthcare, consulting, and non-profit educational industries.

Raymond Patchett, MSOD, served as the City Manager of Carlsbad, CA from 1997-2007. Currently, he is Principal at Patchett & Associates, providing clients with OD consulting, leadership consulting, teambuilding, and conflict resolution expertise.

Sarah Peacey, MSMOB, is a management consultant with KPMG's People and Change Advisory Services practice based in Chicago. She specializes in behavioral change management, talent acquisition, program/project management, and social media integration. Peacey serves on the board for the National Asian Pacific Islander Network, one of KPMG's diversity employee resource groups. Currently, she is a doctoral candidate in Benedictine University's Organization Development program.

Vincent Pellettiere, PhD, has been a Human Resources generalist for 31 years with various industries including manufacturers of plumbing fixtures, plastic dairy and drink containers, coffee/beverage products, hospital health care, precision gears/drives, medical devices, home health care, architectural, and bio engineering industries. He is the former vice president of Human Resources of a Fortune 100 Company's division where he received several high performance recognition rewards. Vincent is currently an assistant professor at Aurora University teaching undergraduate and graduate courses in business management, human resources management, and organizational behavior.

Chris Pett, MSOD, is the Practice Director of Leadership and Organization Development at Patina Solutions in the Chicago area. Additionally, he is the President of Christopher R. Pett Consulting. His internal and external OD work has led to successful operations at organizations of all sizes, including Fortune 100 and 500 companies. Chris specializes in strategic planning, talent and leadership development, organizational assessments, and performance coaching.

Jan Rashid, EdD, is Assistant Superintendent for Instructional Services in Des Plaines School District 62, a diverse K-8 district just northwest of Chicago. Prior to her current role she served in District 62 as Director of Curriculum and Principal of Central Elementary School. She has provided workshops at the local and State level on various topics including: involving teachers in the use of data with the goal of improved student achievement and school improvement, developing teacher leaders, and authentic and whole school approaches to reading and writing instruction. She is also Copresident of the Suburban Council of the International Reading Association (SCIRA) and can be reached at rashidj@d62.org.

Linda Rasins, MSOD, has been a practicing OD professional for over 30 years, and shared her expertise as an instructor at Loyola University. She has run Linda Rasins Consulting since 1997, specializing in talent and organization development, serving such clients as McDonald's Corporation, Exelon, Comcast, United Airlines, and Clorox. Linda also serves as the Chair of the Board of Directors for the Chicago Jazz Philharmonic.

Nazneen Razi, PhD, is EVP and Chief Global HR Officer for Jones Lang LaSalle with over 25 years' experience leading HR departments at national and global firms such as Comdisco and CNA Insurance. Ms. Razi earned a PhD in Organization Development and an MBA from Benedictine University in Lisle, Illinois. She holds a master's degree in English Literature from Osmania University in India. Ms. Razi served as chairman of the board of HRMAC and was on the advisory boards of Menttium and AON Consulting. She currently serves on the Boards of the Chicago Sinfonietta and the Chicago Shakespeare Theater. She can be reached at nazneen.razi@jll.com.

Lorna Rickard is Chief Workforce Architect at Xtivia in Littleton, CO, focusing on services including change management and team, leader, and organizational effectiveness. She also serves as an anthropologist at Power & Systems, providing a better understanding of how to lead human systems. Lorna can be reached at lrickard@xtivia.com.

Cathy L. Royal, PhD, is a System and Organizational Development practitioner. She is owner and senior consultant of Royal Consulting Group and an adjunct faculty member at Colorado Technical Institute. She is also the Executive Director of Your World Travel Consultant Education Foundation. She specializes in Appreciative Inquiry (AI), Leadership Development, and Social Justice and Inclusion. She developed the Quadrant Behavior Theory (QBT)©. QBT is a platform theory that supports leaders and change agents in expanding their understanding of the behaviors that create and sustain exclusion in societies and systems. She works with individuals and systems to enhance their use of self as effective change agents. She can be reached at catroyal@verizon.net.

David Russo, MSEd, is in his sixth year as Middle School Principal of Fairview South School in Skokie, IL. Fairview South serves a diverse section of the village with approximately 640 students in grades K through 8. He is in his 12th year in education, and is devoted to ensuring that young people will be able to relate to a wide range of ideas, personalities, and thought as they continue the process of maturing into young adults. He received his bachelor degree from the University of Illinois at Urbana-Champaign in 1997 and a master's of science in Educational Administration from Southern Illinois University-Carbondale in 1999. He can be reached at drusso@fairview.k12.il.us.

Eric Sanders, MBA, is an OD Economist: an independent consultant who helps leaders and their organizations achieve measurable results through developing their people. He has worked both internally and externally, and has helped clients in many industries, including retail, telecommunications, manufacturing and nonprofits. He is also a faculty member at Benedictine University and the Lake Forest Graduate School of Management. Eric can be reached at eric.sanders@ODeconomist.com.

Edgar H. Schein, PhD, is the Sloan Fellows Professor of Management Emeritus from the MIT Sloan School of Management where he taught from 1956 to 2004. He received his PhD in Social Psychology from Harvard in 1952 and has applied this field to the understanding of career development, organizational culture, process consultation, and the dynamics of interpersonal relations in organizations. He can be reached at scheine@comcast.net.

Katherine A. Schroeder, MA, has been in the organization and individual development profession for the past 20 years. Currently, she is the Director of Organizational Effectiveness for North America at Astellas Pharma where she works globally with senior leaders on change management, high performance, culture change, team effectiveness, and global organizational effectiveness. She has a BA from University of Illinois and an MA in International Relations from University of Denver and is currently working on her PhD in Organization Development at Benedictine University. She can be reached at geoschroeder@gmail.com.

Bev Scott, MA, is Founder and Partner of The 3rd Act, an organization which provides support for life transition planning, particularly targeting individuals planning for retirement. She has over 30 years of OD experience as an internal consultant, external consultant, and university faculty member. Bev has transitioned recently from OD professional to writer and author. She can be reached at bev@bevscott.com.

Tammy Seibert, MBA, MSOD, PCC, is an Organizational Effectiveness consultant at Allstate Insurance. Previously, Tammy has partnered with business leaders in the areas of coaching, leadership development, team effectiveness, change management, talent strategy, mergers and acquisitions, and restructuring and integration. Her experience covers Fortune 500 companies, midsize organizations and nonprofits with international experience in the United Kingdom and key assignments for Canada, Germany, Australia, Mexico, Caribbean, and South America. Tammy can be reached at tseib@allstate.com.

Carol Silk, MBA, is Vice President and Chief Learning Officer for New York-Presbyterian Hospital. She is responsible for the Hospital's Center for Organizational and Leadership Effectiveness Department which services all five campuses in the areas of: training and development, technology learning solutions, organizational development, performance management, talent management, leadership development, and awards and recognition. She can be reached at cas9039@nyp.org.

Robert Sloyan is currently Vice President of Human Resources for Apogee Enterprises (Tru Vue), a U.S.-based manufacturing organization. Previously, he held various HR roles at SBC, Ameritech, and MetLife. He holds a PhD in Organizational Development from Benedictine University (2009). Additionally, he earned an MBA in Finance (2001) and Human Resources (1994) from St. Xavier University. Rob is a regular presenter at academic, human resources, and organizational development conferences. He also teaches at Benedictine University. Rob lives in the Chicago suburbs with his wife Doreen and their three boys. He can be reached at rsloyan@ben.edu.

Jennifer Smith, MSMOB, is the Manager of Global Leadership Development for Molex Inc., a global manufacturer of electrical interconnects based in Lisle, IL. She has responsibility for developing and sustaining a globally diverse talent pipeline through the means of comprehensive management and leadership development framework. In this role, she leads the advancement of education for the organizations high performing, high potential global leaders. Jennifer is an active steering committee member of the Women's Business Council at Molex where her primary focus is career development and advancement for women. She is currently involved with the Executive Learning Exchange, Global Network, and Midwest Chapter of ASTD. She holds a graduate degree in Organization Development and is a certified Six Sigma Green Belt. Her work includes supporting teams within the organization achieve their desired results. She is adjunct faculty at Benedictine University where she lectures on organization behavior and development topics. She can be reached at Jennifer.smith@molex.com.

Peter F. Sorensen, PhD, is Professor and Director of the OD PhD Program and the MSMOB programs at Benedictine University. He is Past Chair of the ODC Division of the Academy of Management, and is currently on the executive board of AOM's Management Consulting Division. He has authored over 200 articles, book, and best papers. He was Guest Editor for the New Millennium issues for *OD Journal* and *OD Practitioner*. Sorensen's recent book is *Strategic Organization Development* with Therese Yaeger. He can be reached at psorensen@ben.edu.

Aimee Stash, MS, RODC, serves as the System Administrator of Organization Learning and Development for Memorial Health System in Springfield, Illinois. MHS is a multihospital health system with 5,800 employees that serves the communities of Central Illinois. In her role at Memorial, Stash is respon sible for all facets of organization development. She can be reached at Stash.Aimee@mhsil.com.

Ginny Storjohann, MHRD, founded Storjohann & Associates in 1994 in the Denver area, specializing in executive coaching, leadership, and organization development. Previously, she has worked in federal government and public service arenas, serving as both an HR professional and OD professional.

Dalitso S. Sulamoyo, is the President & CEO of the Illinois Association of Community Action Agencies, Illinois' largest anti-poverty network of 40 organiza tions. His current research interest is the measurement of OD success rates in Africa. He holds a PhD in Organization Development from Benedictine University. He can be reached at sulamoyo@iacaanet.org.

Sue Sweem, PhD, has over 25 years of experience in HR. Currently, she is HR Director at Optimum Nutrition in Aurora, IL. She has worked at such companies as Walgreens, MasterBrand Industries, and Akzo Nobel Inc. She has also taught at Benedictine University and the University of St. Francis. Sue can be reached at susansweem@aol.com.

Neesa Sweet is the former Director of Learning and Development for the Chicago Sun-Times News Group. She is a past president of the Organization Development Network of Chicago. As an independent consultant, she focuses on leadership, coaching, change management, and communication. Her company is the Braided River Group in Highland Park, IL. Neesa can be reached at NeesaS@aol.com.

Ross Tartell, PhD, is Learning Leader of North America for GE Capital Real Estate. He also serves as an adjunct professor of Psychology and Education at Columbia University in New York. He has over 25 years of HR experience with companies such as Pfizer, specializing in talent management, learning and development, and instructional design. He can be reached at ross.tartell@tc.columbia.edu.

Kit Tennis, PhD, is COO and Senior Consultant for Sanchez Tennis & Associates LLC, specializing in global multicultural diversity and inclusion. His organization has served on billion-dollar organizational expansion efforts. His experience has taken him to such organizations as Hewlett-Packard, Xcel Energy, and St. Thomas University.

Charles "Terry" Terranova, MBA, is Director of Global Change Management at Newmont Mining Corporation in Denver, CO, working in particular with the Safety Task Force. Previously, he has held Management Development and OD Consultant roles at companies such as Charles Schwab, Sun Microsystems, and New York City Transit.

Ruth Urban, MS, Principal in The Urban Group, brings more than 25 years of conflict resolution experience to her independent consulting, facilitation and organizational development practice. She is a Certified Professional Facilitator by the International Association of Facilitators. Ruth can be reached at Ruth@RuthUrbanGroup.com.

Annie Viets, EdD, is an Associate Professor of Management at Prince Mohammad Bin Fahd University in Al Khobar, Saudi Arabia. She is also an OD consultant, a mediator and a former president of the Vermont Mediators Association. She can be reached at mviets@pmu.edu.sa.

Lola Wilcox, MA, has over 20 years of valuable OD experience in such areas as change consulting, government organizations, technology, and energy corporations. Currently Lola is Principal with White Raven Enterprises, LTD, where she specializes on change management, conflict management, and system transformation. She can be reached at LolaLWilcox@gmail.com.

Paula Wilder, EdD, is Senior Partner at WilderWeber Leadership Group, an organization which aims to help leaders create strategic, sustainable change. Paula has been owner of multiple consulting practices in her career. In addition to her doctorate degree in Education, Paula also has a master's degree in Organization Development.

Ken Williams, EdD, is Associate Professor at the School for International Training Graduate Institute in Vermont where he specializes in: cross and intercultural team and organizational development; change management and evaluation of educational programs; organizational inquiry and developing multicultural learning organizations; decision making, leadership, and community collaboration. He is also an independent consultant and has lived or worked in a number of African, Asian, European, Latin American, and Caribbean countries. He completed his doctorate in Educational Manage ment and Administration at Teachers College, Columbia University and his master's degree at the London School of Economics. He can be reached at williamsalex50@gmail.com.

Jason A. Wolf, PhD, is the Director of Organization Development for the Eastern Group of HCA and an adjunct faculty at American University. He brings over 15 years experience both as an internal and external consultant in organization change and high performance, helping to build and grow OD functions in two Fortune 500 organizations. Jason served on the Board of Trustees of the Organization Development Network from 1999-2002. He can be reached at jasonawolf@earthlink.net.

Kathy Woodrich, MSOD, is an independent OD consultant in the Los Angeles area. Currently, she runs Woodrich Consulting, and has worked as a Training and Development Specialist and Performace Technologist at American Express Tax & Business Services and Ameriquest Mortgage Company, respectively.

Christopher Worley, PhD, is a Senior Research Scientist at the Center for Effective Organizations (CEO) at the Marshall School of Business at the University of Southern California. He is a recognized leader in the field of organization development. Prior to coming to CEO, he was Director of the

Master of Science in Organization (MSOD) program at Pepperdine University and remains a primary faculty member in that program. He was awarded the Luckman Distinguished Teaching Fellowship in 1997. Prior to Pepperdine University, Dr. Worley taught undergraduate and graduate courses at the University of San Diego, University of Southern California, and Colorado State University. Dr. Worley has coauthored over 30 books, chapters, and articles. His most recent books, coauthored with Ed Lawler, are *Management Reset* and *Built to Change*. He also authored *Integrated Strategic Change: How OD Builds Competitive Advantage* in Addison-Wesley's OD Series, and with Tom Cummings has coauthored five editions of *Organization Development and Change*, the leading textbook on organization development. His articles on strategic change and strategic organization design have appeared in the *Journal of Applied Behavioral Science, Journal of Organization Behavior, Sloan Management Review,* and *Organizational Dynamics*. He can be reached at cworley@marshall.usc.edu.

Therese F. Yaeger, PhD, is Associate Professor, Benedictine University Organization Development (OD) and Master of Science in Management and Organizational Behavior programs. She is Editorial Board Member of *OD Practitioner*, and she has authored numerous papers and books, including *Strategic Organization Development: Managing Change for Success* (2009). Yaeger is Division Chair of the Management Consulting Division of Academy of Management, and Past President of the Midwest Academy of Management. She can be reached at tyaeger@ben.edu.

CPSIA information can be obtained at www.ICGtesting.com
Printed in the USA
LVOW070736140613

338395LV00004B/83/P